MYSTICAL ORIGINS
of the TAROT

OTHER BOOKS BY PAUL HUSON

Mastering Witchcraft

The Devil's Picturebook

The Coffee Table Book of Witchcraft and Demonology

Mastering Herbalism

How to Test and Develop Your ESP

The Keepsake

The Offering

MYSTICAL ORIGINS
of the TAROT

From Ancient Roots to Modern Usage

PAUL HUSON

With illustrations by the author

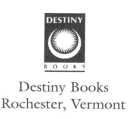

Destiny Books
Rochester, Vermont

Destiny Books
One Park Street
Rochester, Vermont 05767
www.InnerTraditions.com

Destiny Books is a division of Inner Traditions International

Library of Congress Cataloging-in-Publication Data

Huson, Paul.
  Mystical origins of the tarot : from ancient roots to modern usage / Paul Huson; with
illustrations by the author.
      p. cm.
  Includes bibliographical references and indexes.
  ISBN 978-0-89281-190-8
  1. Tarot. 2. Tarot—History. I. Title.
  BF1879.T2H87 2004
  133.3'2424—dc22
                                                                                    2004001131

Printed and bound in the United States

10 9 8 7

Text design and layout by Mary Anne Hurhula
This book was typeset in Adobe Garamond with Galliard as the display typeface

In loving memory of Olga and Carl

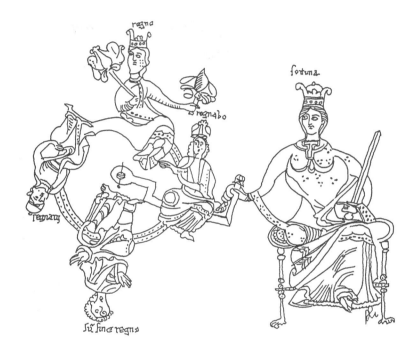

The Wheel of Fortune
The Roman goddess Fortuna was still respected and placated during the Middle Ages as the ruler of human destinies.

CONTENTS

5 THE MEANINGS OF THE SUIT CARDS: THE MINOR ARCANA

6 READING THE TAROT

ACKNOWLEDGMENTS

Thanks are due to the following for their help in preparing this book: Stuart R. Kaplan for providing me material on the Mamlûk cards so long ago; Andrea Pollett for important information about the Mamlûk suit signs; Ron Decker for sharing with me his expertise on tarot symbolism and Etteilla; Giordano Berti for his help in trying to locate the elusive *tarocchi* of Vittoriano Facco; Jess Karlin for his pointers on tarot and magic; Mary K. Greer for a careful reading of an early draft followed by learned and constructive suggestions; the International Playing-Card Society, notably Christopher Rayner, Dr. Michael Cooper, and Barbara Clarke, for their help in locating valuable playing-card research; the staff of the British Library, London, for their diligence in locating material on medieval drama; Susan Jeffers and Mark Shelmerdine for their supportive enthusiasm throughout the long history of this project; Niki Marvin for her love, encouragement, and spiritual fortitude; Mel Raab for coming to my assistance with his timely technical wizardry; Martha Millard for her long-standing faith in the book; Jon Graham for his persistence and tenacity in bringing the book to publication; Vickie Trihy and Bronwyn Becker for their erudite and constructive input to the final manuscript; and last but definitely not least, William Bast, who made everything possible.

PREFACE

King of Spades and Queen of Clubs, after fifteenth-century French playing cards

I have been intrigued by playing cards since I was a toddler, when I came across my first deck and laid them out around the pattern of the rug on the living room floor. I can recall my fascination at the time with these magical symbols: What did they mean? Who were all these interesting, colorfully dressed people? Who was the most important?

Then I discovered the tarot. I drew my first set of tarot trumps (the twenty-two mysterious cards that distinguish a tarot deck from a standard deck of playing cards) on file cards when I was fourteen years old, painted my next complete deck when I was twenty; a third set when I was twenty-six, and a fourth when I was thirty. I guess you could say I was obsessive.

But I am not alone in my obsession. Despite the many attempts to elucidate them, tarot cards have remained one of history's enduring puzzles. What do those enigmatic cards really mean? What mysteries, if any, do they conceal? I think I'm accurate in claiming that until the publication of this book, they have succeeded, quite literally, in concealing certain types of mysteries for around five hundred years.

The idea for this book began life as a revision and update to *The Devil's Picturebook,* a tarot book I wrote some years ago. But as I reread each chapter of *Picturebook*, I realized with somewhat mixed emotions that so much new light had been shed on the history of the subject since I wrote it that if I did write anything at all—and there was plenty to write about—it would have to be an entirely new venture.

Unlike *Picturebook*, in which I speculated broadly on the tarot's possible associations to medieval and Renaissance myth and magic, my aim here is not merely to provide another "how-to" book on cardreading. Rather, I propose to track each symbol in every card of the deck, in both so-called Major and Minor Arcanas (the trump cards and the suit sign cards) to its actual historical origin, and then explore how its meaning in divination evolved from this source, if in fact it did.

In the thirty years since I wrote *Picturebook*, my views on the tarot have changed. Tarot, moreover, has expanded from a subject of interest only to playing-card enthusiasts and occultists to one of worldwide appeal, having gained a considerable amount of academic attention and an enormous presence on the Internet. There you can find an amazing plethora of tarot Web sites, chat rooms, and information resources promoting lively, well-informed, and often diametrically opposed points of view: historical, psychological, Hermetic, divinatory, feminist, postmodern, you name it. Furthermore, a vast collection of books on tarot has now become available. However, although the mysterious cards have arguably become part of mainstream culture—the art of tarot reading recognized as, at minimum, a technique of psychological exploration and the cards themselves finally anchored in an assured historicity by the books of British philosopher Michael Dummett and others—there still remain shadowy areas from which three questions of enormous importance loom unanswered.

- First, what was the origin of the suit card symbols, and what did they stand for?
- Second, what was the source of the trumps, and what was their original import? They were not simply conjured out of thin air.
- Third and lastly, when and why did people begin using the cards for divination—that is, as a means of acquiring spiritual guidance or discovering hidden information?

As we shall see, all the evidence available today suggests that the trumps were added to an already existing game of fifty-six playing cards during the middle of the fifteenth century and for their subject matter drew on imagery readily recognizable by the card players of the time. However, knowledge of that symbolism was quickly lost by the average card player, which allowed for regional changes to creep into the design of the cards as their use in gaming spread throughout Europe. Nonetheless, the archaic and suggestive imagery used in the trumps and court cards resonated with that part of people's psyches from which dreams and visionary experience spring (designated by the pioneering psychologist Carl Gustav Jung as the unconscious mind). This mystical quality may have led naturally to the evolution of the cards as a divination tool, if indeed the trumps were not initially adapted from a preexisting divination device—a notion I shall examine in due course.

Michael Dummett, who is opposed to what he regards as the misappropriation of the tarot by occultists, doubts that the images depicted on the trumps taken as a set contained any special meaning to their earliest users, inasmuch as they were standard subjects of medieval and Renaissance iconography. I, on the other hand, for the very same reason, believe the trumps to have been pregnant with meaning from the start, their symbolism drawn from the world of medieval drama, of miracle, mystery, and morality plays, with a hint of Neoplatonism evident here and there, which lent itself very readily to esoteric uses such as divination. Furthermore, we shall see that the court cards in the so-called Minor Arcana spring from a heady brew of pagan and medieval myth, also handy for the would-be diviner. Moreover, as Dummett himself has so ably demonstrated, the symbolism of the four suit signs seems to have evolved from a source even older than that of the trumps, a source that I believe can be traced to the Persian Empire before the time of the Islamic conquest in 642 C.E. Consequently, they also carry definite meanings exploitable by the diviner.

This brings me to my last great unanswered question about the cards: when, and why, were they first used for divination? Today historical opinion favors the eighteenth century because many historians equate playing-card divination with "cartomancy," a particular form of fortune-telling with cards that was introduced in the late seventeen hundreds. However, an older method of seeking hidden wisdom from playing cards existed as much as three centuries earlier. I contend that this early practice of drawing playing cards singly as lots to answer questions—a type of divination known as "sortilege" and an ancient and widespread practice—introduced the earliest use of cards for divination. Indeed, the French verb still used today for card reading, *tirer* (drawing, as in drawing lots), is a strong indication that playing-card divination had its roots in sortilege. The fact that the term *cartomancy* was invented in the eighteenth century to refer to a newly devised system of divination that made use of extended combinations of cards does not affect my argument.

In our search for the tarot's origins, we will explore a vast and fascinating world of arcane symbolism and a diversity of cultures, and we will witness how the human love of playing games melded with the equally human desire to probe the unknown. The introduction briefly describes how playing cards first arrived in Europe from the Middle East and how tarot decks developed for game playing, then became popular throughout Europe during the sixteenth and succeeding centuries. Chapter 1 explores the cultural origins and symbolism of the four suit signs; chapter 2 is a similar examination of the origins of the trumps. Chapter 3 is devoted to an account of the development of the tarot's use as an instrument of divination. In chapters 4 and 5, I offer an analysis of the first documented divinatory interpretations of the trumps and suit cards. The remainder of the book is addressed to those who wish to explore the tarot in greater depth: chapter 6 presents actual methods of reading the cards. Three appendices provide the most current information available about obtaining and viewing decks: appendix 1 details the variety of historical tarot decks that are available in facsimile; appendix 2 lets the interested reader know where he or she can obtain them; and appendix 3 indicates where the truly devoted tarot enthusiast can see the actual decks described or illustrated in the text.

Finally, a personal note about tarot divination.

Although I received an early training in the Western esoteric tradition, I don't advocate any particular method of tarot divination today, although I am more than willing to offer suggestions. I began reading tarot cards over forty years ago while I was studying with the Society of the Inner Light and later with a group that studied the teachings of the Hermetic Order of the Golden Dawn. From the experience I gathered during that time, I ultimately came to the conclusion that Dion Fortune's more casual approach to the cards was more effective for me than the rigidly formal method advocated by the Golden Dawn. As I see it, cartomantic rules and regulations have been cobbled together from a variety of sources, and I hold to the school of thought that the secret of

A CHRONOLOGY OF THE HISTORICAL TAROT

Fourteenth century: Mamlûk playing cards introduced to Europe, inspire the creation of European playing cards for trick-taking games. European decks generally comprised four suits, each headed by a King and one or two Ministers. The Ministers evolve into Knights, Knaves, and Queens.

Fifteenth century: Tarot decks created by adding twenty-two pictorial trump cards to standard Italian deck of fifty-six cards showing Mamlûk-derived Coins, Cups, Swords, and Batons as suits. Imagery for the trumps is drawn from medieval sources. Painted decks are created for the nobility: the Viscontis of Milan, the D'Estes of Ferrara, the commissioners of the Charles VI Tarot. The Cary-Yale sheet of tarots is printed in Milan.

Sixteenth century: Printed tarot decks produced in Florence, Bologna, Ferrara. Printed tarot cards now spread to France, Switzerland, Belgium, and Spain. Captions and roman numerals added to the trumps. Tarot decks widely used to play card games.

Seventeenth century: Papal states clamp down on use of "inappropriate" trump imagery, leads to substitute cards for Female Pope, Pope, Emperor, and Empress in the Tarot of Bologna and the minchiate of Florence. Tarot of Besançon replaces Female Pope with Juno and Pope with Jupiter. The Belgian Tarot gives rise to the Tarot of Paris and the Viéville Tarot.

Eighteenth century: Rise in popularity of the Tarot of Marseille. Egyptian symbolism used to explain its origin. Tarot cards now used for complex cartomancy as well as card games.

Nineteenth and Twentieth centuries: Hebrew kabbalist symbolism and astrology incorporated into the tarot. Explosion of decks made exclusively for cartomancy.

successful divination lies within the diviner. Actually, I believe anyone who wants to read the cards is not only free to, but must evolve a personal method for himself or herself, for reasons I will make clear. If you have the talent, it will make itself known to you soon enough. However, if you take the art of tarot reading seriously (and expect others to), it might behoove you to know something about the actual historical roots of your chosen field.

Which, in a nutshell, is what this book is all about.

Introduction

Of Playing Cards and Tarot Decks

I sing of knights and ladies, of love and arms,
Of courtly chivalry, of courageous deeds . . .

LUDOVICO ARIOSTO,
ORLANDO FURIOSO, CANTO 1, 1532.

Tarot cards and what we think of today as regular playing cards are not quite the same thing, although they are close cousins of one another. The tarot appeared out of the blue as a colorful variant of the standard northern-Italian playing-card deck in Milan or Ferrara sometime during the middle of the fifteenth century.

Until twenty years ago, nobody could put a finger on exactly where what we consider to be standard European playing cards originated, let alone tarot cards. There had been many theories, but nothing definite by way of proof. The best bets were that they came from China, Persia, or India, all of which have their own different types of playing cards, but nobody could piece together just how European playing cards evolved from these exotic roots. Solid documentary evidence for the existence of playing cards in Europe, mostly in the form of bans against them, indicated that they were well known by the 1370s. The earliest known mention of them is an injunction against gambling with cards, issued in the canton of Bern in 1367. The earliest known actual description, however, was written ten years later, in Basel, by a Dominican monk known to history as Johannes von Rheinfelden.

Rheinfelden's homily *Tractatus de moribus et disciplina humanae conversationis* (A Treatise on Morals and Civilizing Teachings to Be Drawn from Frequently Used Things) dealt with popular games, such as card playing, based on the feudal structure of medieval society, and noted their usefulness as a source of moral instruction. Among other card games, he described a collection of fifty-two cards used for games involving trick taking. These cards were divided into four different sequences of symbols or "suits," thirteen cards to a suit. Each suit consisted of cards numbered from one to ten, with each numbered card bearing its own symbol, and three "court" picture cards also bearing symbols: a King and what our monk referred to as two *Marschalli* (officers), which sound like they could be the ancestors of our standard Queen and Knave cards.

Now, what symbols marked these cards to represent the suits, our Dominican monk didn't say, although suit sets as diverse as Herons, Hounds, Falcons, and Falcon Lures, or Roses, Crowns, Pennies, and Rings, are known to have been used in early northern-European card decks. We now know that the suit signs that became standard in the lands that became Switzerland (Roses, Hawkbells, Shields, and Acorns) and later in Germany (Hearts, Hawkbells, Leaves, and Acorns) developed around 1450 and 1460 respectively. The French suit signs (Hearts, Clover Leaves, Pikes, and Paving Tiles) appeared in about 1480. These later gave rise to the suits of our "regular" decks of cards: Hearts, Clubs, Spades, and Diamonds.

However, it wasn't until as recently as 1980 that Michael Dummett, Wykeham Professor of Logic at Oxford University from 1979 to 1992, demonstrated that remnant and telltale traces of suit and deck structure found in French and German playing cards indicate that they undoubtedly evolved from the suits that were popular in Italy, Spain, and Portugal at the end of the fourteenth century: Cups, Coins, Swords, and Batons or Cudgels. Of even greater significance, Dummett also made a convincing case for the Islamic Near East as the actual place of origin of the prototypical deck of cards that gave rise to all the other European decks.

THE MAMLŪK CARDS

In 1939 a deck of fifteenth-century hand-painted cards from Egypt was discovered in the Topkapi Sarayi Museum in Istanbul. At the time the decks were created, Egypt was governed by the Mamlûks, a dynasty of Egyptian sultans originally descended from Circassian Turkish slaves brought to Egypt to form a standing army in the thirteenth century C.E.

The game played with these Mamlûk cards was known in Arabic as *Mulûk wanuwwâb* (the Game of Kings and Deputies).

The Istanbul discovery remained unnoticed until it was finally brought to light in a paper written by the cards' discoverer, L. A. Mayer, which wasn't published until 1971. The four suits displayed in the Islamic deck consist of Cups, Coins, Swords, and what were believed to be Polo Sticks. In 1980 Dummett fairly conclusively demonstrated that they all showed more than a significant similarity to the suit signs of early Italian playing cards.

Ace of Cups, Ace of Coins, Ace of Polo Sticks, and Ace of Swords, after fifteenth-century Mamlûk cards

The curved shapes of the Mamlûk Swords make much better sense if we think of them as scimitars, the weapon of choice among medieval Islamic warriors. Likewise, polo sticks—which are what those angular, crisscrossing, and in some instances dragon-headed objects on the Mamlûk cards are believed to be—were known to be heraldic emblems in the world of Islam. The game of polo being unknown in Europe in the fourteenth and fifteenth centuries, these polo sticks were transformed into batons, cudgels, or scepters by European card makers.

Arabic names for the Coin and Cup suits hint that the Mamlûk cards were used for gambling. Indeed, an existing record states that the Mamlûk sultan al-Malik al-Mu'ayyad won money in a game of cards in

   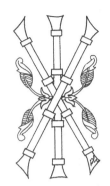

Left—Two of Swords (scimitars), after a fif-teenth-century Mamlûk card. Right—Two of Swords, after a Tarot of Marseille pattern. Notice how the curve of the scimitars is repeated in the curving sword design of northern Italian tarots.

Left—Three of Polo Sticks, after a fifteenth-century Mamlûk card. The dragon-head motif will show up later in European tarot decks, notably in the Marseille Two of Cups. Right—Three of Batons, after a Tarot of Marseille pattern. Notice the crisscross Baton motif inherited from the Mamlûk Polo Stick.

about the year 1400. The word *denari* or *danari,* still used in Italian for the Coin suit, is derived from the Arabic word for the gold Mamlûk *dînâr* coin. The Cups of the Mamlûk cards are named *tûmân,* and *tûmân* is actually the word for a Persian gold coin that was worth at one time ten thousand *dînâr* coins. The money-derived names also suggest that the Islamic card makers may have copied their playing cards from the oldest playing cards we have on record—Chinese "money cards" made for gambling that make use of three or four suits: Coins or "Cash"; Strings of a Hundred Coins (in which the coins are strung together through holes in their center and look like banded rods); Myriads of Strings (representing tens of thousands of coins and repre-sented by highly stylized oriental personages); and in some packs, Tens of Myriads. We shall examine the puzzle of why Islamic playing-card makers might choose to replace these four suits with Coins, Cups, Swords, and Polo Sticks later.

Significantly, Islamic playing cards are mentioned in three fifteenth-

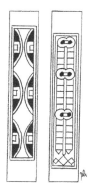

Chinese "money-suited" Dongguan Pai *cards from a modern deck using three suits. The cards illustrated are Six Cash (Coins) and Six Strings of Coins (Batons). These cards are still used for gambling. Not so much "cards" as narrow, disposable strips of paper, they come in packs of 120, comprising three "decks." Each deck of forty is rarely used more than once or twice.*

century Italian manuscripts known as the *Chronicles of Viterbo,* which state: "In the year 1379 there was brought to Viterbo the game of cards, which in the Saracen language is called *nayb.*" In fifteenth-century Italy we find the term *naibi* used for playing cards in general, and in many Spanish-speaking countries they're still called *naipes,* from which we probably get the Old English term for a scoundrel, *jackanapes.* As Dummett concludes, the entry in the *Chronicles* supplies the only plausible etymology for these odd words, especially when it becomes evident that the word *nayb* in Arabic means "deputy" or "minister" and refers to two of the court cards in the Mamlûk deck.

THE CREATION OF THE COURT CARDS

Because of the Islamic prohibition against the depiction of the human figure, the Mamlûk King and two Deputy cards simply show a suit sign, a calligraphic inscription in Arabic that describes the title of the card, and sometimes a flowery aphorism.

When the cards were reinterpreted by European card makers, however, no such Islamic prohibition of images applied, so we now have representational court cards headed by very obvious kings wearing crowns.

The earliest decks used in Italy, Spain, and Germany initially contained

The malik at-tûmân, *King of the Ten Thousand (Cups), after a fifteenth-century Mamlûk card. The inscription is the only indication that this card is a king.*

only two court cards in each suit in addition to the King: a Superior Officer and an Inferior Officer, deriving from the corresponding Deputies of the Mamlûk deck. The Queen appeared later in German and French decks as a substitute for the Mamlûk Superior Officer, while the

Queen and King of Batons, after the fifteenth-century Visconti-Sforza tarocchi deck. The childlike faces are typical of the style of the painter who created them, Bonifacio Bembo, a favorite designer at the court of Milan.

Inferior Officer was renamed Knave. Italian card makers liked the idea of this newly invented Queen and gave her a place of her own in the card court, entitling her *Reina* or *Regina*. They then bestowed the name of *Cavallo* (Knight) on the Superior Officer and, like the French, demoted the Inferior Officer to a male Knave or sometimes a female Page, whom they called *Fante, Fantesca,* or *Fantiglia.*

Knave and Knight of Batons, after Bembo's fifteenth-century Visconti-Sforza tarocchi deck. Again, notice how Bembo makes them both look like children in costume.

Some card players apparently became carried away by this idea of court cards. The fifteenth-century painter Bonifacio Bembo was commissioned by his noble Milanese patron Francesco Sforza to paint *six* court cards for each suit. In addition to what we now regard as the four customary courts, he included a *Fantesca* and a female Knight in each suit. Luxurious cards hand painted for wealthy patrons, some illuminated with gold and silver leaf and worth considerable sums of money, now allowed artists considerable freedom to invent their own suit signs and indulge creative flourishes. These cards would have been little used for gaming but, rather, kept as fine art objects and stored in custom-made wooden caskets. Maybe this accounts for the number of them that have survived, whereas examples of early printed tarot cards are very rare.

THE NAMING OF THE COURT CARDS

The French notion of naming the court cards of their decks emerged in the early to mid-1400s, about the time the tarot trumps first appeared. The court cards' names would have been bywords for the French nobility, as the names were taken from popular medieval romances written in the thirteenth and fourteenth centuries. Indeed, many of the male court card names in French card decks are drawn from a medieval grouping of heroes known as the Nine Worthies, three of whom derive from the legendary world of biblical Judaism, three from classical paganism, and three from legendary Christendom. The seventeenth-century poet and dramatist John Dryden describes them in his translation of the poem *The Flower and the Leaf:*

> *Nine Worthies were they called, of different rites,*
> *Three Jews, three pagans, and three Christian Knights, . . .*

Originating in *Les Voeux du paon*, "The Vows of the Peacock," a tale written in 1312 by one Jacques de Longuyon, the Nine Worthies were

Hector, Caesar, and Alexander, after a fourteenth-century French illustration of the Nine Worthies. Notice how Caesar is crowned with the closed crown of an emperor, whereas Alexander wears the open crown of a king.

the incarnations of an idealized, chivalric past that was considered to have existed between five and seven hundred years earlier. As with the stories of the Grail and the Arthurian cycle, *Les Voeux* seems to have represented the nostalgic fantasies of a fourteenth-century aristocracy about a time and set of ethics that never really existed outside their own minds and maybe in the otherworld of Jungian archetypes.

The Worthies themselves were an assorted collection of heroes: King David of Israel, the patriarch Joshua, the Jewish patriot Judas Maccabeus, Hector of Troy, Alexander (the Great) of Macedon, Julius Caesar, the emperor Charlemagne, King Arthur, and Godfrey of Bouillon—first ruler of the short-lived Christian kingdom of Jerusalem.

The Worthies' likenesses appear all over Europe, in council chambers, law courts, man-

King David (looking rather star-tled), after a fourteenth-century French illustration of the Nine Worthies. Notice that he bears his harp, a symbol that we shall be encountering later, as a heraldic emblem on his shield.

King Arthur and the emperor Charlemagne, after a fourteenth-century French illustration of the Nine Worthies. Note how Arthur holds a banner with three crowns, the flag of his kingdom of Logres, while Charlemagne supports a shield bearing the imperial eagle of the Holy Roman Empire and fleurs-de-lys, indicating his double role as Holy Roman Emperor and king of the Franks.

uscripts, tapestries, and frescoes, in books of heraldry once the printing press was invented, and of course, in French playing cards. In what has come to be known among playing-card historians as the standard Paris card pattern, the Kings are named after the Worthies Alexander, Caesar, Charlemagne, and David. These heroes were considered to represent the four great empires of the world's history as conceived in medieval times—those of the Greeks, Romans, Christians, and Jews. The Queens usually bear the names Rachel, Argine, Pallas, and Judith, while the Knaves are named Lancelot, Ogier, Paris, or Joan of Arc's champion La Hire, and Hector or Roland. Other playing-card patterns, such as the Rouen pattern, differ in their court card names, which tend to be—to quote playing-card historian Ronald Decker—"bewildering in their diversity, obscurity, and their very decipherment" and seem to reflect only the whim of the designer rather than an underlying theme like the Paris pattern's. However, understanding the relationship between the court cards and the Worthies illuminates much that has hitherto been obscure about their interpretations in cartomancy.

THE CREATION OF THE TAROT TRUMPS

Just what were the games being played with these fifty-six-card decks whose court cards bore the names of legendary heroes? Besides the trick-taking games mentioned by Rheinfelden in the 1370s, we know for a fact that in 1423 playing cards of some kind were commonly being used for gambling in northern Italy. The fire-and-brimstone monk Bernardino of Siena preached in Bologna at that time against cards—among other things—branding them an invention of the devil, and calling for the townsfolk to burn them in a "bonfire of vanities." The year 1423 is generally considered too early for these cards to have been tarots, but they were no doubt decks printed by woodblock on card—a process that had only just been invented—and hand colored by stencils, rather than the expensive hand-

Trump and court cards, after a fifteenth-century Italian wood-block imprint

painted decks favored by the nobility. Examples of the type of tarot card that just might have provoked the monk's pious indignation if they had existed this early can be seen in uncut sheet form in the National Gallery of Art in Washington DC and the Budapest Museum of Fine Arts.

On the other hand, Bernardino was probably railing against the regular decks of four-suited Italian cards, as it isn't until almost twenty years later that we find actual documented evidence of the existence of what we today think of as proper tarot cards.

The consensus among playing-card historians is that the twenty-two trump cards of the the tarot deck were introduced to add an extra dimension to the trick-taking game already in existence. We don't know exactly who created the first set of trumps or whether the earliest tarot decks were mass-produced in small numbers or created as one-off decks by individual artists. However, we do know that in the year 1442 an entry was made in a "wardrobe register," or account book, belonging to the aristocratic D'Este family in the Marquis of Mantua's court at Ferrara, referring specifically to the commissioning from a painter of four decks of *trionfi* (triumphs), containing "Cups, Swords, Coins, and Batons and all the figures of four packs of trump cards." Essentially, the trumps were an extra suit of twenty-two picture cards added on to the Italian suit cards, which, when played, could beat any card from any of the other four suits. Today the French and Italian words for a trump are *atout* and *atutti* (to all), perhaps implying their superiority to all the other suits. It was the addition of the trumps that changed the regular northern-Italian suited deck of fifty-six cards into a tarot pack.

Playing-card historians today favor the notion that costly tarot decks painted for educated northern-Italian nobility like the D'Estes and the Viscontis were the first to be produced, around 1445. From here their popularity would have spread to the lower ranks of society through the use of printing, first by woodblock, then by etched copperplate. On the other hand, the first tarot decks may actually have originated alongside the standard decks made for mass production sometime between 1440 and 1445, drawing on subject matter which at that time would have been perfectly recognizable to any card player. This is something we shall be looking at in greater detail later.

Art historians have long debated the identities of the designers of the exquisite, hand-painted tarot decks of the aristocracy of northern Italy. Today the painters Bonifacio Bembo and those working in the studio of the Zavattari brothers are among the favorite contenders, based on two distinct styles of painting that can be discerned in the Visconti-Sforza cards from Milan.

Michael Dummett, however, believes that the willingness of the Ferrarese D'Este family to entertain flights of fancy indicates that tarots may have originated in their court at Ferrara rather than among the Milanese Viscontis. The D'Este nobles involved themselves deeply in chivalric tales about Emperor Charlemagne's paladins, the mystique of which they tried to recapture in elaborate jousting tournaments as well as in the tarot cards they are known to have commissioned. The Museo delle Arti e delle Tradizioni Popolari in Rome possesses eight cards from a D'Este deck, one of which is a Lovers trump thought to depict Ruggiero, a mythical Saracen knight who converted to Christianity, embracing the equally mythical warrior maiden Bradamante, both of whom the D'Estes believed were their actual ancestors. Ruggiero and Bradamante's tale is recounted in Ludovico Ariosto's epic sixteenth-century sword-and-sorcery poem *Orlando furioso,* which embroiders on the Charlemagne legend but spreads its canvas farther south to include Italy as well as France and Germany.

Mars, after the fifteenth-century Mantegna engraving. The chariot he rides in appears to be the same chariot represented in the tarot trumps.

As with the D'Este cards, other Renaissance Italian card makers and their patrons initially illustrated their trumps with a variety of images different from those that are today considered the canonical sequence. The 1491 deck of the Sola-Busca family is a good example of this, featuring for their trumps a Fool and twenty-one warriors and kings from antiquity. So is the so-called Mantegna Tarot, a set of fifty tarot-type engravings once attributed to the illustrious artist Andrea Mantegna but now dated by art historians to about 1470 and thought to have been executed by an as yet unidentified Ferrarese engraver.

The German painter and engraver Albrecht Dürer, inspired by the Mantegna Tarot when he visited Italy in 1494, produced several tarot images of his own two years later, interpreting them in a characteristic Gothic style. We shall be returning to the "Mantegna" images later when we study tarot's uses as an instrument of divination.

TAROT IN THE SIXTEENTH CENTURY

Early in the sixteenth century, tarot cards began to be referred to in Italy as *tarocchi* (plural of *tarocco*), and the word *trionfi* disappears from documented reference. Italian playing-card collector Andrea Pollett suggests that the term *tarocco*, which has long perplexed playing-card historians, derives from the archaic Italian verb *taroccare*, which he associates with the Arabic word *taraqa* (to hammer). According to Pollett, *taroccare* referred to a technique that goldsmiths employed to cover a surface with gold leaf and then hammer diamond-shaped patterns into it, a technique used in many of the backgrounds of the Visconti cards and others.

In 1534 the French satirist Francois Rabelais referred to a game he called *tarau* in a list of games played by Gargantua, a character in one of his novels, indicating that the Italian word *tarocco* had begun its transformation into what today we know as *tarot*. In fact, during the sixteenth century the game of tarot spread beyond northern Italy and became popular throughout France, Switzerland, Belgium, and Spain. The French towns Rouen and Lyons printed literally thousands of decks from woodblocks in

*Trump cards, after a fifteenth-century wood-block imprint (probably Milanese).
Notice the figure of the cleric reading a book at the top left. This could well be the
Female Pope disguised as a young man.*

what has come to be known today as the Marseille pattern. One of the earliest, Milanese, prototypes of this pattern may today be seen in the Cary Collection at Yale University, an uncut partial sheet of fifteenth-century wood-block printed cards. The pattern was possibly introduced to France from Milan by French soldiers returning from the French occupation of the city sometime between 1494 and 1525.

Because it was so widely reproduced, the Marseille pattern represents what most people today would regard as the conventional tarot deck: fifty-six cards in four suits (Coins, Cups, Swords, and Batons), each of which contains fourteen cards—ten "pips" numbered from ace to ten and the four court cards, Knave, Knight, Queen, and King. To these are added twenty-one roman-numbered pictorial trumps (the Juggler, Female Pope, Empress, Emperor, Pope, Lovers, Chariot, Justice, Hermit, Wheel of Fortune, Fortitude, Hanged Man, Death, Temperance, Devil, Tower, Star, Moon, Sun, World, and Judgment) and one unnumbered trump (the Fool). Indeed, the trump cards of the famous deck designed by Pamela Colman Smith for A. E. Waite in 1909 are based upon the Marseille pattern.

Prior to the sixteenth century, however, the tarot trumps were uncaptioned and inconsistently numbered. Presumably, tarot players were expected to remember trump names and order. Only with the arrival of the seventeenth century do we find trump cards with names regularly printed underneath the image and a roman numeral at the top, providing an explicit sequence for the novice player. Thereafter, while some card makers bowed to pressure from the church and attempted to find substitutes for what censorious Catholic authorities considered to be the offensive images of the Emperor, Empress, Female Pope, and Pope, generally speaking, the form and order of the trump sequence when used in game playing has remained more or less consistent over the centuries.

FURTHER DEVELOPMENTS

During the sixteenth century the card makers of Florence created another important deck of playing cards that made use of tarot imagery. Known as *minchiate,* these decks diverged in various ways from tarocchi. To begin, several of the tarocchi trumps were replaced. The vexatious card known as the Female Pope became a less controversial Grand Duke, the Empress became a Western Emperor, the Emperor an Eastern Emperor, and the Fool vanished altogether. In addition, the minchiate introduced cards representing the twelve signs of the zodiac, the four Pythagorean elements—earth, air, fire, and water—and four of the traditional Seven Virtues apparently missing from the tarocchi, namely Prudence, Faith, Hope, and Charity. I say "apparently" because, as we shall see, it may turn out that Prudence was present in disguise, operating under an assumed identity. These additional trumps were shoehorned in near the end of the

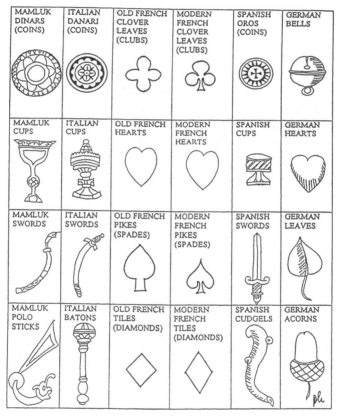

Mamlûk suit signs and their European derivatives. It's customary among historians to derive the trèfle, *the cloverleaf French suit sign that we call a Club, from the Italian Baton. However, it's my belief (along with cartomancers of the French school) that it's far more likely that the cross-shaped Clover Leaf represented the pattern to be found on the interior of the Italian Coin. As for the reason the Diamond developed from the Baton, you'll have to read the section dealing with the suit of Batons in chapter 5 to discover that!*

usual tarot trump sequence, swelling the minchiate decks to a hefty ninety-seven cards. Like the tarot, of which it was a variation, the minchiate game consisted of trick taking. Each card had a specific numerical value assigned to it. The sum total of the card values within the tricks taken by each player was toted up at the end of every game to determine the winner. Although the zodiac and the elements frequently assume an important place in European esoteric systems, their incorporation as extra trumps into the minchiate seems simply to have been a means to add complexity to the game rather than to endow it with any special esoteric significance.

Meanwhile, alongside the development of tarocchi, minchiate, and French and Belgian tarots, playing cards continued to evolve. German card makers crafted exquisitely engraved decks of various descriptions, and decks of cards using the so-called French suit signs—Clubs, Hearts, Spades, and Diamonds—were becoming increasingly popular. Partially, this popularity must be attributed to the economics of mass production: the French suit signs were far simpler and less work-intensive to produce than the engraved, hand-tinted ones, requiring only forty stenciled suit cards and twelve printed and stenciled court cards.

French cards using the Rouen pattern had been introduced to England around 1450, although they all but disappeared during Oliver Cromwell's Protectorate during the seventeenth century. Indeed, Cromwell's game-hating puritans considered card play an invention of the devil, believing the court cards to be "idols and false gods; which since [the card makers] would seem Christians, [they] have changed to Charlemaigne, Launcelot, Hector and such like names. "

After the puritans were swept from power in 1659, English playing cards made their appearance once more, again using the French suits. These would evolve into the familiar, stylized pattern of "regular" playing cards in use all over the world today.

This then, in much-abbreviated form, is what we know about the documented history of the pre occult tarot. Today, aside from the decks produced for divination, tarot cards still exist in a variety of regional forms: French, Italian, Sicilian, Swiss, Belgian, and German. These decks are still in use as game cards. In many cases the Italian suit signs have been exchanged for the French variety and the original trumps' designs replaced by pictures of animals or scenes from nineteenth-century family life, as in the modern French tarot or the German and Hungarian card decks known as *Tarock*.

From the point of view of the first tarot readers, whoever they may have been, it was the old imagery that was worth close attention. Much like their ancient Chinese forerunners, the medieval and renaissance patterns became invested with elaborate occult and talismanic values. Divination being a large subject, we shall go into that in greater depth later. Indeed, the story of tarot's evolution doesn't end at the point we're leaving it here. We'll be picking up the thread again in chapter 3, where tarot moves into the arcane world of eighteenth- and nineteenth-century occultists who rediscovered the tarot and put it to use for their own purposes. For now we'll turn our attention to finding out exactly what the original tarot card imagery may have meant. We shall discover that there may be more of the genuinely magical and mystical about some of the cards' original roots than was ever dreamed of by those latter-day occult philosophers. Our quest will lead us to the very portals of the fire temples of ancient Persia.

1

THE ORIGIN
OF THE SUIT SIGNS

Before we explore the original meanings of the tarot trumps, we should attend to the riddle that, historically speaking, first presented itself: the origin of the suit cards, or as tarot readers refer to them, the Minor Arcana (*arcana* being a term meaning "secrets" introduced to tarot in 1870 by the journalist and occultist Jean-Baptiste Pitois, writing under the pseudonym of Paul Christian).

What significance did the Italian and French suit signs have when they were first introduced, if they had any at all and weren't just random, handy tokens for differentiating four sequences of cards with which to play games? Were the suits just arbitrarily plucked out of thin air, or is there something more profound to them?

Aside from various facetious or hostile interpretations that have been proposed down the centuries—facetious or hostile on account of playing cards' association with gambling—the first serious attempt to attach a meaning to the four suits was made in 1704 by Claude-François Ménestrier, a Jesuit antiquarian from Lyons.

This avid iconologist was responsible for the idea, still current among some playing-card enthusiasts, that the French suits reflected the feudal social structure of Europe in the late Middle Ages and early Renaissance. In Ménestrier's analysis, the suit of Hearts represented the church, Spades (Pikes) the arms-bearing aristocracy, Diamonds (Paving Tiles) the merchant class, and Clubs (Trefoils) the peasantry. Given that Johannes von Rheinfelden had associated card play with the feudal structure of medieval society in his fourteenth-century treatise, Ménestrier's theory might seem plausible. However, Rheinfelden is just as likely to have been referring to the internal hierarchical structure of the suits—from the lowest Ace to the highest King—as a reflection of feudal society rather than to any hierarchical structure ascribable to the suit signs themselves.

Furthermore, Ménestrier was unaware that the French suits were a fairly new invention that had been derived, via the Italian suit signs, from those of the Mamlûk packs. Nonetheless, Ménestrier's interpretation was so widely accepted that the matter of the suits' meanings remained unquestioned until it passed into the hands of eighteenth- and nineteenth-century students of the occult, whose ideas, it now turns out, don't stand up to close scrutiny, either.

Probably the most important and persistent of these later notions dates from the end of the nineteenth century, when it became popular to interpret the suit signs in light of a supposed connection between Celtic mythology and the European Grail and Arthurian cycles.

According to proponents of this theory, the four magical talismans that belonged to the pagan gods of Irish Celtic legend—the cauldron of the Dagda, the sword of Nuada, the stone of Fál, and the spear of Lugh—are considered the prototypes of certain talismanic objects that appear in medieval tales concerning the Holy Grail, that elusive object often described as the legendary chalice with which Jesus was said to have celebrated his Last Supper and which was subsequently used to collect his blood as he hung dying on the cross. In these tales, which are usually quests interwoven into the medieval stories of King Arthur and his Knights of the Round Table, the Holy Grail is frequently borne by a procession of maidens carrying three other ritualistic objects. Proponents of the "Celtic" theory maintain that these objects—said to be a dish, a sword, and the spear that the centurion Longinus thrust into Jesus's body on the cross to ensure his death—evolved from the four Celtic talismans.

However, the notion that there were exactly four sacred objects, "Hallows" as the writer and mystic A. E. Waite dubbed them, in the Grail procession is contested by scholars today. There is no dish or sword in some accounts of the legend. In others there are more than four ritual objects, including candlesticks, knives, and lamps. Furthermore, when it comes to correlating the Celtic/Grail objects and the tarot suit signs, a dish is not really a coin (or a stone, for that matter), nor is a spear a baton. Finally, the idea that the talismans of Celtic legend or, indeed, the Grail legend should have given rise to the tarot suit signs must now be considered untenable in view of their recently proven derivation from the Mamlûk deck.

Another enticing theory about the suits' origins was that propounded by Jessie Weston, an Arthurian scholar at the turn of the century. Partly persuaded by Waite's beliefs about the subject, she maintained that the tarot suits were evidence of the survival of a secret pagan cult into the Middle Ages, a thesis she set forth in her popular book *From Ritual to Romance*. Waite, however, took issue with her on this, hinting that the source of the symbols probably lay in the unorthodox Christianity of the Albigensian heretics of the thirteenth century, which he also associated with the Grail. Neither Weston nor Waite offered any evidence for their conclusions, however.

Although these theories have not withstood the test of time, the Grail theme has entered today's cartomantic idea pool, largely due to the important part it plays in the imagery of the immensely influential tarot deck designed to Waite's specifications that we shall encounter later. Accordingly, tenuous and unsupported though these Grail links with the tarot may be, I shall be touching on them from time to time when we examine card interpretations.

Now, having surveyed some of the historically discredited theories of the suits' origins, maybe we should start our quest for the suit signs where they first appear in recorded history, where the Mamlûk deck led us.

Those polo sticks, for instance.

We will recall that the four Mamlûk suits consisted of Cups, Coins, Polo-sticks and Swords. Now, Polo-sticks happen to figure prominently as marks of distinction in Mamlûk heraldry. Coats of arms were among the prerogatives of the military dignitaries known as *emirs* in Mamlûk culture. Although the coat of arms itself was bestowed by the sultan on the emir, the emir was allowed to choose his design for himself. Among the many and varied marks of distinction used in these Mamlûk coats of arms were indeed cups, indicative of service as a cup-bearer, round disks or plates, indicative of service as a taster, polo-sticks, for service as a polo-master, and swords as the emblem of an armor-bearer.

So taken at face value, these heraldic emblems would appear to be the most obvious explanation of the Tarot suits. Or would they? Why choose those particular emblems to mark the suits, one finds oneself wondering? Was it simply the artististic whim of the card maker, anticipating the diverse choice of suits that would later appear on early German playing cards? But if that were the case, then why do we not find more varied suits among Mamlûk decks made by other card makers, bearing emblems other than just these four; such as the equally popular heraldic emblems saddles, pen-boxes, napkins or bows, for instance? Why would these four and just these four be chosen to become what we might call the "standard Mamlûk pattern?" Maybe some further meaning underlay their selection. Maybe we should delve a little deeper into the sources of the symbols themselves. So, once again, let us turn to those Polo-sticks.

SUFIS AND THE SUIT SIGNS

The word *polo* is believed to derive from a Tibetan word, *pulu* (ball). Earliest records of the game indicate that it was played by Persian tribes sometime before King Darius I and his troops formed the first great Persian Empire in the sixth century B.C.E.

Darius I of Persia, "the Great King." Also referred to as "the King of Kings," Darius was one of the seven Persian princes who agreed that he should be king whose horse was the first to neigh.

From Persia, polo spread to Constantinople, then Turkestan, and on to India and the Far East. The game migrated to Egypt with the Arab conquests of the eighth century C.E. and became an integral part in court life there. The polo stick became an important motif in Islamic heraldry, and in the sect of Shi'ah Muslims that came to be known as Sufis.

In its evolution, Sufism was influenced by a variety of doctrines besides Islam: early Christian monasticism, the Indian Buddhism that flourished throughout the East long before the conquest of Islam, and Greek and Roman Neoplatonic philosophy, which entered Islam around 800 C.E. The pantheistic type of Sufism that came to prevail in Persia emphasized mysticism—ecstatic and visionary experience. The Deity was seen as the sole reality, beyond all names and definitions. Not only was It considered absolute being, It was also considered to be absolute good and absolute beauty, too. The very nature of beauty was believed to consist of the desire for manifestation, and the cosmos itself was thought to be the result of this desire. Well-known Sufi tradition has the Deity say, "I was a hidden treasure, and I desired to be known, so I created creatures in order that I might be known."

Arifi of Herat, a fifteenth-century Sufi, entitled a book about ecstatic, self-sacrificing love *The Ball and the Polo Stick,* and he uses the game of polo as an allegory for his mystical teachings. The *Rubaiyat* quatrains of the eleventh-century Sufi poet and Persian astronomer-mathematician

Omar Khayyám also allude to the game of polo to illustrate the helplessness of humankind, humanity being the ball, and fate or the Deity the polo player and his stick:

> *The Ball no question makes of Ayes and Noes,*
> *But Here or There as strikes the Player goes;*
> *And He that toss'd you down into the Field,*
> *He knows about it all—HE knows—HE knows!*

Other suit sign images also occur in the *Rubaiyat*. The cup image is used repeatedly throughout the poem, and it is an evocative, powerful icon. In a couple of instances, the allusion is made to the magic seven-ringed cup that belonged to the legendary Persian king Jamshid, in which past, present, future—indeed everything in the world—was revealed to him. Coins are also alluded to when the poet judges "money, better than a thousand promises" and equates coins to "a cup, a lover, and music on the field's verge" to be grasped today rather than exchanged for the vague promise of heaven later. Actual money, moreover, is to be spent on friends rather than hoarded and left behind for one's enemies.

Are these intriguing images proof that the Sufi culture can claim to have originated the suit signs of the Mamlûk cards? The Sufi writer Sayed Idries Shah claimed that the tarot had Sufi roots, although he failed to give any convincing details to substantiate his claim. On the other hand, polo predated the Sufis, so the suit symbols may have a much earlier, Persian, provenance.

Moreover, as I mentioned earlier, the word *tûmân* as applied to the Mamlûk Cup suit appears to derive, somewhat confusingly it would seem, from the Persian word *tûmân*, meaning "ten thousand." According to the renowned fourteenth-century Moorish scholar and historian of the Islamic Empire Abd-ar-Rahman ibn Khaldûn, the *dînâr* (the Mamlûk Coin symbol) was a gold coin at the time he was writing. In fact the *tûmân* was said to be worth ten thousand *danânîr* (plural of *dînâr*), which seems to be quite a substantial amount of money. By the 1890s, however, the *tûmân*'s exchange value appears to have dwindled to an amount worth about six British shillings; use of the coin was ultimately discontinued in 1932. So apparently the term *tûmân* points to the use of the deck for gambling rather than to the Cup symbol itself.

Yet such linguistic clues alone cannot place the Persians at the scene of suit origins. To accomplish this, we must refer to a Platonist and traveling lecturer of the second century C.E. who provides us with an unexpected nugget of what may turn out to be golden information. It will involve us in a lightning-quick tour to Africa, Italy, France, ancient Greece, and back to Persia once more.

THE FOUR CARDINAL VIRTUES

Around the year 160 C.E. in the North African city of Oea, Apuleius of Madaura, author of the famous magical romance *The Golden Ass,* was forced to defend himself on a charge of sorcery that had been cooked up to bolster a dubious lawsuit against him and that used his known interest in the occult sciences as a smear tactic.

Apuleius quoted Plato in his defense, who stated that "magic" (which Plato defined as the legitimate worship of the gods performed by the Zoroastrian Magian priests of his era) was taught to young Persian crown princes by four tutors, each chosen from among all the other Persian elders for his outstanding display of virtue. The important point for our purposes is that, of these tutors, one was considered the wisest elder, one the most just, one the most restrained, and one the bravest.

If one pauses to consider, it becomes evident that Apuleius's elders are the exemplars of what later came to be known as the Four Cardinal Virtues: Prudence (Wisdom), Justice, Temperance (Restraint), and Fortitude (Bravery or Strength). Now it also happens that the symbols most frequently associated with the Cardinal Virtues from classical times

The Four Cardinal Virtues depicted as winged angels, after Luca della Robbia

through the Middle Ages into the Renaissance are identical with the four suit signs of the Italian tarocchi, something first noted, as far as I am aware, by Gertrude Moakley, a scholar whose important contributions to tarot research we shall be glancing at in the following chapter. You may see the symbols displayed, among other places, by the fifteenth-century ceramicist Luca della Robbia on the ceiling of the Cardinal of Portugal's chapel in the beautiful Florentine church of San Miniato al Monte. In each of the four corners of the vaulted ceiling, an angel carries one emblem apiece: the circular mirror (Coin) of the Cardinal Virtue Prudence; the sword of Justice; the cup of Temperance; and the rod of Fortitude.

That this attribution of the virtues to the suits was not just an Italian conceit but current in other parts of Europe, too, is suggested by a popular sixteenth-century book of games, *Cento giuochi liberali et d'igegno* (One Hundred Liberal and Ingenious Games). Authored by one Innocenzio Ringhieri, it was dedicated to the subsequently famous Italian princess from Florence who married into the French royal family, Catherine de Médicis. (As Queen of France, she was later to place her fate entirely in the hands of diviners like Nostradamus and the astrologer Luca Ganrico.)

First printed in Bologna in 1551, Ringhieri's manual was reprinted in Venice and in French translation in Lyons in 1553, then again in Bologna in 1580. It detailed a hundred games and entertainments that made use of dice, chess, and playing cards, including some with such intriguing names as *delle figure Celesti* (dealing with astrological signs) or—alarmingly—*dell Incantatore o dell Serpi* (dealing with snake charming) or *del Chiromante* (dealing with palm reading) or, most intriguing of all, *dell'Inferno* (dealing with hell)! More important for us, however, is the game the book describes as the Magnificent Game of the King, which involves using Italian playing cards in which the suits are considered to represent the Cardinal Virtues. As we might expect, Mirrors (Coins) are said to stand for Prudence, Swords for Justice, Cups for Temperance, and Columns for Fortitude.

Perhaps even more significantly, the Nine Worthies that we encountered in the previous chapter were considered to be the medieval embodiments of the virtues: Fighting Spirit (Fortitude), Wisdom (Prudence), Law (Justice), and Civility (Temperance). Indeed, the Four Cardinal Virtues were thought to be the essential ingredients of *prouesse,* which doesn't mean just "prowess" but something far more elevated and spiritual than mere machismo, namely, the highest goal aimed at by the medieval knight. Furthermore, the Cardinal Virtues turn out to be an important theme that runs through the Major Arcana of the tarot deck.

So we must pose the question, if the Cardinal Virtues are so important to our argument, where did they originate?

Most historians ascribe their source, prior to their adoption into Christianity by the Dominican scholar Thomas Aquinas, to Greek philosophy. Writing in the fourth century B.C.E., Plato assembles the Cardinal Virtues into a unit in his *Laws* and *Republic:* "Wisdom [Prudence] is the chief and leader," he writes, "next follows Temperance, and from the union of these two with Courage [Fortitude] springs Justice." Aristotle, Plato's pupil, added variations of his own. Philo of Alexandria, the Jewish Platonist philosopher of the first century C.E., compared them to the four rivers that ran out of Eden, which is poetic and maybe esoterically meaningful, but hardly helpful in pinpointing the virtues' geographical source.

However, if we assume that Apuleius quoted Plato correctly, it is conceivable the four virtues predate Greek philosophy, and the Great King of the Persians had to possess all four in good measure if he were to effectually govern. And that assertion brings us back to the Persian Empire once more.

THE FOUR CASTES OF ANCIENT PERSIA

The Persian Empire of the Achaemenids was founded around 550 B.C.E. on the ruins of the Assyrian Empire, in the geographical area we know today as Iraq and Iran. Vast and all-encompassing, it reached from Egypt in the west to the river Indus in the east. Twenty-nine years after the empire's founding, Darius I, known to history as Darius the Great, became Persia's first "Great King." Zoroastrianism, said to have been inculcated by the prophet Zoroaster or Zarathustra, became Persia's official religion. After the Arab conquest of Persia in 642 C.E., the practice of Zoroastrianism and a variety of other religions such as Buddhism, Judaism, and Christianity continued to exist alongside the dominant religion of Islam. This state of affairs lasted into the seventeenth century.

Indeed, there exists a highly informative seventeenth-century Persian text that goes by the name *Dabistan-ul-mazahab,* a translation of which was published in 1901 under the title *The School of Manners,* although *School of Religious Doctrines* would perhaps have been more appropriate. The English translators of the text believed the author to be Mohsan Fani, a Sufi of Persian extraction living in India and born around 1615 C.E. However, Joseph H. Peterson, who has written extensively on religious and esoteric traditions, ascribes the book to the pen of a seventeenth-century Persian, a

Shi'ah mullah named Mir Du'l-fequar Ardestani, whom Peterson believes based it on the teachings of Azar Kayvan, a sixteenth-century Zoroastrian high priest.

Be that as it may, whoever wrote the *Dabistan* presents sketches of what he considered were the great religions currently being practiced in Persia during the seventeenth century. Most pertinent for us is the account of Magism, that is, Zoroastrianism, which, as we have noted, had its beginnings in the seventh or sixth century B.C.E. and had survived in Persia since that time.

Fani/Ardestani begins his account of Zoroastrianism by recounting, among other things, the exploits of the legendary culture hero of the Persians, Mahabad, exploits lost in the depths of mythological time. To Mahabad he attributes the organization of cities, villages, streets, colonnades, and palaces, the introduction of commerce and trade, and the division of humankind into four classes or castes. These were:

Class 1: The priestly class of Magi. This was divided into *Hirbeds* or disciples, *Mobeds* or masters, and *Destur Mobeds,* masters of masters. The author of the *Dabistan* describes this class as ascetics and learned men, selected for maintaining the faith and enforcing the sentence of the laws; he also refers to them as *Húristár, Birman,* and *Birmun.*

Class 2: Kings and intrepid warriors, chosen to devote themselves to the cares of government and authority, to promoting equity, policing, and curbing aggression. Members of this caste are named *Núristár, Chatraman,* and *Chatri,* which words are said to mean "standard" or "distinction."

Class 3: Farmers, cultivators, artisans and skillful men, styled *Súristár* or *Bas,* said to imply "cultivation" and "improvement."

Class 4: The *Rúzistár* or *Sudin,* composed of people destined for "employment" and "service."

The *Dabistan* is quite obviously describing a social system with remarkable similarity to the four castes of Hinduism, a concept that the Persian religion apparently shared with its Hindu cousin. We know that the Persian tribe of the Magians, referred to as *Húristár* by the *Dabistan,* functioned as officiating clergy in the Persian Empire, essential to the fire cult of the god Ahuramazda, "the Wise Lord." By all accounts, they performed the sacrifices, prophesied the future, made libations, and chanted the invocations and theogonies of the deity. They wore white robes, with fur caps peaked

A Persian magus, after a Zoroastrian votive plaque from around the seventh century B.C.E. Notice the ceremonial rods of office he carries.

forward, and carried bundles of rods in their hands as their symbols of office.

Is it possible that the *Húristár,* these wise and ascetic magi who enforced the sentence of law, came to be represented by the rods that they carried, something that may be borne out by their carved representations such as the one in the figure above? And might it be that the *Núristár,* who promoted equity, were represented by a sword or scimitar; that the *Súristár,* who cultivated and improved, were represented by a cup; and the *Rúzistár,* who served, by a coin? Do these classes of Persian society constitute the origins of the four virtues in which the young kings of Persia had to be schooled? Have we found, in fact, the origins of the Four Cardinal Virtues and their symbols? If so, then the four Italian suit signs might well acquire a fairly ancient provenance, ironically of a quite literally Magian, and therefore "magical," origin.

The question nevertheless remains: how were these archaic symbols transmitted to the Mamlûk antecedents of our playing cards? We don't know. However, we can theorize again.

The Mamlûk deck from the Topkapi museum can be dated to the fifteenth century C.E. Earlier examples of Mamlûk cards are now known to exist, but only as isolated cards. They can, however, be dated to somewhere between the twelfth and thirteenth centuries. Now, under Islamic rule Persia emerged as a major cultural center between the eleventh and thirteenth centuries. Although disrupted by savage Mongol invasions in the thirteenth and fourteenth centuries, Muslim rule was later reestablished under the auspices of the Ottomans in Asia Minor and Egypt and the Safafids in Persia. So it may well be that the Mongols were responsible for introducing Chinese playing cards to Persia in the first half of the thirteenth century.

It is also conceivable that the Persians, who already possessed playing-card games known as *As-nâs* and *Ganjifa,* created the prototype of the Mamlûk decks by substituting the symbols corresponding to the four classes of ancient Persian society for the money signs found on the Chinese gambling cards used by the Mongols. When this new four-suited Persian card game ultimately spread through the Islamic world in much the same manner that the game of chess is known to have done, the symbolic rods of the Magian priests would have been exchanged in the Mamlûk decks for more familiar polo sticks, in much the same manner that the Mamlûk polo sticks were later transformed (back!) into batons by European card makers. Only the Shi'ah Sufis, with their ties to pre-Islamic Persia and their penchant for religious eclecticism, would seem to have preserved the import of the polo stick as a symbol of divine power, as witnessed in the works of Arifi and Omar Khayyám. Indeed, the fact that the Sufis were not only familiar with, but in accord with, certain Zoroastrian beliefs is hinted at in the the description of the wine that Omar Khayyám drinks, which in Islam is a forbidden drink, so is referred to as "Magian," that is, pertaining to the Zoroastrians, who were permitted to drink it.

Whether the Persian origin of the European suit signs can ultimately be proven or not, it's interesting to note that both this theory and Ménestrier's align the suits' symbols with hierarchical social classes. It is also true that both theories beg further investigation for evidence of their validity. However, cartomancers may note that if the suit symbols are indeed of Zoroastrian provenance, they may also carry an association with the four elements held sacred by the Magian priests, fire, air, water, and earth.

And if, for the sake of argument, we say that the four standard Italian suit signs of the tarot represent the four Pythagorean elements, what would a fifth suit, if we may refer to the tarot trumps as that, be said to represent other than the mysterious fifth element—quintessence—a notion current among fifteenth-century Italian students of Neoplatonic philosophy? In Pythagorian terms we would be talking here about the element of the ether or spirit, the fifth point of the pentagram that rules the other four, the archetypal, spiritual world that lies above and below the world of appearances. This is, in fact, a concept we shall see amply illustrated in the following chapter, where we shall discover how spiritual and indeed, quite literally, "mysterious" the trumps really were.

2

THE ORIGIN
OF THE TRUMPS

Historians have long quibbled over whether the twenty-two trumps of the tarot were initially created as a sequence by themselves—as a separate card game perhaps—or were added on ad hoc to the Italian deck of fifty-six to make an existing game more complex.

Judging from the facts that no decks consisting solely of twenty-two trumps have survived and that the early uncut printed sheets of tarot cards and various Visconti and D'Este painted decks all show trumps and suit cards united, it seems more likely that somebody had the bright idea of making the regular game of fifty-six Mamlûk-derived playing cards more complex by adding to it twenty-one special, high-ranking cards (and one special nonranking card).

Whether it was an unknown wood engraver and card maker or Bembo himself or artists from the Zavattari studio or someone in the Visconti court who provided the idea of the trump suit, we don't yet know. Nor do we know who selected the cards' imagery. However, whoever he or she was, the inventor may (or may not) have had a fondness for the works of the Italian writer Giovanni Boccaccio and his friend, the poet and humanist scholar Francesco Petrarca, otherwise known to us as Petrarch.

In 1966, then New York Public Library cataloger Gertrude Moakley followed up a clue provided by Alessandro di Francesco Rosselli, a sixteenth-century Florentine dealer in graphic arts. Rosselli had declared in his catalog of 1528 that aside from other card games, he also stocked *The Game of the Triumphs of Petrarch*. Moakley advanced the ingenious theory that Rosselli was actually referring to tarot cards and that the title of the game derives from *I trionfi* (The Triumphs), the name of a poem written between 1352 and 1374 by Petrarch. As a matter of fact, it turns out that the poet did have a special relationship with the Visconti court, which may or not be significant.

PETRARCH'S *I TRIONFI*

Born in 1304 in Arezzo, Italy, the son of a legal clerk who was exiled for political reasons, Francesco Petrarch spent his early life at Avignon in France, at that time the seat of the papacy. Although he followed his father's wishes and studied law at Montpellier and Bologna, Petrarch's burning passion was literature, and particularly the study of Latin literature—an interest he shared with his friend Giovanni Boccaccio. As a talented and dedicated scholar and poet, Petrarch attracted international fame and in 1341 was crowned with the laurel wreath of Poet Laureate in Rome. In Avignon, Petrarch wrote numerous sonnets, the most famous being a series of love poems addressed to an idealized but unattainable married nineteen-year-old woman, Laura de Noves, who died of the plague during the Black Death in 1348.

Petrarch led a wandering life, moving from city to city searching out Latin manuscripts and writing his essays, poems, and letters. In 1353 he settled for a while in Milan and lived as the guest of the powerful Visconti family. It was there that he began composing the poem entitled *I trionfi* in 1356, again on the theme of his undying love for Laura, continuing to work on and revise it until his death eighteen years later in 1374.

Now, fourteenth-century Italians used the term *triumphs* to describe the decorated floats or pageant carts that were drawn in procession through streets at religious or secular festivals. These processional triumphs generally illustrated allegorical themes. Each successive allegory won or "triumphed" over the one illustrated by the previous float.

There are six allegorical triumph carts in Petrarch's poem. The first is a traveling float illustrating the triumph of Cupid over men and gods, representing the triumph of love, notably Petrarch's own love for Laura. Cupid's triumph is followed by the triumph of chastity over Cupid and fickle fortune, illustrating Laura's chaste and proper refusal of Petrarch's love (she was a married woman, after all). The third float in the procession illustrates the awful triumph of death over Laura during the plague; the fourth, the triumph of Laura's bright fame over grim death; the fifth, the inevitable triumph of Old Man Time over Laura's fame; and the sixth and ultimate triumph, the triumph of eternity over time, in which Laura and Petrarch are finally able to enjoy everlasting bliss together.

Many paintings and engravings have been created illustrating *I trionfi* since the poem was first published, although none that I know of have utilized all the images that appear in it. The images that do appear in illustrations, however, are highly suggestive of some of the tarot trumps.

Gertrude Moakley's association of the tarot trumps with *I trionfi* is extremely persuasive, although it doesn't solve all the riddles of the trumps, at least not those of the Marseille-pattern deck. Petrarch's poem accounts for the trumps Love, Temperance, Fortune (the Chariot), the Pope, Emperor, Empress, Death, Time (the Hermit), Hades (the Devil), the "Quick Revolving Wheel" (the Wheel of Fortune), the Sun, the Moon, and Eternity (the World). Unaccounted for are the images of the three virtues, the Fool, the Juggler, the Female Pope, the Hanged Man, the Tower, the Star, and Judgment.

However, Petrarch's works may nevertheless turn out to be important in our search for the source of all the trumps, even if *I trionfi* cannot be said to have given rise to them all. What Moakley did not develop in her theory is the fact that Petrarch also authored a variety of other books, one dealing with the Four Cardinal Virtues and another, *De hominis illustribus* (About Illustrious Men), chronicling the pontificates and reigns of various Roman emperors and popes, including, in passing, the legendary pontificate of Pope Joan. Unfortunately, even if we posit that the trump images were taken from the collected works of Petrarch and maybe Boccaccio, the Fool, the Juggler, the Hanged Man, the Tower, the Star, and Judgment are still unaccounted for. What source could these possibly have?

Rather than rummage through recondite symbolisms like those of alchemy or astrology as has been the custom among tarot sleuths in the past, I propose that we turn our attention entirely in the opposite direction and search for these images in far more obvious places. Specifically, we must look at what one might call the mass entertainment of that era: the medieval drama, from where, as we shall see, Petrarch obviously drew the "triumph" conceit for his poem in the first place. As Glynne Wickham notes of the era in his *History of the Theatre:* "Echoing in some respects a Roman 'triumph,' these pageant theatres (superbly illustrated in Italy by Mantegna, Petrarch, and others) became a commonplace from the Atlantic seaboard to the Baltic."

It is these pageant theaters, rather than Petrarch's works, that unlock the riddle of the origin of the trump cards. I shall describe the plays that were performed in them in some detail, to demonstrate just how illuminating they become when placed in context with the cards.

MEDIEVAL DRAMA

In early Christian Europe, the problem of how best to proselytize the illiterate Teutonic and Celtic masses became a major headache for Pope Gregory the Great and his missionaries from Rome. Aside from incorporating old pagan beliefs and practices into the fabric of the new Christian religion, one of the chief ideas suggested to Gregory by his advisor Augustine was to use the arts to capture the people's imaginations—the architecture, sculpture, and paintings of cathedrals, the poetry and music of the liturgical rituals. In the ninth and tenth centuries, drama was added to the list of inducements, primarily through the offices of the Benedictine monasteries that developed it. And this is where we discover the location of our genuine tarot "mysteries."

Mystery Plays

Most historians concede that Christian mystery plays were the first and most important of the forms that medieval drama took. Some derive the term *mystery*, not from anything to do with secrets, but rather—like the French word *mystère*—from the Latin *ministerium*, meaning a church service; others believe it stems from the French word *métier*, meaning the function of the craft guilds who referred to their trades as "mysteries" and who performed the mystery plays when they ultimately passed into secular hands.

The mystery play originated in the practice of setting the Christian liturgy to music to be sung antiphonally, that is, in the form of a dialog between two sections of the choir. For example, one half of a Benedictine choir might sing the introductory words of the Easter Mass: "Quem quaeretis in sepulchro?" (Whom do you seek in the tomb?)—the angel's question to the two Marys when they came searching for Jesus' body on Easter Sunday—and the other half would respond. These antiphons were performed first in Switzerland, France, and England. However, it did not take the church long to discover that this kind of musical entertainment proved popular and instructive. Plays could be written to fit other liturgical events too, such as Christmas, the adoration of the Magi at Epiphany, and Jesus' ascension into heaven. And so mystery plays came to be performed annually, growing in complexity over the years by the addition of new scenes and material.

By the thirteenth century, the story they unfolded was that of man's creation, fall, and redemption as portrayed in the Christian liturgical year. In every year's drama, Lucifer would be cast out of heaven, Eve would be created from Adam's rib, and the tree of knowledge would be transformed into the cross at Calvary. Jesus would be born and adored by the Three Wise Kings following their star; he would perform his miracles and die on the cross betrayed by Judas. The Marys would weep. Jesus would descend into hell to smash down its doors, defeat Satan, and release the unredeemed from limbo. He would then rise dramatically from the tomb to ascend to heaven in his mandorla—the almond-shaped nimbus of light that frequently surrounds the figure of the glorified or ascended Christ in liturgical art—to join God the Father and the Holy Spirit in order to judge all of those who had been subjected to the tyranny of death—popes, emperors, lovers, warriors, hermits, beggars, and even jugglers.

By the early fourteenth century, when Petrarch and Boccaccio would have been able to witness them, these dramas were being performed by secular tradesmen as well as by the clergy. While the plays were still performed in churches, the secular productions were loaded onto huge wagons called pageant carts that rumbled off to open areas like marketplaces. There the plays, in chronological order, would be enacted, pageant after pageant, beginning with the biblical creation of the world and ending with the Last Judgment. In Italy, the land of Petrarch's birth, these pageant wagons came to be referred to as trionfi.

According to Martial Rose, who researched and restaged mystery plays in the 1960s, the pageant carts would be led through four or five gaps in an outdoor circular auditorium of raked bleachers. Those representing heaven and hell would be brought into position first and left in place through the entire performance.

These wagons were two-tiered towers. On heaven's battlements Jehovah, the archangels, and the angelic choir would appear. On hell's tower the devils would set watch on the battlements during the "Harrowing" play. Beneath or beside hell's tower, limbo would be located, represented as a grating or prison. (In Roman Catholic theology, limbo was a region between heaven and hell to which were consigned the souls of men who died before the coming of Christ, and those of infants who died before baptism.) Close to limbo would be placed the gaping jaws of Hell-Mouth—a dragon's head belching flames—through which actors portraying devils and damned souls would pass by trapdoor to the ground level beneath the pageant.

Limbo and Hell-Mouth, after a sixteenth-century manuscript illustration of a mystery play. Jerusalem is represented onstage to the left, but out of sight in the illustration. The ship moored in the left foreground sits on a painted square, representing the sea. Behind it the barred, burning tower containing prisoners represents the tower of limbo. To the far right, in the tower of hell, the souls of the damned suffer tortures in a blazing cauldron and bound to a wheel, while Satan surveys the scene with satisfaction, mounted on a dragon atop a pole.

This pageant system of production proved highly popular throughout Europe, but ultimately the plays ended up being presented on long fixed platforms with individual settings or "mansions" for each scene. The stage effects accompanying the plays could now be made complex and spectacular. Actors could be lifted above the playing area or descend from heaven. Fireworks were used for diabolical effects: the devils are described as belching fire from their mouths and horns. A sixteenth-century eyewitness to one of these spectacles wrote:

> The secrets of Paradise and Hell, are utterly prodigious and capable of being taken by the spectators for works of genuine enchantment. For one saw there Angels and other characters descend from on high, sometimes visibly, sometimes invisibly and appearing all of a sudden.

The Devil trump, after Viéville's French card, 1650

Lucifer rose from Hell riding on a dragon, without anyone knowing how. The rod of Moses, dry and sterile, suddenly bloomed with flowers and fruit. The souls of Herod and Judas were lofted into the Air by devils.

Morality Plays

The rapid increase of semiprofessional groups of actors and entertainers, known as jongleurs, from 1425 onward added to the number of plays offered to the public. Most of these were what have come to be known as morality plays. They appeared first around 1400 but, unlike the mystery play, were not tied to any particular day of the liturgical calendar.

Fifteenth-century devil's costume for a German mystery play

Devils' masks for an Austrian mystery play

Although not liturgically inspired, morality plays usually adopted the ritual format of a fall from grace followed by redemption. Dramatized allegories, their characters were abstractions, their protagonist humanity itself. They coupled the Christian concept of sin with allegorical figures taken from classical pagan mythology, figures like the goddess Fortuna.

Three themes were dominant in morality plays: the so-called psychomachia, a term borrowed from an allegorical poem of the same name by the fourth-century Spanish poet Aurelius Clemens Prudentius, to describe the conflict of the virtues and the vices for man's soul while he is still alive; the summoning, portraying the arrival of Death at man's last hour; and the judgment, a debate over the fate of the soul of the deceased, with Mercy and Peace on one side and Truth and Justice on the other.

Given the popularity of these themes in fifteenth-century drama, the tarot trumps Death, the Wheel of Fortune, the Judgment, and the three Virtue trumps may well have derived from the morality plays, although, maybe significantly, another work of Petrarch's, *Things to be Remembered*, written in 1343, also dealt specifically with all four of the Cardinal Virtues.

The *Dance of Death*

With regard to the derivation of the Death trump, we may look to what may well be the first morality play to emerge as a drama distinct from the liturgical cycle, namely that known in various forms as *The Dance of Death, Dance Macabre,* or *Dodentantz.* This play illustrated the all-conquering power of the Grim Reaper, something that the Black Death—that world-wide epidemic of bubonic plague—had recently made overwhelmingly obvious in the devastation it inflicted on Europe between 1347 and 1364. The play's perennial message was primarily directed at the wealthy and frivolous of the age in the hope of refocusing their gaze on more spiritual matters.

Death comes for the emperor, pope, and king, after Von Wyl's sixteenth-century Dance of Death. *Notice the courteous attitudes displayed to Death by his victims, which avail them not at all, as we shall see in chapter 4!*

The earliest pictorial representation of the Dance of Death, painted sometime around 1424 on a cloister wall of the Cemetery of the Innocents in Paris, depicted members of all social classes—from pope and emperor down to beggar, fool, and hermit—engaged in a stately dance with skeletons and corpses, the dead escorting the living to the tomb. The original painting was destroyed in 1669, but woodcuts depicting the Dance were made by the Paris engraver Guyot Marchant, and its explanatory verses have also been preserved, which we will see later.

Numerous German versions of the Dance, to which we will have further recourse when we examine the trumps in detail, also exist as woodcuts in books and in murals. Highly renowned in the world of art, the Dance is also depicted in engravings of lost drawings by Hans Holbein the Younger published in 1538, as well as the horrifying panel painted by Brueghel around 1562.

Quite obviously, most of the images on tarot trumps I through XIII could have been drawn directly from the Dance of Death. The unnumbered card, the Fool, who appears in some illustrations of the Dance, also turns out to be a stock character in medieval drama, whose job was to clown, address the audience and other actors, and make satirical comments about the inscrutable ways of the Deity. Again, we shall explore his function further when we come to examine the trumps individually.

As for the origin of the tarot Wheel of Fortune, the goddess Fortuna— or Dame Fortune, as she came to be known—featured repeatedly in the morality plays.

Dame Fortune enthroned opposite Dame Wisdom, after sixteenth-century French engraving. Fortune carries her famous wheel, on which rides humanity; Dame Wisdom (Prudence), on the other hand, consults her mirror, in which she surveys the entire cosmos. Her mirror is represented in the tarot by the Coin suit.

Fortuna originally entered the medieval scholarly consciousness through the writings of the sixth-century Roman Neoplatonist, Anicius Manlius Severinus Boethius. A patrician scholar who was ultimately condemned to death on a concocted charge of treason, Boethius lived from about 480 to 524 C.E. His Latin translations of Aristotle and his works on Greek arithmetic, astronomy, geometry, and music became enormously important during the Middle Ages. Possibly of even greater popularity than his translations, however, was a work entirely of his own that he entitled *The Consolation of Philosophy*, which we shall also look at later. Even the poet Dante is said to have drawn comfort from it after the death of Beatrice, his particular beloved. Dame Fortune plays a major role in the *Consolation*, together with her wicked wheel, which every member of humanity rides and whose turning determines fate. Significantly, she also appears in the tarot trumps and, as we shall see, in a variety of other devices used for divination.

Miracle Plays

The third category of play that concerns us in identifying the trumps' origin is the miracle play. These dramas generally featured religiously edifying

Pope Joan with her child, after fifteenth-century German woodcut

stories similar to those recounted in *The Golden Legend*, a thirteenth-century compilation of pious tales, generally gruesome and blood soaked, about saints and martyrs or sinners often saved from eternal damnation through the intercession of the Virgin Mary. An example of such a story may be found in a German miracle play written in 1480 that deals with the mythical life and death of one Frau Jutten, otherwise known to the world as Pope Joan, the only female pope the Catholic Church has yet seen. We shall consider poor Joan's tale in due course.

THE FOUR LAST THINGS

Finally, we should consider Catholic Church doctrine itself, if not as a direct source, then at least as a reinforcement of the meanings of four of the trumps, namely Death, the Devil, Judgment, and the World. It happens that these cards, if the World trump is considered to be a representation of heaven, constitute a depiction of those four most important events in a believing Roman Catholic's spiritual life, known as the Four Last Things—important because nobody can escape death or judgment, and the choice of heaven or hell is one each soul must make.

Hieronymous Bosch included the Four Last Things in his fifteenth- or early sixteenth-century painted panel entitled *The Table Top of the Seven Deadly Sins and the Four Last Things* presently hanging in the Prado Gallery, Madrid. His depictions of Judgment and Hell show significant similarity to the imagery of the Judgment, Devil, and Tower trumps.

THE TALE THE TRUMPS TELL

It is my contention, then, that whoever selected the original pictures for the tarot trumps used imagery drawn directly from mystery, miracle, and morality plays, most especially *The Dance of Death*. The origins of these images in popular culture also lead me to believe that the trumps were probably introduced in the mass-produced "folk" decks before being custom-made by celebrated painters for noble families.

In the custom-made painted decks, alterations to the trump's designs—such as omission of unpleasing references to hell in the form of the Devil and Tower trumps—could be incorporated. A variety of elements pertaining to the aristocratic families who commissioned the painted cards' manufacture, ranging from heraldic mottoes to the portrayals of family members themselves in the trumps, could also be added to provide layers of relevance for the intellectual delight of the Viscontis, D'Estes, and other owners. These painted decks, however, I believe to have been based upon the original Roman Catholic "drama" imagery of decks printed for the common people, by whom it would have been most appreciated.

So if we set aside the Neoplatonic and literary glosses of the aristocratic, painted cards, the trumps basically tell the story of the soul's journey through life into the afterlife, an archetypal and perennial story recounted in Christian imagery typical of the late medieval period. A tale such as this, told at a time such as this, so soon after the catastrophic Black Death, and dealing with issues of eschatology, worldliness, fortune, death, salvation, and resurrection, would have been totally comprehensible to any card player of the late Middle Ages and early Renaissance. Viewed in this light, tarot trumps can certainly be said to fulfill the pronouncements of the fourteenth-century Dominican monk known to historians as Johannes von Rheinfelden: that playing cards could be morally instructive.

However, we can be sure that the card makers and engravers responsible for each new generation of printed folk tarots would have felt at liberty to incorporate elements from any source that they felt supplied suitable reference material, provided it remained close to the recognizable and standard pattern of the district that was expected by card players. This practice may account for such idiosyncratic details as the zodiacal signs of the Crab and the Twins creeping into the Moon and Sun trumps respectively, and the similarity between tarot imagery and symbols shared by such early Renaissance block-books, house-books, almanacs, calendars, and horoscopes as those of the late-fifteenth- and early-sixteenth-century German engraver Erhard Schön. We shall have recourse to Schön's work later, on account of the light it sheds on the Renaissance connotation of some of the trump images.

But a question that has long baffled students of the tarot still remains unanswered. It goes to the heart of the very inscrutability of the cards that allowed them to become the pegs on which so many groundless fancies could be hung.

Schön's houses of the horoscope, 1515. Tarot trump images are displayed in houses 5, 7, 8, 9, 10, 11, and 12, indicating their close association in sixteenth-century minds with divinatory practices such as astrology.

If the trumps did initially carry some kind of message or meaning, how is it that by 1550 that meaning had vanished, leaving the cards merely enigmatic pictures, tokens to play games with? The sixteenth-century Ferrarese poet Flavio Alberti Lollio, who at that date published a tirade against the indignity of subjecting himself to the vicissitudes of gambling games in general and tarocco in particular, complained that the derivation of the word *tarocco*, and the images on the cards themselves, made no sense at all to him:

> What else do they mean by the Juggler and the Fool, than swindler and trickster? What other meaning have the Popess, the Chariot, the Traitor, the Wheel, the Hunchback, Strength, the Star, the Sun, the Moon, Death and Hell, and all the rest of this motley crew? And that fantastic and bizarre name tarocco—is it without an etymology?

Lollio was a man who hailed from Ferrara, a town that had hosted the creation of a variety of painted D'Este tarots in the previous century. You would have thought that he, a poet, of all people, might recall the trumps' meaning. Apparently not. It seems that something particularly potent and iconoclastic had been at work to effectively blot the memory out.

The answer to this puzzle may surely be found in the religious turmoil that ravaged Europe during the sixteenth century. With the arrival of the Reformation—that rebellion against the hegemony of Roman Catholicism begun by Martin Luther—and the bitter internecine wars that followed, the religious drama of the pageants quite literally vanished in France, Italy, and England. The stories that the pageants told were, after all, originally intended as instruments of conversion to the Catholic faith and therefore offensive to the rising Protestant authorities. In 1548, in fact, *all* religious plays were banned by the Parliament of Paris. Under the patronage of the nobility, Italy now led the humanist revival of interest in classical antiquity, which included the playwrights of Greece and Rome. The old religious dramas were banished from the minds of the educated as so much medieval rubbish, and with them went the knowledge of what the tarot trumps originally represented.

However, though the meanings of the trumps appear to have been largely forgotten by most of the card players who used them—they were, after all, only a card game initially—the symbolism undoubtedly would have continued to appear meaningful and potent to a few. In view of the church's documented hostility toward what it perceived as blasphemous use of the trump images in gaming, apparently some of its ministers should be included among those who continued to discern the cards' symbolism. Their attitude undoubtedly would have been the same as that of the Dominican preacher who castigated the use of dice, playing cards, and triumphs in the 1480 and 1500 document *Sermones de ludo cum aliis* (Sermons on Games Together with Other Matters). He fairly frothed with rage when he declared that "nothing is so abhorrent to God as the game of triumphs," chiefly because it had the effrontery to depict the emperor, the pope, the Cardinal Virtues, planets, and angels, even God himself, for its purposes (see trump XXI in chapter 4 to explain this last gripe). And it would be particularly odd if such potent symbolism was dismissed as mere trivial decoration by others who also fancied they knew about such matters but were not necessarily representatives of the church, which leads us to the subject matter of our next chapter.

3

OF CARTOMANCY AND THE TAROT

THE ANCIENT ART OF SORTILEGE

In the introduction we followed the evolution of the tarot from its initial appearance as a deck of playing cards in fifteenth-century Italy through its growth in popularity as a game of cards to France and Europe in the sixteenth and seventeenth centuries. Now it's time to pick up the thread once more and examine how these, by now enigmatic, cards fared in the eighteenth and nineteenth centuries. We shall see how, captivated by what I shall call their archetypal resonance, eighteenth- and nineteenth-century illuminati and occultists of various persuasions came to perceive them as instruments of divine revelation, ascribing them first an ancient Egyptian provenance, then a kabbalistic one. This has led to their

Ibis-headed Thoth, Ancient Egyptian god of wisdom, and creator of the tarot according to such eighteenth-century French cartomancers as Jean-Baptiste Alliette, otherwise known as Etteilla

CHRONOLOGY OF THE DOCUMENTED OCCULT TAROT

Circa 1750: Tarot is being used for divination in Bologna.

Ca. 1753: Etteilla claims tarot divination is revealed to him by a man from Piedmont.

1773–1781: Antoine Court de Gébelin links the tarot with Egyptian symbolism.

1785–1791 Etteilla promotes his "rectified" tarot. His pupil d'Ooducet develops Etteilla's system through the eighteen hundreds.

1855–1856: Éliphas Lévi links the tarot with the Kabbala and the Hebrew alphabet.

1857: Jean-Alexandre Vaillant associates tarot suit cards with the decans.

1870: Paul Christian links tarot to astrology and the decans.

Ca. 1888: The Golden Dawn's tarot associates the suit cards with the decans, the trumps with the kabbalistic Tree of Life. Its deck later becomes the prototype for those of Paul Foster Case and Aleister Crowley.

1910: Arthur Edward Waite publishes his tarot deck with the collaboration of artist Pamela Colman Smith. It later becomes the prototype for many Anglo-American decks.

enshrinement at the center of variety of occult philosophies. The tarot is still widely promoted as a vital key to the practice of high ceremonial magic, although its chief claim to fame today probably rests in its use as a tool for divination, which is as a good a place as any for us to pick up our tale. But first we should examine exactly what we mean by the term *divination*.

Divination as a practice has its roots in very ancient history, in Babylon and Egypt and China. All the oldest civilizations indulged in it; figuring out one's future seems always to have been a major human preoccupation. With regard to this, the practice of reading prophetic meaning into the random selection of signs or symbols was known to the ancient Greeks as *manteia,* which provides part of the base of our word for playing-card divination, *cartomancy*—or *cartonomancie,* as the word was first coined. The Romans called this art of occult investigation *divinatio* (divination), a word undoubtedly related to the word *divinus* (divine), implying finding out what the gods had in store for us.

In the past almost anything could be, and was, used to divine by: the entrails of sacrificial animals, the features of the human body, the stars, the weather, the elements, flights of birds. Sometimes the will of the gods was discerned by casting or drawing lots, *sortes* in Latin, which were symbols or runes or alphabetical letters inscribed on bones, dice, or slips of wood. Every system worked differently, but basically each symbol or sign was associated by tradition with a certain meaning when it showed up. These meanings could be strung together and interpreted by the diviner— who was frequently the priest or priestess of a cult or religion—to provide answers to a specific question. Our word *sorcery* comes from these *sortes,* and the Latin word *sortilegium* (sortilege) means divining by picking up lots in this manner.

In medieval Europe a type of sortilege that could be practiced by the literate man or woman became popular. It was called bibliomancy: people obtained supernatural guidance by opening certain books at random. Keeping their eyes shut, they would draw their oracle by pricking a line of text with a needle and interpreting it as the answer to their question. Generally, the books used were those considered in some way special, such as the Bible, the *Iliad,* or the *Aeneid.* Significantly, it is from the pages of these books that the characters depicted on many of the court cards of the Minor Arcana are drawn. This type of divination came to be called *sortes Biblicae, sortes Homericae,* or *sortes Virgilianae.* Later, other methods of selecting random texts from books were adopted: dice, for instance, could be rolled to indicate chapter and verse numbers or small pivoted wheels could be spun to select verses that contained the particular answer sought. No less a pillar of Christian society than Saint Augustine, in Book VIII of his *Confessions,* confessed to using sortilege in times of crisis. Significantly perhaps, Petrarch also made use of it, using as his instrument of divination a pocket-sized copy of Augustine's same *Confessions,* which he carried with him at all times. As literary scholar Mary Carruthers points out in her book on the function of memory in medieval society:

The very custom of using books for "sortes" is an interesting example of regarding books as personal sources whose function is to provide memorial clues to oneself, divine influences being able to prophecy through the images of letters on the page just as they can during sleep through the images written in the memory.

Using Playing Cards for Divination

Our first literary allusion to divination by playing cards dates back to the fourteenth century. Tarot historian Gerard Van Rijnberk discovered a reference to it in a fourteenth-century epic poem, later printed in Milan in 1519, and entitled *Spagna istoriata* (History of Spain). Canto XX recounts that Roland (Orlando), in order to discover the whereabouts of the enemies of Charlemagne, has recourse to a magic circle in which he lays out a deck of cards. This, of course, is only fiction in which playing cards appear as divination devices. Our first actual examples of playing cards being used for sortilege date from a hundred years later, during the fifteenth century, where cards are employed in conjunction with versified oracle books similar in principle to the *I Ching*, or Book of Changes. This was an ancient Chinese oracle book, tentatively dated to the twelfth century B.C.E., that was consulted by the random selection of dried yarrow stalks to build up a six-lined figure indicating a verse or set of verses. Our case in point, however, is a German oracle book entitled *Ein Loszbuch ausz der Karten gemacht,* (A Lot-Book Made from Playing Cards), which was written in the 1480s to accompany a deck of cards using the German suit signs Hawkbells, Hearts, Leaves, and Acorns.

Fifteenth-century German playing cards used for divination purposes, after illustrations in Eyn Loszbuch ausz der Karten gemacht. *From the left, the King of Leaves (King of Swords), the Ober of Leaves (Knight of Swords), the Unter of Leaves (Knave of Swords), and the Banner of Leaves (Ten of Swords).*

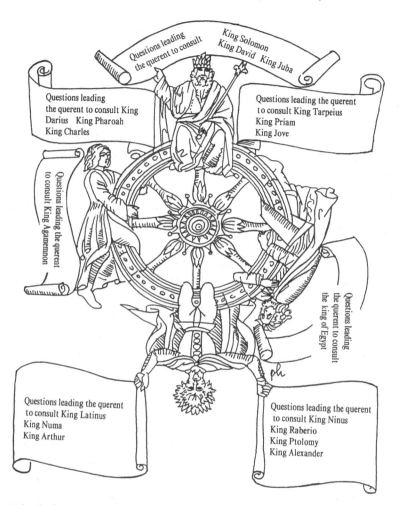

Questions leading the querent to consult King Solomon King David King Juba

Questions leading the querent to consult King Darius King Pharoah King Charles

Questions leading the querent to consult King Tarpeius King Priam King Jove

Questions leading the querent to consult King Agamemnon

Questions leading the querent to consult the king of Egypt

Questions leading the querent to consult King Latinus King Numa King Arthur

Questions leading the querent to consult King Ninus King Raberio King Ptolomy King Alexander

The Wheel of Fortune, after Spirito's illustration. I have indicated the gist of the writing on the scrolls in English, which in the original is written in barely decipherable Italian.

Indeed, such lot-books seem to have been highly popular among educated Germans of the fifteenth century. Often their pages are illustrated with depictions of Fortune's Wheel, as they are in similar Italian lot-books of the following century, such as Sigismondo Fanti's *Triompho di Fortuna* (The Triumph of Fortune) and Lorenzo Spirito's *Il libro della ventura overo Il libro de la sorte* (The Book of Luck or The Book of Fate) of 1501. Spirito's book required the use of dice and involved questions arranged around a Wheel of Fortune; the questions led to a variety of legendary or imaginary kings, whose names in turn led to a variety of oracular answers.

Many lot-book covers bore circles around which twenty-three letters of the alphabet were inscribed. In some the circle itself could be spun like a roulette wheel to pick out a letter; in others a pivoted pointer fulfilled the function. The letters would lead to an oracular verse inside the book that would answer the inquirer's question, either directly or after a further procedure involving dice or cards. The oracles invariably consisted of verses or morality tales.

Up to this point we have discussed the origin of the trump cards solely in light of the evolution of card games. However, combine the fact that the subject matter illustrated on the early trumps was drawn from just the kind of drama-derived moral, philosophical, or religious milieu dear to the hearts of the creators of the lot-books with the fact that the Wheel of Fortune appears so reliably in tarot trumps and lot-books, and I think it fair to conjecture that these facts taken together may indicate some similarity of purpose shared by the trump sequence and such sortilege devices. Whether or not this was in fact the case, whatever the source of these new cards, the significance of their spiritually charged symbolism quite apparently was never lost upon those who had eyes to see. As we noted earlier, the sixteenth-century German engraver Erhard Schön made use of seven of the trump images to illustrate the astrological houses of his printed "Horoscope." And sooner or later people began to use tarocchi images and images very like them for sortilege as well as for gambling.

There are, for instance, those tarotlike engravings already alluded to, dated to about 1470 now and once attributed to Andrea Mantegna. They are printed on flimsy paper and seem much too large for playing ordinary card games. They exist in two versions, known as the E-series and the S-series, differing only in minor details from one another. The unknown Ferrarese artist who created them made fifty images (rather than twenty-two or seventy-eight), five ranks of ten, and they too carry alphabetical letters as well as numbers. The first rank depicts the social order of precedence in medieval and early Renaissance times, progressing from a beggar to an artisan to a servant, passing through king and emperor, ending with the pope. The second rank shows the Arts as the nine classical muses led by the god Apollo; the third rank depicts the seven liberal arts of medieval scholasticism, plus astrology, philosophy, and theology; the fourth rank depicts the three disciplines of astronomy, chronology, and cosmology, followed by the Seven Virtues. The fifth and most sublime rank shows the seven planetary gods, then the sphere of the fixed stars, followed by the Primum Mobile, or ether, and finally the Prima Causa, or first cause of everything. In other words, the Mantegna tarocchi presents the entire cosmic ladder in typical Neoplatonic fashion, from beggar to God, in fifty steps that would be comprehensible to the educated fifteenth-century mind. It is in the first rank, the images depicting the social order of precedence, that we can detect similarities to the tarot trumps. Undoubtedly, the artist was drawing inspiration here from existing tarocchi, whether of the painted aristocratic variety or the printed folk kind.

Differing opinions have been advanced as to who, if anyone, originally commissioned the Mantegna images, and for what purpose. Playing-card historian Detlef Hoffmann has conceded that they were most likely used to provide a stimulus for profound discussions between educated people rather than to play idle games. The images certainly look as though they had been created for a philosophical game of Nontrivial Pursuit rather than merely as emblems for a deck of playing cards. Historian Heinrich Brockhaus, who made a detailed study of the images in the 1930s, theorized that they may have been created to provide amusement for Pope Pius II, Cardinal Johannes Bessarion, and German philosopher Nicholas of Cusa—the last two of whom were strongly influenced by Neoplatonism in their theologies—during a seven-month ecclesiastical council held at Mantua between June 1459 and January 1460.

Would these clerics have included sortilege in their list of potential amusements, then? Like Nicholas of Cusa, Cardinal Bessarion undoubtedly took at least a passing interest in divination. We know that *De sortibus,* a fifteenth-century treatise on sortilege, was dedicated to him by a Sienese professor of canon law, Marianus Socinus. Indeed, Pius II is said to have stated that he would prefer to read Socinus's work on sortilege than to plow through Socinus's commentaries on other, more boring theological subjects. Lynn Thorndike in his seminal *History of Magic and Experimental Science* commented that "something akin to shaking dice seems to have appealed to the volatile and practical Piccolimini (Pius II) more than poring over the dry wording and involved logic of a technical legal discussion." For his part, Nicholas of Cusa was fond of using games as metaphysical metaphors, viewing play as a uniquely human activity that ultimately could lead the participant to the Absolute. He himself invented a game around the year 1463 entitled *The Game of Spheres* that was played on nine concentric circles drawn on the ground. These resembled the standard medieval diagrams of the planetary spheres, and although we do not understand the rules of the game, it seems to have involved the Hermetic doctrine of God's being an infinite sphere whose center is everywhere and circumference nowhere.

Despite such tantalizing hints that the fifteenth-century inhabitants of Milan or Ferrara might have used their newly printed trump cards for divination, we have no documented evidence that they did so. They may have, or the twenty-two images may simply have been appropriated from the medieval drama and used to create a fifth suit of "triumphs" with which to elaborate the regular Italian trick-taking game of cards. In either case, there is a slim dividing line between a game of hazard on which you place a bet and a game of hazard that you interpret as an indication of what fate has in store for you. In both procedures, Dame Fortune ultimately decides the issue.

Matteo Maria Boiardo, a fifteenth-century poet and author intimately involved with, and indeed patronized by, the D'Este court at Ferrara, did devise a special tarot deck around the year 1475 with eccentric suit signs, eccentric trumps, and verses to go with each card. These verses essentially assigned meanings to each card—a significant step toward using the cards as oracles—but we don't find our first definite mention of anyone using standard Italian tarocchi trumps by themselves for anything like sortilege until 1527.

Teofilo Folengo, an Italian poet also known to his readers as Merlini Cocai or Coccalo, was born in Mantua in 1496. He was educated at the University of Bologna, before entering the Benedictine Order as a monk. Folengo's fame rests on his poetry, which belongs in the category of verse known as "macaronic," that is, composed in a jumble of languages—in Folengo's case Latin, Italian, and a Mantuan dialect. His importance to tarot history lies in one of his poems, the oddly entitled *Caos del triperuno* or *Tri per uno* (The Chaos of Three for One). It was written under his pseudonym, Merlini Cocai, published in Venice in 1527, and contains a set of five sonnets that make use of the names and imagery of all twenty-two trumps.

The verses are interspersed between the dialog of two men, Triperuno and Limerno (the latter being another of Folengo's literary pseudonyms). Limerno has been commanded to recite poetry for the queen and has written sonnets for four people, two women and two men, all of whom have been dealt trump cards. The cards form the basis for each sonnet and a description of the character of the person to whom they have been dealt.

The meanings assigned to the cards are all fairly obvious, face-value ones: Justice means justice and the Lovers, or Love, as the card was called then, means love, and so on. The Tower is referred to as *Foco* (fire), and Judgment is called the Angel, both recognized name variants of the time. However, the important fact for us is that the cards are referred to as *sortes*, "destinies," or otherwise "lots," and used to form character sketches.

Folengo's use of the cards to devise sonnets began something of a craze among sixteenth-century Italian aristocracy for a game that came to be known as *Tarocchi appropriati* (Appropriated Tarots). Here trump cards were selected by one player and presented to another, who would interpret them thematically by a process of idea association to create verses about himself or herself, about another person, or most popularly, to praise certain well-known ladies around the court.

But what of the question-and-answer type of sortilege like that practiced by Augustine, Petrarch, or users of the lot-books? Cocai and the practitioners of *Tarocchi appropriati* used only the trumps. What of the suit cards? Did they find a use too?

In 1540, thirteen years after the appearance of Cocai's poem, also in Venice, a method of divination devised to make use of only the Coin sequence of the suit cards crops up in the form of an elaborately produced book entitled *Le sorti di Francesco Marcolino da Forlì, intituolate Giardino de Pensieri* (The Oracles of Francesco Marcolino da Forlì, entitled Garden of Thoughts).

Marcolino details a method of drawing nine cards from the Coins suit as lots (*sortes* again) to provide answers to a series of fifty questions, much in the manner of the German lot-books. The inquirer is directed to draw one or two of the Coin cards unseen. These cards would identify oracular verses printed elsewhere in the book that were to be read as an answer to the question asked.

Marcolino's method of drawing *sortes* definitely falls into the category of sortilege. Furthermore, it is an indicator that, alongside more intellectual practices like that which must have accompanied the Mantegna tarocchi, at a popular level the suit cards were also being used for fortune-telling. Ruth Martin provides supportive evidence for early magical use of the tarot in her study *Witchcraft and the Inquisition in Venice, 1550–1650*, which details how only a handful of years later, women prosecuted as witches in Venice are reported in court records to be using tarocchi trumps in their spells, something that Godfrey Lelend, the gypsy-lore scholar, also reported to be the case in and around Florence two centuries later. So, not forgetting the appearance of Erhard Schön's significant "Horoscope" engraving, there can be no doubt that during the sixteenth and seventeenth centuries the tarot was already being viewed as an occult device.

By the mid-eighteenth century, the famous rake Giacomo Casanova was reporting in his diary of 1765 that his Russian peasant mistress resorted to reading playing cards every day, but we don't know whether or not these cards were tarots. Fairly conclusive, however, to the question of whether or not tarocchi had a tradition of divinatory usage prior to the late eighteenth century is the 1989 discovery of a manuscript in the library of the University of Bologna. Announced by Franco Pratesi, an expert on early Florentine cards and tarocchi, and subsequently dated to some time prior to 1750, the manuscript gives a list of cartomantic interpretations for thirty-five Bolognese tarocchi cards along with a rudimentary method of laying them out.

The 1750s turn out to be particularly significant in the documented history of tarot divination due to the efforts a Parisian algebra teacher who created a new identity for himself by reversing his surname, Alliette, and establishing himself as the world's first professional card reader.

EGYPTIAN MAGIC AND THE BOOK OF THOTH

According to what purports to be Etteilla's own account of the matter, it was during the early 1750s that he first learned the art of telling fortunes with French-suited playing cards from three aging cartomancers, one of whom hailed from Piedmont in northern Italy.

In the book that appeared under Etteilla's imprint in 1791, *Etteilla, ou L'art de lire dans les cartes* (Etteilla, or The Art of Reading Cards), he disparaged these card readers' rudimentary art of "card drawing," as he termed it, which he describes, not inaccurately, as being little better than the old practice of sortilege, of "drawing lots from Homer, Virgil or the Bible." He felt that there was a potential in the art that was being neglected.

Etteilla began divining in 1753 with the reduced deck of thirty-two French-suited cards used to play the game Piquet (plus an extra home-made card that he named an "Etteilla," the prototype of what today's card reader calls the significator). However, Etteilla claims that he had to wait four years until his Piedmontese teacher led him to the tarot in 1757, declaring that these were the cards that truly contained all the secret wisdom of the ancients.

This was, as we shall see, an idea that was soon to gain wide acceptance.

A few years after Etteilla's alleged revelation, at some period between 1773 and 1781, a French-Swiss Protestant pastor named Antoine Court de Gébelin came across a group of friends playing cards with a tarot deck, which he claimed never to have set eyes on before. Drawn to the unusual imagery of the cards, Court de Gébelin, who fancied he knew something about arcane matters, suddenly recognized in them symbols of the lost religion of ancient Egypt.

Nobody contradicted this interpretation, as nobody knew very much about ancient Egypt in the eighteenth century, except what could be gleaned from a few classical Greek and Latin writings. Most notable among these was a collection known as the *Corpus Hermeticum,* thought by Renaissance philosophers and magicians to contain deep Egyptian secrets in the form of dialogues between Thoth and other Egyptian gods. We shall look at the *Corpus* in more detail presently, as it becomes an important element in our tarot story.

So in 1781 Court de Gébelin expounded an imaginative history of tarot that would influence scholars for many years and propel the cards into entirely new and exotic arenas. Found in volume VIII of his sprawling nine-volume history of the world begun in 1773 and entitled *Le monde primitif analisé et comparé avec le monde moderne* (The Primitive World Analyzed and Compared with the Modern World), Court de Gébelin's theory claimed that the tarot was the remains of a book written by ancient Egyptian priests and introduced to Europe by Gypsies after their purported exodus from Egypt. (Gypsies, who in reality had an Asian origin, had initially promoted the idea that they were bands of persecuted Egyptian Christians to win favor in the Christian courts of Europe, and the word *gypsy* itself is a garbling of the word *Egyptian*.) Of course, we now know that tarot cards predated the appearance of Gypsies in Europe by many years.

But why did Court de Gébelin plump for ancient Egypt rather than, say, Persia, one may ask?

From the time of Pythagoras in the sixth century B.C.E. and throughout the duration of both the Roman and Islamic Empires, Egypt had been singled out by philosophers as the place where the deepest insights into the history of humankind could be obtained, so Court de Gébelin was only following a long tradition. As the Rosetta stone had not yet been discovered or deciphered, Egyptian hieroglyphics were believed to contain a huge treasure trove of information about prehistory and other obscure matters. In Court de Gébelin's day, with the grip of the Roman Catholic

Church loosening and the Age of Enlightenment in full swing, just about anything that wasn't considered seditious by the state could legitimately be considered fair game for speculation, and speculate people certainly did. Court de Gébelin himself was deeply preoccupied by the question of origins, particularly the origins of the human race and languages. Furthermore, in addition to practicing as a pastor, he was a Freemason and a follower of the teachings of the mystics Martines de Pasqually and Louis Claude de Saint Martin. Illuminist societies like some of the lodges of the Freemasons were breeding grounds for discourse on the mysteries of great civilizations of the past and the origins of humankind.

Court de Gébelin was aided in his antiquarian research by a person he referred to as "M. le C. de M***," who has only recently been identified by Oxford historian Robin Briggs as a military man, Louis-Raphaël-Lucrèce de Fayolle, Comte de Mellet and lieutenant of the king of France's bodyguard. Though de Mellet was not known to be a Freemason, he may well have met Court de Gébelin through membership of one of the several groups engaged in esoteric studies to which the pastor belonged. Moreover, it was de Mellet, whose essay on the tarot Court de Gébelin incorporated into his book, who fleshed out Court de Gébelin's idea that would become of paramount importance to later cartomancers: that the twenty-two mysterious picture cards known as trumps in the tarot deck were associated in some way with the twenty-two letters of the Hebrew alphabet. In actual fact, were the trumps to be connected with an alphabet, one would think it far more likely to be the Latin alphabet, bearing in mind their fifteenth-century European origins.

With the publication of Court de Gébelin and de Mellet's work, almost overnight, it seems, tarot became the bible of would-be magi, hailed as the key to all the secrets of the ages. Most important, it appears to have provided the impetus for Etteilla to enter the public arena and claim center stage.

Between 1785 and 1791, Etteilla began publishing his own ideas about tarot, apparently building on the Egyptian theory laid down by de Mellet and Court de Gébelin, although he claimed that he had known about the cards' Egyptian origins since 1757 and that Court de Gébelin had merely relayed all that he wrote about from an "amateur," presumably de Mellet. Etteilla, meanwhile, had concluded that the actual root source of the deck was the *Book of Thoth,* a mythical book of magic said to belong to Thoth, the ibis-headed Egyptian god of wisdom, later known to Arabic alchemists and Renaissance magicians as Hermes Trismegistos (Thrice-

Great Hermes). What's more, Etteilla supplied the amazing detail that the book had been engraved for posterity by seventeen Hermetic adepts, priests of Thoth, on plates of gold 171 years after the Great Flood, and that these plates had been the prototypes for tarot cards.

Etteilla set about designing his own tarot deck based upon these notions and began telling fortunes with them in addition to his Piquet pack. So successful did he ultimately prove in his practice that his decks became known as "Egyptian" tarots to distinguish them from what were then generally referred to as "German" tarots (which we would call Tarocks) and also from "Italian" tarots, that is, decks consisting of the traditional French, Swiss, Belgian, or Italian patterns. Ironically, fashionable Parisian society came to consider only "Egyptian" tarots suitable for proper cartomancy.

The first Etteilla deck, probably a reproduction of Etteilla's own engraved one, was published in 1789, two years before his death in 1791. In 1826 a second appeared, introducing titles that evoke Masonic concepts. These can still be seen in B. P. Grimaud's *Grand Etteilla ou Tarots Egyptiens* deck. A third appeared in 1838, heralded as the *Grand Livre de Thot,* happily coinciding with the appearance of an explanatory booklet entitled *Le grand Etteilla ou L'art de tirer les cartes* ascribed to one "Julia Orsini," proclaimed "the Sibyl of the Faubourg Saint-Germain." A fourth, this time promoted as the *78 Tarots Egyptiens—Grand jeu de l'Oracle des Dames,* appeared between 1865 and 1870. This last deck of "Etteilla" cards, completely redrawn and exuding a nineteenth-century Gothic aura that contrasted with the dowdy, rather inept look of Etteilla's original deck, again altered the symbolism of several of the cards as well as various interpretations.

ETTEILLA'S SYSTEM

Etteilla's importance to tarot reading today chiefly resides in his interpretations of what (anachronously here) I shall call his Minor Arcana, which I shall deal with shortly. His first set of sixty-four interpretations (two per card, depending on whether it was drawn upright or reversed) included those that he had used for his thirty-two-card French-suited Piquet deck, to which he now had to add ninety-two new interpretations to account for the twenty-four extra suit cards and twenty-two trumps.

As for his interpretations of the trump cards, which are of less importance to us, he seems to have taken a number of them from de Mellet, specifically the attribution of the first trumps to various stages of the biblical creation of the world. This meant that Etteilla reversed the customary trump sequence and worked backward, beginning his deck with the trump generally known as Judgment, which he redesigned and entitled "Chaos." As for the other trumps, Etteilla followed the logic that if they were indeed the remnant of the *Book of Thoth,* that is, of Hermes Trismegistos, the interpretations should correspond to teachings contained in the *Corpus Hermeticum,* that collection of Neoplatonic philosophical manuscripts from Egypt under the Roman Empire that had been kicking about Europe in various translations since 1460.

Where a match between a tarot card and a Hermetic concept wasn't possible, the Hermetic concept prevailed and the medieval tarot symbolism was discarded. Furthermore, Etteilla insisted that his entire deck should be quite literally recognized as pages from the *Book of Thoth,* and he rearranged the order of the cards according to this theory, shuffling them in the process and numbering them from one to seventy-eight as follows: trump I displayed five concentric rings to represent Chaos, which was said to represent the male inquirer or Etteilla; trump II depicted the Sun and Light, and represented Enlightenment or the element Fire depending on its upright or reversed position; trump III depicted the Moon and Plants, representing Opinion/Water; trump IV depicted the Stars and Sky, representing Deprivation/Air; trump V depicted Man and the Four-Footed Animals, representing Journey/Earth; and so on through the entire "rectified" trump sequence. The Fool or Alchemist shows up, not unnaturally, representing Folly.

As for his suit cards, Etteilla followed Court de Gébelin in equating all *Trèfle* (Trefoil) cards (and their meanings) with his Coin suit (contrary to many present-day cartomancers who identify Coins with Diamonds); he identified all *Coeur* (Heart) cards with his Cup suit; all *Pique* (Pike) Spade cards with his Sword suit; and all *Carreau* (Paving Tile) Diamond cards with his Baton suit.

The English magus Samuel Liddell MacGregor Mathers followed the same equation of suits in his 1888 booklet about the tarot. Arthur Edward Waite, the English mystic whom we have already encountered (and a frequent critic of Mathers who played an even larger role than Mathers did in the subsequent development of tarot divination), acknowledged in his 1910 *Pictorial Key to the Tarot* that the divinatory meanings of the tarot suit cards were the same as the French suit sign cards, but confusingly stated that Coins were the prototypes of Spades, and Swords of Clubs. This is oddly self-contradictory, as his suit card interpretations do follow those of Etteilla, and indeed, Waite followed Etteilla in equating Cups to Hearts, Swords to Spades, Wands to Diamonds, and "Pantacles" to Clubs in his earlier, pseudonymous, *Manual of Cartomancy*, first published in 1889.

To my knowledge, nobody yet knows where Etteilla obtained his original Piquet interpretations, which accounted for the French suit cards seven through ten and which he used later for his tarot Minor Arcana. They predate the declarations of Court de Gébelin and de Mellet by eleven or twelve years, so there seems no question of his having borrowed them from a printed source. They do, however, bear resemblance to some of Pratesi's mid-eighteenth-century Bolognese tarot interpretations which we shall be referring to in later chapters, as do the meanings Etteilla would later ascribe to some of his trumps.

Regarding their authenticity as a traditional system, generally speaking, Etteilla's interpretations seem too quirky and heterogeneous for him to have just made them up. When cartomancers invent an interpretive system, as in the instance of the one invented by the nineteenth-century occultist Papus (Gérard Encausse), it usually displays some kind of internal logic, guiding principle, or inner consistency—philosophical, numerological, or astrological, perhaps—which certainly cannot be said of Etteilla's interpretations.

Etteilla did later supplement his studies of the *Corpus Hermeticum* with numerology, astrology, and alchemy, and his interpretations for all the tarot suit cards from two through ten might conceivably have been influenced by meanings attributed by astrologers to the thirty-six divisions of the zodiac known as "decans" (which the *Asclepius*, one of the books of the *Corpus*, mentions but does not detail). However, the meanings of the decans and Etteilla's Minor Arcana cards are, for the most part, at odds. Etteilla claimed to have learned his Piquet lore from those three elderly fortune-tellers. I believe the likelihood is that he did, and that he was genuinely following some kind of traditional set of interpretations current for playing cards in eighteenth-century Europe.

Maybe they came from Piedmont?

Maybe his interpretations of the French aces and seven-through-ten number cards all derive from traditional sources, while those of cards two through six come from his other research? One can't tell. We probably can rule out, however, the notion that they were borrowed from some other system of divination. Etteilla's last published work, *Etteilla, ou L'art de lire dans les cartes,* contains a remarkable passage stating that Etteilla had at one time believed card reading derived from a process of sortilege using thirty-three wooden wands devised by a Greek named "Alpha," but which origin he had long since come to regard as a myth! Historians Decker, Depaulis, and Dummett surmise that Etteilla's story may have been a confused account of a system of geomancy that reached France via Moorish Spain.

Geomancy is a type of sortilege that makes use of symbolic figures built out of four layers of single or double dots—rather like the *I Ching,* but derived from Arabic sources. However, it possesses only sixteen figures, not thirty-three, and none of their meanings, however and whichever way you twist them, appears to fit the original list of card interpretations Etteilla produced for the number cards of his Piquet pack.

Be that as it may, there's no mystery about where Etteilla's interpretations of the court cards came from. Although the various names for the French court cards were by no means consistent over the centuries, those known to playing-card specialists today as the standard Paris pattern make Etteilla's (or his mentors') source quite apparent. As we noted earlier, each court card was drawn from medieval legends and romances popular at the time the cards were invented and, therefore, has a personality and a story associated with it. Obviously, the depictions of these characters lend themselves to sortilege, as indeed the books did that recounted so many of their exploits, namely the Bible, the *Iliad* of Homer, and the *Aeneid* of Virgil.

Etteilla and later French cartomancers invariably ascribed three of the court cards—King, Queen, and Knave—to certain types of people, but as far as I know, nobody knows where the fortune-telling characteristics of the tarot Knights came from, probably for the simple reason that French-suited packs contained no Knights. However, other legendary characters were ascribed to court cards in other deck patterns, such as that of Rouen, so it's possible that the tarot Knights borrowed personas from this pool of characters, specifically those of Knaves. The word *knave,* by the way, originally meant a boy or a candidate for knighthood and was synonymous with *valet, page, infant, damoysel, bachelier,* or *childe* (as in "Childe Roland to the dark tower came"). In modern cartomancy, however, the card can signify a young person of either sex, incorporating the role of the female page, the *Fantesca* or *Fantiglia* that sometimes appears in the "feminine" Italian Coins and Cups suits.

The year of Etteilla's death in 1791 saw the anonymous publication of the *Dictionnaire synonimique du Livre de Thot* (Thesaurus of the Book of

Thoth), which Decker, Depaulis, and Dummett have concluded was actually authored by a pupil of Etteilla's, retired army officer Pierre-Joseph Joubert de la Salette. Obviously intended as the companion volume to Etteilla's deck, the book explains all the meanings of the cards, upright and reversed, card reversals being a practice that seems to have been first documented if not introduced by Etteilla. Inspired by this work, another pupil of Etteilla's, Melchior Montmignon d'Odoucet, issued a work in three volumes between 1804 and 1807 called *Science des signes, ou Médecine de l'esprit, connue sous le nom d'art de tirer les cartes* (The Science of Signs, or Medicine for the Mind, Known under the Name of the Art of Card Drawing). It is ultimately these two books, La Salette's and d'Odoucet's, that laid the groundwork for most Minor Arcana interpretations today.

Aside from these interpretations, of course, the other enormous contribution Etteilla and his school made to the art of tarot divination was to advance it from the practice of simple sortilege—the drawing and interpreting of single cards—to the use of spreads and layouts of multiple cards to be read as "sentences" or entire complexes of ideas. It is this latter method that is generally practiced by today's card reader.

Etteilla had a host of disciples and imitators, but it took the ingenuity of Éliphas Lévi, the pen name of Alphonse-Louis Constant, a talented and imaginative nineteenth-century Roman Catholic ex-deacon turned writer and illustrator, to enlarge upon de Mellet's suggested link between the twenty-two letters of the Hebrew alphabet and the twenty-two enigmatic trump cards and to add a layer of kabbalistic Jewish bricks on top of Court de Gébelin's and Etteilla's Egyptian story. In this manner, Lévi launched the tarot on its evolution from an instrument of gaming and fairly humble sortilege to its present status as an indispensable tool for the student of the Christian Kabbala and high ceremonial magic.

THE KABBALA AND ÉLIPHAS LÉVI

The Kabbala is a Jewish theosophy claiming an excessively ancient origin of a supernatural, angelic nature, but now thought by scholars to have evolved in twelfth-century Spain and Provence, possibly from Gnostic and Pythagorean—as well as the obvious biblical and rabbinical—sources. It was later incorporated into Renaissance Christian Neoplatonism, where it became a "Christian" Kabbala, intended originally as a means to convert Jews to Christianity (which it didn't). Indeed, the noble young Florentine philosopher Pico della Mirandola felt that "no Hebrew Kabbalist can deny that the name Iesu, if we interpret it according to Kabbalistic principles and methods, signifies God, the Son of God, and the wisdom of the Father through the divinity of the Third Person." Well, as the endurance of the Jewish faith testifies, deny it they did.

In any case, the mysterious Kabbala might seem as plausible a source as any for the original and equally mysterious tarot trump images, if evidence of a link to them could be discovered. Lévi thought Court de Gébelin and de Mellet had provided him with one. Or twenty-two, to be precise.

ALEPH	DOCTRINA	SERAPHIM	I THE JUGGLER
BETH	DOMUS	CHERUBIM	II THE FEMALE POPE
GIMEL	PLENITUDO	THRONES	III THE EMPRESS
DALETH	PORTA	DOMINATIONS	IV THE EMPEROR
HE	ECCE	POWERS	V THE POPE
VAU	UNCUS	VIRTUES	VI THE LOVERS
ZAIN	ARMA	PRINCIPALITIES	VII THE CHARIOT
HETH	VITA	ARCHANGELS	VIII JUSTICE
TETH	BONUS	ANGELS	IX THE HERMIT
YOD	VIRI FORTES	HEROES	X THE WHEEL OF FORTUNE
KAPH	MANUS	THE FIRST MOTION	XI FORTITUDE
KAPH final		THE FIXED STARS	
LAMED	DISCIPLINA	SATURN	XII THE HANGED MAN
MEM	EX IPSIS	JUPITER	XIII DEATH
MEM final		MARS	
NUN	SEMPITERNUM	THE SUN	XIV TEMPERANCE
NUN final		VENUS	
SAMEKH	ADIUTORIUM	MERCURY	XV THE DEVIL
AYIN	FONS, OCULUS	THE MOON	XVI THE TOWER
PE	OS	SOUL	XVII THE STAR
PE final		SPIRIT	
TZADDI	IUSTITIA	MATTER	XVIII THE MOON
TZADDI final		THE FOUR ELEMENTS	
QOPH	VOCATIO	MINERAL	XIX THE SUN
RESH	CAPUT	VEGETABLE	XX JUDGMENT
SHIN	DENTES	ANIMAL	0 THE FOOL
TAU	SIGNUM	MICROCOSM	XXI THE WORLD

The relationships between Hebrew letters, Renaissance cosmology, and the trumps, as deduced by Éliphas Lévi from Athanasius Kircher

To the kabbalist, each of the twenty-two Hebrew letters and the numbers from one to ten signifies a unique spiritual power. By matching up the twenty-two tarot trumps with things that Lévi believed the Hebrew letters originally represented, he obtained what he considered a "kabbalistic" interpretation for each card. Through the skillful sleuthing of Decker, Depaulis, and Dummett and a clue offered by Waite in his 1938 autobiography, we now know the sources of Lévi's innovation. He apparently blended ideas taken from Court de Gébelin's *Le monde primitif* with those of Athanasius Kircher, a seventeenth-century Jesuit philologist and polymath. In his book *Oedipus Aegyptiacus,* Kircher had equated the letters of the Hebrew alphabet, and the Latin translations of the names of these letters, with the entire Renaissance cosmos of angels, zodiac signs, planets, and elements.

We shall be seeing the consequences of this equation later, when we examine the trumps in detail.

And what of the suit cards? There were fifty-six of them to account for somehow, and Lévi was certainly not content to accept Etteilla's idiosyncratic system. Instead, he looked again to the Kabbala, specifically to the four-lettered name of God known as the Tetragrammaton, and also to the medieval grimoire (magician's manual) known as the *Key of Solomon.*

The name of the God of Israel that is rendered as "Jehovah" in the Bible is spelled JHVH in Hebrew, with only four Hebrew letters: *Yod, Heh, Vau,* and *Heh* final. To magically minded kabbalists, this name was the supreme wonder-working Word of Power, the correct pronunciation of which could be used to perform any number of miracles. There were actually many of these names, including one of seventy-two syllables derived from the Biblical verses contained in Exodus 14:19–21 and known to kabbalists as the Shemhamphorash. It will come into our tarot tale shortly.

During the course of his kabbalistic studies, Lévi had come across a tradition reported in the sixteenth century by Henry Cornelius Agrippa of Nettesheim, an important chronicler of Renaissance magic, whereby each of the four letters of the Tetragrammaton could be assigned to one of the four Pythagorean elements, thus:

J (*Yod*)–Fire

H (*Heh*)–Water

V (*Vau*)–Air

H (*Heh* final)–Earth

In his popular 1855 book *The Doctrine of Transcendental Magic*, Lévi then made the claim that each of the four tarot suit signs also corresponded to a letter of the Tetragrammaton, in effect giving the following scheme:

J - Fire–Batons or Wands

H - Water–Cups

V - Air–Swords

H final - Earth–Coins or "Pantacles"

Lévi gave no coherent explanation for how he arrived at the relationships between letters and suit signs, but that did not keep him from presenting the correspondences as fact in his 1860 *History of Magic*:

It has been said in the Doctrine of Transcendental Magic that the name Jehovah resolves into seventy-two explicatory names, called Shemhamphorash. The art of employing these seventy-two names and discovering therein the keys of universal science is the art which is called by kabbalists the Keys of Solomon. As a fact, at the end of the collections of prayers and evocations which bear this title there are found usually seventy-two magical circles, *making thirty-six talismans, or four times nine,* being the absolute number multiplied by the tetrad. Each of these talismans bears two of the two-and-seventy names, the sign emblematical of their number and that of the four letters of Tetragrammaton to which they correspond. *From this have originated the four emblematical tarot suits: the Wand, representing the Yod; the Cup, answering to the He; the Sword, referable to the Vau; and the Pentacle, in correspondence with the final He. The complement of the denary has been added in the tarot, thus repeating synthetically the character of unity.* (Italics added)

None of what Lévi says about the seventy-two magical circles and thirty-six talismans is quite true, at least not for any *Key of Solomon* that I have ever seen, but this is what Lévi claimed. Furthermore, in the L. W. de Laurence edition of Mathers's translation of *The Greater Key of Solomon*, a version of the above can be found, but now ascribed to the hand of Solomon like the rest of the book, though credited to Lévi's translation:

I have done great things by the Virtue of the Schema Hamphorasch, and by the Thirty-two Paths of Yetzirah.

Number, weight, and measure determine the form of things; the substance is one, and God createth it eternally.

Happy is he who comprehendeth the Letters and the Numbers.

The Letters are from the Numbers, and the Numbers from the Ideas, and the Ideas from the Forces, and the Forces from the Elohim.

The Synthesis of the Elohim is the Schema.

The Schema is one, its columns are two, its power is three, its form is four, its reflection giveth eight, which multiplied by three giveth unto thee the twenty-four Thrones of Wisdom.

Upon each Throne reposeth a Crown with three Rays, each Ray beareth a Name, each Name is an Absolute Idea. There are Seventy-two Names upon the Twenty-four Crowns of the Schema.

Thou shalt write these Names upon Thirty-six Talismans, two upon each Talisman, one on each side.

Thou shalt divide these Talismans into four series of nine each, according to the number of the Letters of the Schema.

Upon the first Series thou shalt engrave the Letter Yod, symbolized by the Flowering Rod of Aaron.

Upon the second the Letter He, symbolized by the Cup of Joseph.

Upon the third the Letter Vau, symbolized by the Sword of David my father.

And upon the fourth the He final, symbolized by the Shekel of Gold.

These thirty-six Talismans will be a Book which will contain all the Secrets of Nature. And by their diverse combinations thou shalt make the Genii and Angels speak. (Italics added)

The first section of this "Yetziratic" tract is something Lévi could well have concocted out of the *Sepher Yetzirah,* a primary text of the Kabbala, various translations of which were extant at the time he was writing. The Cup of Joseph and the Flowering Rod may have been derived by Lévi from volume IV of Court de Gébelin's *Le monde primitif,* although there Moses is incorrectly identified as the rod's owner. (True, Moses had his own wonder-working rod, but it was Aaron's rod that flowered as a means of settling the question of which tribal chief should lead the twelve tribes of Israel.)

Wherever Lévi came up with the quotation, from some unknown kabbalistic text or his own fertile brain, it is Levi's system—in which the nine fire signs of the zodiac are attributed to Batons, the nine water signs to Cups, the nine air signs to Swords, and the nine earth signs to Coins—grafted onto Etteilla's system, that provides the basis for most tarot divination today.

THE GOLDEN DAWN ATTRIBUTIONS

While Etteilla was clearly the central force in France for disseminating the "Egyptian" system of tarot card interpretation, in England it was the Order of the Golden Dawn that put Lévi's "Kabbala" theory to work.

The Hermetic Order of the Golden Dawn, to give it its full title, was a secret society devoted to the study of the occult arts founded in London in 1888 by Wynn Westcott, MacGregor Mathers, and William K. Woodman, three English Freemasons and latter-day Rosicrucians. The Order's teachings consisted chiefly of a blend of Agrippa's *Occult Philosophy*, its own version of the *Enochian* magic of Queen Elizabeth I's astrologer John Dee, the magical kabbalism of Éliphas Lévi, certain yogic practices, sundry contemporary interpretations of ancient Egyptian magic, and the practice of a variety of divination systems, including the tarot. This was all taught within a framework of hierarchical Rosicrucian grades of initiation typical of the eighteenth century.

During the years of its existence, if you include those of the many temples and societies it spun off, the Golden Dawn drew into its fold such personalities as the Irish poet William Butler Yeats; author Algernon Blackwood; actress Florence Farr; poet-magus Aleister Crowley; kabbalists Dion Fortune, Israel Regardie, and Paul Foster Case; mystical writers Evelyn Underhill and Charles Williams; and last but definitely not least for our purposes, Arthur Edward Waite. Although it began its life as a society bent merely on the theoretical study of the occult, with its growth in membership it expanded its goals to encompass the achievement of practical occult powers and mystical illumination. It claimed to be able to turn its initiates into twentieth-century magi.

The Golden Dawn's version of the tarot was available only to magic-practicing initiates of the higher grades in a second, "inner" order: the Order of the Rose of Ruby and Cross of Gold. This Order tarot offered "rectifications" of its own (such as exchanging the positions in the deck of Justice and Fortitude), redesigns of the court cards and several of the trumps, and exotic new titles for all the cards. It assigned the trumps to Hebrew letters in a way different from Lévi's, however, correlating them with the twenty-two channels or "paths" that link the sephirothic spheres on the kabbalistic Tree of Life, a diagram representing the cosmos. In Hebrew Kabbala there are various versions of the Tree, but the Golden Dawn used the one popularized by the Christian kabbalists of the Renaissance. When it came to the Minor Arcana, the Order followed Etteilla's interpretations but melded them with a fresh source of esoteric symbolism it had discovered: the thirty-six decans of the zodiac.

The Decan System of Rulership

What exactly is a decan, you may ask. Well, a decan is an astrological concept at least five thousand years old, genuinely dating from the time of ancient Egypt. However, today's astrologers and cartomancers owe their decans to the Islamic variant of this concept.

According to Arab and medieval astrologers, each of the twelve signs of the zodiacal band may be divided into three ten-degree arcs. These are called the first, second, and third decanates or decans of the sign. Thus there are thirty-six decans in the zodiac. Each is considered to be ruled by the sun, the moon, or one of the five planets recognized by ancient astrologers. The succession of these celestial bodies through the zodiacal signs is the so-called Chaldean one, in which the planets' ranking is determined by their apparent speeds as they cross the sky, Saturn being the slowest, the moon the fastest. The planets Neptune, Uranus, and Pluto were unknown when the system was invented, but the sun and moon were both counted as planets, making seven in all.

Now, two of these decan systems are commonly used by astrologers, but the Golden Dawn only made use of the one that ascribes Mars to the first decan of Aries, and from here carries on in a repeating Chaldean series—Mars, the sun, Venus, Mercury, the moon, Saturn, Jupiter, Mars, and so on—throughout the thirty-six decans as follows:

ZODIAC SIGN	DECAN 1	DECAN 2	DECAN 3
Aries	Mars	Sun	Venus
Taurus	Mercury	Moon	Saturn
Gemini	Jupiter	Mars	Sun
Cancer	Venus	Mercury	Moon

ZODIAC SIGN	DECAN 1	DECAN 2	DECAN 3
Leo	Saturn	Jupiter	Mars
Virgo	Sun	Venus	Mercury
Libra	Moon	Saturn	Jupiter
Scorpio	Mars	Sun	Venus
Sagittarius	Mercury	Moon	Saturn
Capricorn	Jupiter	Mars	Sun
Aquarius	Venus	Mercury	Moon
Pisces	Saturn	Jupiter	Mars

Like the planets and stars, decans have been associated with a variety of images since Egyptian times. Recent researches by Marco Bertozzi and Gianluigi Magoni suggest that the decan images used by Arab and medieval astrologers, like those of the ancient Egyptians, are derived from the shapes of constellations and star clusters neighboring the constellations of the zodiac. *Picatrix,* a book of astrological magic translated from Arabic into Latin dating from the fourteenth century or earlier, recommended using these images as talismans for a variety of purposes. Two centuries later Agrippa also advocated using them as talismans in his *Three Books of Occult Philosophy.*

Agrippa's *Occult Philosophy* may have sparked the Golden Dawn's idea to marry the thirty-six decans to the thirty-six tarot suit cards (minus the aces and court cards), or it may have been Paul Christian, a student of Lévi's, whose 1870 book *Histoire de la magie* (History of Magic) presented a complex astrological interpretation of the suit cards (quite unlike the Golden Dawn's, however) alongside an Egyptian development of the trumps. Whatever you may think of the Golden Dawn system, though, the decans do add dimension to Etteilla's, possibly traditional, cartomantic interpretations. Indeed, they add seventy-two more variables (counting reversed cards) of a more Hermetic caliber, based on genuinely ancient astrology. However, there's no evidence that I know of that the numbered suit cards ever had any connection with decans before Christian and the Golden Dawn gave them one. Perhaps they did. Another thing we just don't know.

When it came to the court cards, the Golden Dawn Tarot also rearranged them, turning the Knaves into "Princesses" and renaming the Knights on horseback "Kings" and the Kings "Princes." The rationale for this shuffle was, once more, the kabbalistic Tetragrammaton formula, although the Princesses may have been suggested by Italian decks, which, as already noted, sometimes replace the male *Fanti* with female *Fantesca* in the feminine suits of Coins and Cups.

Without burdening the reader with unnecessary explanations of the "Four Worlds" of the Kabbala, suffice it to say that the court cards of the Golden Dawn Tarot were expressly designed to portray divine power manifesting in each world. King cards are said to portray this divine power manifesting in the archetypal world of pure Deity, *Atziluth,* as the mature, masculine *Yod* of the Tetragrammaton *JHVH.* As such, the kings are depicted dynamically, mounted on horseback. Queens are seated on thrones to portray divine power manifesting in the archangelic, creative world of *Briah* as the mature, feminine *Heh.* Princes (Knights) ride in chariots, portraying the young, masculine *Vau* that unites the power of the King and the Queen by manifesting in the angelic, formative world of *Yetzirah.* Princesses (Knaves), portraying the divine power manifesting in the world of action and matter, *Assiah,* are depicted as young, bare-breasted, and standing, uniting the powers of King, Queen, and Prince through the young, dynamic, feminine *Heh* final. Quite apparently, aside from requiring a commitment to kabbalistic doctrine, this scheme significantly complicates the simpler and older cartomantic court card classifications as different types of people.

Some historians believe that the Order tarot was Mathers's invention; others believe that Westcott devised it. Golden Dawn historian Darcy Küntz, for example, published a booklet containing photographs of the sixteen original Golden Dawn court cards and subtitled it *"As drawn by William Wynn Westcott and Moïna Mathers."* Moïna was MacGregor Mathers's wife and a student at the Slade School of Fine Art. She was also, quite literally, the first member to be initiated into the Order, in March of 1888, a month after its founding. So if the depiction of the Golden Dawn tarot can be attributed to Moïna Mathers, then presumably her husband may have had a hand in inventing it, including the detailed decan ascriptions of the suit cards. But Mathers makes no mention of decans in his pamphlet *The Tarot,* which was published in 1888 (although he does refer in its pages to Jean-Alexandre Vaillant, the author of the 1857 text *Les Rômes: Histoire vraie des vrais bohémians* (The Romanies: A True History of True Gypsies) who proposed that Gypsies were responsible for introducing the tarot to Europe and suggested ascribing the two through ten suit cards to the decans). Instead, Mathers simply uses Etteilla's suit card interpretations, word for word mostly, giving any negative, ill-omened interpretations to reversed cards.

On the other hand, the Order tarot may have been the creation of neither Westcott nor Mathers. Some historians now surmise that the inspiration for the Golden Dawn itself can be traced to the brain of one Kenneth Mackenzie, a scholarly occultist who may have been responsible for the rudimentary enciphered notes on which the Golden Dawn rituals and teachings were based. Mackenzie was a member of the Societas Rosicruciana in Anglia, a Rosicrucian society that later came to count both Westcott and Mathers among its membership, and this may have been the link that gave them access to Mackenzie's papers after his death in 1886—and possibly to descriptions of a revised tarot.

No tarot deck designs traceable to Mackenzie apparently survive, however, although he did inform both Westcott and Mathers that he was at one time considering writing a book on the subject. His interest in it also appears in an account he wrote for his Rosicrucian society's journal, the *Rosicrucian and the Red Cross,* detailing questions he asked Éliphas Lévi on the occasion of a visit to Paris in 1861. This connection between Mackenzie and the French magus might explain the attributions of the suit cards to the elements and Tetragrammaton, but the the origin of their attribution to the decans still remains a mystery. I think it probable that Westcott devised the court cards and maybe the trumps, leaving the suits to Mathers, who, taking the hint from Vaillant and Christian, married them to the decans.

Waite seemed to change his mind about the tarot over the years. Although under his own name he generally adopted a critical attitude to what he deemed vulgar fortune-telling, that didn't prevent him, somewhat disingenuously one might think, from publishing a variety of "how-to" fortune-telling books. Most notable among these is the 1889 book entitled *A Handbook of Cartomancy, Fortune-Telling and Occult Divination* that Waite published under the pseudonym Grand Orient and reissued later with minor changes as the *Manual of Cartomancy.* Here he gives the customary interpretations of regular playing cards under the heading "The English Method of Fortune-Telling by Cards" (which correspond by and large to those revealed by Robert Chambers in his *Book of Days* of 1864) but declines in a chapter on the tarot to reveal the interpretations of the tarot suit cards "because they would involve the statement of certain facts on occult divination which have never been made public."

Presumably, Waite was referring to the Golden Dawn decan attributions, which in 1889 he believed to be a genuine tradition handed down from antiquity via the Golden Dawn's "secret chiefs"—the hidden high-grade adepts alleged to govern the order in much the same way as Madame Blavatsky's mahatmas were said to govern the Theosophical Society. However, in 1910's *The Pictorial Key to the Tarot,* which Waite wrote under his real name, he declares that inasmuch as the Minor Arcana suit cards are essentially the same as a deck of regular playing cards, they therefore possess only fortune-telling or gambling potential rather than deep esoteric secrets. Furthermore, he now happily includes the order's decan-derived interpretations (although not identified as such), as well as Etteilla's fortune-telling interpretations, which like those in Mathers's 1888 book, are quoted practically verbatim from Etteilla.

One wonders whether Waite, at this stage disillusioned by the Golden Dawn's pretensions to antiquity, now felt free to disregard his initiatory oaths of secrecy and disclose the decan interpretations of the tarot imparted by the Order. Whatever the truth may have been, along with publication of his own book on tarot divination in 1910, Waite was also to oversee the republication of another book on the same subject that he had seen fit to revise, and to which he had added a critical, though friendly, introductory preface. This was *The Tarot of the Bohemians,* by Dr. Gérard-Anaclet-Vincent Encausse, otherwise known to the world as Papus.

PAPUS AND HIS "BOHEMIAN" TAROT

Second only to Éliphas Lévi, Encausse is a prime contender for the prize for being the most influential popularizer of the occult during the nineteenth and beginning of the twentieth centuries. Aside from practicing as a physician, he wrote voluminously about esoteric matters under the Papus pseudonym. This odd name, according to Lévi, whom Encausse greatly admired, belonged to one of the genii to be found in a Greek theurgic tract. Known to occultists as the *Nuctemeron of Apollonius,* the text had been used by Lévi to conjure up the shade of the dead philosopher Apollonius of Tyana in 1854. The genius Papus is said to rule the first hour of the day and, very suitably for Encausse, to personify the practice of medicine.

Having been refused initiation into the order of Freemasonry, Papus subsequently seems to have compensated for the slight by either founding, or becoming a member of, most of the prominent occult orders that flourished in France in his time. He briefly became a member of the Paris branch of the Golden Dawn in 1895.

Like his fellow occultists, Papus took a keen interest in the tarot. He subscribed to the by now popular theory that Gypsies were responsible for its introduction from the East, and that the cards were the "Bible of Bibles," the "Book of Thoth Hermes Trismegistus, the Book of Adam, the book of the primitive Revelation of ancient civilizations."

His own books on the tarot—*Le tarot des Bohémiens* (The Gypsies' Tarot, translated in its various English editions as *The Tarot of the Bohemians*) and *Le tarot divinatoire* (The Divining Tarot)—though popular, were essentially a synthesis of the thoughts of other occultists about the subject, and although Papus attempted to establish his own system of card interpretations, it was unconvincing and unenlightening. He was ultimately forced to recur to the old and established interpretations of Etteilla. What Papus did supply, however, aside from a tarot deck designed to his own specifications, were new methods of laying the cards out for divination purposes. He also insisted that the Minor Arcana was as important in its way as the Major, a point with which Waite concurred.

Papus's name will crop up again in our tarot tale, notably in chapter 6. Now, however, having laid the groundwork, it's time to turn our attention to the tarot cards themselves, individually and in detail.

4

THE MEANINGS OF THE TRUMP CARDS: THE MAJOR ARCANA

In the past it seems to have been the custom for those who wrote about interpreting tarot cards to begin with the Major Arcana. Maybe this was because the trumps were considered to be more important, and there was more to be said about them. Or maybe, like so much else about the tarot, it was simply traditional. Etteilla and d'Odoucet did it that way, and so did Mathers, and so did Waite; I see no reason not to follow their example.

In this chapter, therefore, we shall be delving into the imagery of each tarot trump and its meaning at the time that it was incorporated into the deck. To begin, we should recall that the trumps follow a definite sequence that has changed very little over the centuries. This in itself tells us certain things about them. They commence with worldly matters and then progress to more important, otherworldly concerns as they rise in their order of progression. It may be on this account that a tradition exists whereby the trumps I–V are known as the Lesser Trumps, and trumps XVII–XXI as the Greater Trumps.

To account for later variations in trump design, we must also bear in mind that the original sources of the imagery were probably lost sight of by the second half of the sixteenth century, so designers of new decks were free to add their own frills. Most did so without departing too far from a recognizable pattern, but also without a true understanding of what they were depicting.

For the insight it can provide, I shall be including the various titles by which the early decks of tarots have been known down the years, including the Latin ones found on a sixteenth-century Venetian hand-painted wood-block partial deck in the Leber Collection at the Municipal Library of Rouen, France.

We shall also glance at the various documented divinatory meanings that were attached to the trumps by early occultists. I won't try to analyze the chains of reasoning that led the cartomancers to their conclusions here. As most of them were ignorant of the images' original symbolism, many of their interpretations appear to be well off the mark, except for those attached to the more obvious cards such as the virtues. Etteilla's trump interpretations are a prime example of this—an incredible muddle, in accordance with the radical rearrangement of the trumps' sequence and, in many cases, their imagery. In Etteilla's case then, I shall be omitting most (but not all) of his Major Arcana interpretations as, with few exceptions, they appear to be more than anything the product of his imagination. We shall concentrate rather on the interpretations of Court de Gébelin's collaborator the Comte de Mellet, Éliphas Lévi, Paul Christian, MacGregor Mathers, the Golden Dawn, Waite, and those fragmentary notes discovered by Franco Pratesi. In this manner, we will also be able to discern the bouncing of various ideas from cartomancer to cartomancer down the decades, ideas that have now become part of the "received wisdom" of the tarot.

Surprisingly, Court de Gébelin himself didn't have very much to say of concrete value to the cartomancer except to rename ten of the trumps. It was de Mellet, whose tarot essay Court de Gébelin incorporated into his *Monde primitif,* who provided the first published list of trump interpretations, closely followed by Etteilla. Later, Lévi provided his own kabbalistic interpretations in the last chapter of his *Ritual of Transcendental Magic,* all of which he derived from his understanding of Athanasius Kircher's significations of the Hebrew letters, theoretical foundations built, alas, on a mountain of shifting sand. Christian combined Court de Gébelin's Egyptian symbolism with Lévi's kabbalistic designs, adding many interpretations of his own. Mathers combined Court de Gébelin, Etteilla, Lévi, and Christian, adhering to Etteilla's interpretations of the suit cards for the most part. The Golden Dawn likewise drew from all the above, as did Waite, usually adding his own twist. Basically, he published two sets of interpretations, one under his pseudonym "Grand Orient" in his *Manual of Cartomancy,* and a later set under his own name in his *Pictorial Key to the Tarot.* They show a certain amount of overlap, but also some definite divergence, so I'll refer to both for comparison. In the *Manual,* Waite included two further sets of interpretations, described as those pertaining to the "World of Conformity" and those pertaining to the "World of Attainment." Both sets are repetitive and obscure, referring to matters involved with the kabbalistic Christianity Waite had evolved, so I have omitted them from discussion as too divergent from our central theme. Those interested should consult his *Manual.*

In the sections that follow, I shall give first what I believe to be the origin of the trump's image, then its cartomantic interpretations, and lastly, my own suggested interpretations. These are basically mnemonics to help the aspiring cartomancer remember the card's root meanings, that is, the meanings that I have found to be most useful for divination over the years. Of course, you are at liberty to pick and choose from any of the interpretations, including mine if you like. In any case, as we shall see later, when you perform a reading, you'll be obliged to put your own spin on the cards' traditional meanings and find contemporary equivalents. I shall be quoting directly from the cartomancers' original works, with deletions of irrelevant text where necessary; my own comments are enclosed within brackets.

All of the illustrations immediately following the headings for each trump are from Conver's Tarot of Marseille, 1761 which, following Etteilla's lead, is taken as the prototype for many, if not most, divinatory tarot decks.

TRUMP 0, THE FOOL

ALTERNATE NAMES: *LE MAT, IL MATTO, MATTELLO,
IL PAZZO, LE FOL*

Medieval and Renaissance prints and engravings entitled Children of the Planets appear in books of the period, depicting the rule of the seven astrological planets over types of people and their professions. The image of the Fool frequently appears as one of these children, in his case ruled by the moon. He is, in fact, a "lunatic." As a trump, the Fool carries no number, maybe because he stands outside the social order of medieval life. He is the homeless, placeless, frequently mentally ill person, cast adrift and left to beg for charity on the streets. He appears at the early medieval clerical Feast of Fools and in later morality plays, where he was free to move onto and off the stage, addressing the characters and addressing the audience. At some point in the history of theater his presence onstage came to constitute so much of a distraction that he was used as an independent intermezzo between serious scenes. His part was frequently left unwritten; play scripts would simply indicate when the Fool should speak, and it was left up to the actor to improvise. He played a popular and central part in German medieval drama, where he was known as the *Narr*—a congenital idiot who frequently used his obtuseness to his own advantage.

Despite their outcast station in life, cleverer Fools found niches for themselves in the medieval and Renaissance courts of great lords, where, like poor Yorrick, they provided ongoing comedy and jokes to supplement the entertainment provided by the periodic visits of troubadours and jongleurs, Indeed, court fools could attain considerable fame, in the manner of Mattello, who was court fool to Isabella d'Este, the Marchioness of Mantua. His name, derived from the Italian word *matto,* meaning "mad," still turns up in some tarocchi decks.

Theoretically, the Fool was the one person at court immune from retribution for quips he made at anybody's expense. However, like King Lear's Fool, all too often he became a whipping boy for his master, for he was also a scapegoat. In fact, in games played with tarot cards he is sometimes known as the *Skys,* "the Excuse," an expendable card you may play if you want to save a trump you otherwise would be forced to sacrifice by following suit.

In early painted tarot decks you will find him sometimes dressed in penitential white and sometimes in rags. Often the seat of his hose is being torn at by a dog; in one deck his genitals are being exposed by teasing children pulling at his rags. Sometimes he wears feathers stuck in his hair, as in the Visconti-Sforza deck, or sports an ass-eared jester's cap. Indeed, the medieval drama's fool costume traditionally consisted of a tight-fitting hood with long ass's ears at the sides and sometimes a cockscomb trimmed with hawk bells on the top.

The flaps of his coat frequently ended in bells too, and his long, tight trousers were often of variegated colors, the favorite tints being light green and yellow. The Mantegna engravings of 1484 show him simply as a beggar. The seventeenth-century tarocchini deck of Bologna engraved by Mitelli in the pages of a book depicts him as a lunatic (see illustration below).

In most decks the Fool is left unnumbered or counted as zero and placed at the beginning of the trumps, although some place him at the end. The Italians used to say colloquially, "Esser come Il Matto nel tarocchi" (to be like the tarot Fool)—all over the place, at home everywhere and nowhere.

Original Cartomantic Interpretations

Pratesi's Cartomancer (1750): Madness.

De Mellet (1781): Madness. He has no rank.

Lévi (1855): The Hebrew letter *Shin,* the Fool. The sensitive principle, the flesh, eternal life.

Christian (1870): Arcanum 0. The Crocodile. Expiation. The punishment following every error. You can see here a blind man carrying a beggar's wallet, about to collide with a broken obelisk on which a crocodile waits with open jaws. The crocodile is the emblem of fate and the inevitable expiation.

Mathers (1888): The Foolish Man. Folly, expiation, wavering. *Reversed:* Hesitation, instability, trouble arising herefrom.

Golden Dawn (1888–96): The Spirit of the Ether. Foolish Man. Idea, spirituality, that which endeavors to rise above the material. [That is, if the subject inquired about is spiritual.] But if the divination be regarding ordinary life, the card is not good, and shows folly, stupidity, eccentricity, and even mania unless with very good cards indeed.

Grand Orient (Waite, 1889, 1909): The Fool signifies the consummation of everything, when that which began his initiation at zero attains the term of all numeration and existence. This card passes through all the numbered cards and is changed in each, as the natural man passes through worlds of lesser experience, worlds of successive attainment.

Waite (1910): The Fool. Folly, mania, extravagance, intoxication, delirium, frenzy. *Reversed:* Negligence, absence, apathy, nullity.

Suggested Interpretation

Mania. Intoxication. Infantilism. Innocence. Unpredictability. Anarchy. *Reversed:* Stupidity. Nullity. Apathy. Sloth. Mental illness.

TRUMP I, THE JUGGLER

ALTERNATE NAMES: THE MOUNTEBANK, THE THIMBLE-RIGGER,
THE QUARTERPENNY, *LE PAGAD, LE BATELEUR, IL BAGATINO,
IL BAGATTO, IL BAGATTEL, IL BAGAT, IL CIABATTINO*

Elevated by Lévi to the title and status of Magus, this card originally depicted a medieval street entertainer, also known at the time as a *prestigiator* or *tregatour,* performing his sleight of hand and tricks of legerdemain, which would, of course, be attributed to the power of *nigremance,* that is, genuine magic.

However, despite all his vaunted occult skills, even the Juggler is not immune from Death's sting. John Lydgate, an early-fifteenth-century cleric (and maybe author of miracle plays), wrote somberly in his poem *Daunce de Macabre* (Dance of Death) of the participation in the dance of one famous *tregatour,* a certain John Rykell:

> *Maister John Rykell, sometyme tregitoure*
> *Of noble Henry kynge of Englonde,*
> *And of Fraunce the mighty conqueroure,*
> *For all the sleightes and turnyngs of thyne honde,*
> *Thou must come nere this daunce to understonde . . .*
> *Lygarde de mayne now helpeth thee right nought.*

The skillful Juggler has long entertained the world with one principal sleight of hand, which is depicted in this tarot trump. The cups-and-ball trick uses several, usually three, inverted cups and one ball that is

seemingly placed under one cup. The cups are then switched around rapidly with one another, and the unwary onlooker is encouraged to bet money on which cup the ball is under. So successful is this illusion that it continues to be used in the twenty-first century: I recently saw it being performed by a contemporary Italian *Bagatto* on the Accademia Bridge in Venice. The young man was using three small box tops and a ball of crumpled paper. An unwary German tourist was encouraged to win money on the first and second rounds, but the money was all taken back, plus some, in the third.

Customarily, a bag with strings was used to aid this trick, a piece of paraphernalia that can be seen reposing on the right-hand side of the Juggler's table in many tarot trumps of the Marseille pattern. This was a handy place from which to acquire and dispose of the ball. In some tarot decks we see it worn at the Juggler's waist. In this way the word *Taschenspieler* (pocket player) became a common term for such a sleight-of-hand artist in Germany. The Juggler also appears like this in woodcuts used to illustrate "Luna and her Children" from fifteenth-century German block-books entitled *The Work of the Planets*. The Juggler may be seen here at his table bamboozling a gullible little group of onlookers. But it is the onlookers who are the planetary children in question, for they are simpleminded bumpkins being taken for fools, and there-

fore considered to fall under the moon's influence. The Juggler is similarly displayed in the fifteenth-century *Housebook of Wolfegg Castle*.

The card in the fifteenth-century tarocchi deck in the Metropolitan Museum of Art also depicts this favorite Juggler's trick, as does Hieronymus Bosch.

The seventeenth-century Tarot of Paris actually shows the Juggler befuddling the Fool with the trick.

As the Vice in later morality plays, the Juggler was represented as the devil's invisi-

ble boon companion, whose function was to belabor other unsuspect-
ing players mirthfully with a device
made of two wooden lathes bound
together at the base, which gave out
a sharp slapping sound when
wielded. This was his "slapstick"
(whence, of course, our comedy
term). In Italian and French com-

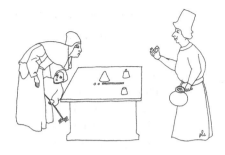

media dell'arte, the slapstick was inherited by Arlecchino or Harlequin,
who are the Juggler's later incarnations.

As the archetypal trickster, the Juggler is also of course a great
chatterbox. As Getrude Moakley pointed out in 1966, the Italian tarocco
titles for the Juggler—*Pagad* or *Bagatto*—could derive from the word
bagatt, meaning "gossip," in the Milanese Italian dialect.

Occasionally, as in the Mantegna engravings and the nineteenth-century Milanese pattern of tarocchi introduced by the card maker
Gumppenberg, the Juggler is pictured as an artisan or cobbler instead of
a sleight-of-hand artist. We can also find him depicted in this manner
among the Children of the Planets, but here the prints illustrate the influence of the Juggler's own ruling planet, Mercury, the archetypal trickster
and wheeler-dealer. Mercury's name itself derives from the Latin *merx*
and *mercator,* the basis for our word *merchant,* implying one involved in
barter and selling.

Original Cartomantic Interpretations

Pratesi's Cartomancer (1750): Bagattino, married man.

De Mellet (1781): The Mountebank.

Court de Gébelin (1773–82): The Thimble-Rigger.

Lévi (1855): The Hebrew letter *Aleph,* the Juggler. The Magus. Being, mind, man, or God; the comprehensible object; unity; mother of numbers; the first substance.

Christian (1870): The Magus: Will. Arcanum I expresses in the divine world the Absolute Being who contains and from whom flow all possible things; in the intellectual world, Unity, the principle and synthesis of numbers; in the physical world, Man, the highest of all living creatures.

Mathers (1888): The Juggler or Magician. Willpower, dexterity. *Reversed:* Will applied to evil ends, weakness of will, knavishness.

Golden Dawn (1888–96): The Magus of Power. The Magician or Juggler. Skill, wisdom, adaptation, cunning, always depending on the cards around it and whether or not it's reversed. Sometimes occult wisdom.

Grand Orient (Waite, 1889, 1909): The Juggler. Skill, subtlety, on the evil side, trickery. Also occult practice.

Waite (1910): The Magician. Skill, diplomacy, subtlety, snares of enemies, the inquirer—if male. *Reversed:* Physician, magus, disgrace.

Suggested Interpretation

Skill. Dexterity. Diplomacy. *Reversed:* Deceit. Quackery. Swindling.

Trump II, the Female Pope

Alternate names: The Popess, Pope Joan, the High Priestess, *Junon, La Papesse, La Papessa*

First dubbed the High Priestess by Court de Gébelin, this card has always presented a great puzzle to students of the tarot and generated some of the most frenzied speculation. Various theories have been advanced about its origins, and several of them have merit and so are worth examining.

Stuart Kaplan, in his *Encyclopedia of Tarot,* proposes the idea that the trump may represent the papacy itself, and takes as his source for this image the sixteenth-century Italian painter Giorgio Vasari's *Allegory of Papal Triumph,* painted to celebrate the victory of Spain, Venice, and the papacy over the Turks at the Battle of Lepanto. Vasari's painting depicts a standing woman wearing the papal triple-crowned tiara and carrying the Keys of Saint Peter.

The problem with Kaplan's interpretation is a simple one. The trumps already have a symbol for the papacy, namely Trump V, the Pope. What need for another?

Gertrude Moakley, in her persuasive 1966 *Tarot Cards Painted by Bembo,* advances the theory that in the Visconti-Sforza painted tarocchi, at least, the Female Pope is a relative of the Visconti family, a nun of the Umiliata order named Sister Manfreda, who was in fact elected pope by the small Lombard sect of Guglielmites at the beginning of the fourteenth century.

She was, of course, burned at the stake as a heretic by the Inquisition in 1300, and the church later proceeded against the first Visconti Duke of

Milan for his very slight connection with the sect. Moakley's analysis of the family history behind the Bembo cards is extremely thorough, although I find it curious that the Visconti-Sforzas would have wanted one of their more eccentric relatives, especially one who had been burned as a heretic, portrayed on an expensive deck of playing cards and thus memorialized. Moreover, the Female Pope also appears in three wood-block-printed fifteenth-century decks that we know of, and I find it less likely that these represent Sister Manfreda than that the Bembo depiction of Sister Manfreda, if that is who she is, was a version of the already established icon of the Female Pope.

Robert O'Neill, in his intriguing *Tarot Symbolism,* proposes that the mysterious lady is in fact the Egyptian goddess Isis. In the 1909 deck that Pamela Colman Smith designed for Waite, the Female Pope is portrayed wearing a horned lunar crown and carrying an equal-armed solar cross on her breast. Here Waite was following the description of the card Lévi had provided in his *Ritual of Transcendental Magic,* which the French magus declared was inspired by an illustration he believed to be an image of Isis that he had come across in an old Protestant book of anti-Catholic propaganda. O'Neill, on the other hand, traces what he believes to be the Female Pope's Isis identity to a mural painted on a wall in the Vatican, in the Appartamento Borgia. Unfortunately the figure in the mural looks nothing like the Female Pope, save for the inclusion of a small open book that she demurely scans with downcast eyes. Furthermore, she wears a simple coronet, not a triple-crowned papal tiara. The Isis connection to this card may one day turn out to have some basis in fact, but unfortunately O'Neill's iconographical "proof" falls short of being convincing.

O'Neill also offers an alternative notion that the trump may represent a sibyl. One of these pagan seeresses does indeed appear in the mystery plays among the various Old Testament prophets who foretell the birth of Jesus. However, again we have a problem with the imagery. The details provided by Martial Rose of the sibyl's costume in mystery plays performed at the Feast of the Circumcision in the cathedrals of Laon and Rouen describe her as crowned, with hair streaming and an expression of mad inspiration on her face—not exactly our serene Female

Pope. The mosaic pavement of the cathedral in Siena constructed in 1482 and 1483 also depicts ten sibyls (and yes, these mysterious women do carry books or scrolls—the so-called Sibylline Books, in fact), but no, they look nothing like the Female Pope as she's portrayed in any tarot deck I know of.

Of course, the Florentine minchiate avoids the entire problem. There, in the same way that we have the Emperor of the East and the Emperor of the West, we also have two Popes, which was indeed the case at one time, one in Rome and one in Avignon. Perhaps there was never meant to be a Female Pope at all? There was just a slight mistake in gender? I think not. The old trump was too well known and too notorious to be dismissed like that.

The lady's big book, however, is interesting and possibly significant. It brings me to my last theory, which I believe to be the correct one—that is, that the card represents exactly what it says it does: Pope Joan.

As Kaplan points out, Joan was believed to have reached her position of eminence through her erudition, hence the big book that she holds in many tarot cards. Aside from her usurpation of the papacy, an exclusively masculine domain, the church may have considered Joan's greatest sin to be her learning, represented by the large book.

And as Dummett notes, both Pope and Female Pope trumps are known to have given offense to papal authorities, who finally prevailed in German-speaking areas of the Holy Roman Empire in the seventeenth century and had the cards replaced by figures of Jupiter and Juno, respectively. The choice of the name Junon or Juno is interesting, being about as close to the name Joan as you can get.

It is true that Joan has since been judged by scholars to be a figment of antipapal imagination, and the English clergyman responsible for the hymn "Onward, Christian Soldiers," Sabine Baring-Gould, in his compilation of medieval legends, *Curious Myths of the Middle Ages,* proposed that her legend was a Greek Orthodox confection designed to throw discredit on the papal hierarchy. However, medieval chroniclers Jean de Mailly, Anastasius the Librarian, Marianus Scotus, and Sigebert de Gemblours all write of her, as do Petrarch and Boccaccio. The Dominican monk Jean de Mailly was the first to mention her in his *Chronicle,* around 1255, and her existence was widely and long accepted. She was said to have been elected to the papacy in 855 as Pope John VIII. Chronicler Martin Polonus gives the following details of her story:

> After Leo IV, John Anglus, a native of Metz, reigned two years, five months and four days. And the pontificate was vacant for a month. He died in Rome. He is related to have been a female, and, when a girl, to have accompanied her lover in male costume to Athens; there she advanced in various sciences, and none could be found to equal her. So, after having studied for three years in Rome, she had great masters for her pupils and hearers. And when there arose a high opinion in the city of her virtue and knowledge, she was unanimously elected Pope. But during her papacy she became pregnant by a servant. Not knowing the time of birth, as she was on her way from Saint Peter's to the Lateran she had a painful delivery, between the Coliseum and Saint Clement's Church, in the street.

Some versions of the story recount that the child and mother died on the spot, some that she survived and was imprisoned, and others that the child was spirited away to become the Antichrist of the last days. Later Protestant writers were not satisfied that the father of the baby should have been only a servant: some made him a cardinal, others Satan himself.

Fiction or not, the most likely reason poor Joan finds herself accompanying Death in the tarot trump parade is that she actually made dozens of appearances in German miracle plays specifically about her, an example of one being *Frau Jutten,* written in 1480 by the cleric Theoderich Schernberg. According to Baring-Gould, "Jutt" was one of Joan's many aliases, and indeed the play tells the story of an ambitious woman who assumes male clothing, attains high ecclesiastical office, and finally becomes Pope. She is, alas, unmasked, does rigorous penance, but is ultimately saved from hell by the intercession of the Virgin Mary. Joan's iconographic source in medieval drama is, in fact, the *only* reason for her inclusion in the trumps parade that makes any sense to me.

Giovanni Boccaccio included Joan among the ranks of great women of antiquity and sang her praises, albeit qualified, in his *De mulieribus claris* (About Famous Women), which he wrote around 1361, supposedly inspired by his friend Petrarch's *De viris illustribus* (Lives of Illustrious Men). Today, in fact, many cartomancers see her as an archetype of feminist issues.

Original Cartomantic Interpretations

De Mellet (1781): Juno. Pride, symbolized by her peacock. Idolatry.

Court de Gébelin (1773–82): The High Priestess.

Lévi (1855): The Hebrew letter *Beth,* the Female Pope. The house of God and Man, the sanctuary, the law, gnosis, Kabbala, the occult church, the duad, wife or mother.

Christian (1870): Arcanum II. The door of the occult sanctuary. Knowledge.

Mathers (1888): The High Priestess. Science, wisdom, education. *Reversed:* Conceit, ignorance, unskillfulness, superficial knowledge.

Golden Dawn (1888–96): The Priestess of the Silver Star. High Priestess. Change, increase and decrease. Fluctuation (whether for good or evil is shown by cards connected with it.)

Grand Orient (Waite, 1889, 1909): High Priestess. Nature, including generation and reproduction, fertility, change.

Waite (1910): The High Priestess. Secrets, mystery, the unrevealed future. The woman who interests the inquirer, if male; the inquirer herself, if female. Wisdom and science. *Reversed:* Moral or physical ardor, conceit, surface knowledge.

Suggested Interpretation

Radical theories. New paradigms. *Reversed:* False revelations. Incorrect conclusions.

TRUMP III, THE EMPRESS

ALTERNATE NAME: *L'IMPERATRICE*

As the wife of the Emperor, the Empress partakes in various Dances of Death. "I thought I had a lot of power. . . . Oh, let me live on, I implore you!" she begs the Grim Reaper in the Lübeck play. In a lighter vein she also appears in Boccaccio's *De mulieribus claris* (About Famous Women) as the Empress Irene of Byzantium, immediately after Pope Joan. On the other hand, if the Emperor Trump represents Frederick III (a subject we shall explore in the next card), then the Empress is his wife, Leonora of Portugal, whom he married in 1552.

In the fifteenth-century Milanese deck in the Cary Collection, both the Empress and her husband carry shields bearing an eagle, the heraldic device of the Holy Roman Empire and an image carried into the Visconti-Sforza deck.

In fact, not until 1855 does she exchange her imperial crown for the stellar crown of modern tarots. At this date, Éliphas Lévi transforms her into the "woman clothed with the Sun and crowned with twelve stars"—of the biblical Book of Revelation—and names her Venus-Urania, later altered by Christian to Isis-Urania. In 1909 Waite added a further touch by transforming the eagle on her shield into the astrological symbol for Venus.

In terms of archetypal significance, one might

follow Boccaccio's lead and say that all the famous women rulers of antiquity are represented by this trump's image: Isis, Jocasta, Hecuba, Clytemnestra, Penelope, Dido, Olympias, Mariamne, Cleopatra, and Irene, the eighth-century Empress of Byzantium. Today we should see her as the supreme archetype of female secular authority and political power at work on or behind the throne.

All the cartomancers who followed the lead of Lévi, who had matched the trumps with Kircher's Hebrew alphabet and come up with the letter *Gimel,* meaning "the Camel," adopted "plenitude" as an interpretation for the Empress.

However, if Boccacio's work is borne in mind, Jocasta, Clytemnestra, Olympias, and Irene herself show very different faces from that presented by Waite's romanticized image.

Original Cartomantic Interpretations

De Mellet (1781): The Queen.

Court de Gébelin (1773–82): The Queen.

Lévi (1855): The Hebrew letter *Gimel,* the Empress. The word, the triad, plenitude, fecundity, nature, generation in the three worlds.

Christian (1870): Arcanum III. Isis-Urania: Action. In the divine world, the supreme power balanced by the eternally active mind and absolute wisdom; in the intellectual world, the universal fecundity of the Supreme Being; in the physical world, nature in labor, the germination of the acts that are to spring from the will.

Mathers (1888): The Empress. Action, plan, movement in a matter, initiative. *Reversed:* Inaction, frittering away of power, lack of concentration, vacillation.

Golden Dawn (1888–96): Daughter of the Mighty Ones. Empress. Beauty, pleasure, success, luxury; sometimes dissipation, but only with very evil cards.

Grand Orient (Waite, 1889, 1909): Empress. The sphere of action; the feminine side of power, rule, and authority; woman's influence; physical beauty; woman's reign; also the joy of life, and excesses on the evil side.

Waite (1910): The Empress. Fruitfulness, action, initiative. *Reversed:* Light, truth, the unraveling of involved matters, public rejoicings; according to another reading [Mathers], vacillation.

Suggested Interpretation

Female political power. Beneficence. Plenitude. *Reversed:* Waste. Vacillation. Overindulgence. Abuse of female political power.

TRUMP IV, THE EMPEROR

ALTERNATE NAMES: *L'EMPEREUR, L'IMPERATORE, L'IMPERADORE*

"I don't know whom to call for help against Death, who has me in his power!" complains the Emperor in the *Dance of Death* that once adorned the Cemetery of the Innocents in Paris.

At its foundation, the Holy Roman Empire was supposed to be the realization of the ideal of the Imperium Christianum, at once the heir of the ancient Empire of Rome and, at the same time, the secular counterpart of the church. As we have noted, Charles the Great, King of the Franks, subsequently known to history as Charlemagne, was crowned the first Holy Roman Emperor of the West in 800 C.E. Over the succeeding centuries, the imperial crown was fiercely fought over, until in 1452 the Holy Roman Emperor's powers were diminished and limited to German lands only. The Empire subsequently came to an end in 1806.

It is possible that the Emperor trump portrays Charlemagne, although the costume he wears in the Marseille pattern is not, as Moakley noted, one that Charlemagne would have worn, but rather that of a European archduke of a later period. As Moakley also pointed out, card makers were more likely to portray an emperor reigning at the time trumps were invented, possibly Emperor Frederick III. He lived from 1415 to 1493 and was crowned emperor by Pope Nicholas V in Rome in 1452, the last emperor in fact to be crowned there. On the other hand, the trump could equally well represent Sigismund, who received the Iron Crown of Lombardy in

Milan in 1431 before being crowned Holy Roman Emperor at Rome in 1433.

In medieval and Renaissance iconography, the Emperor symbolized secular rule as opposed to religious rule, and he turns up in the engraver Erhard Schön's 1515 horoscope woodcut as a symbol for the tenth house of the astrological chart, known to astrologers as the House of Dignities.

In astrology the sky is divided into twelve portions by means of great imaginary circles that cross the north and south points of the horizon, through which the stars and planets pass every twenty-four hours. Not to be confused with the signs of the zodiac, each of these divisions is called a "house." The tenth house is considered to represent, among other things, the profession of the individual to whom the chart belongs. Doubtless the image on the trump in the fifteenth century would have carried this connotation to those who knew anything about astrology. Today the tenth house also carries the notion of the inquirer's honor, fame, promotion, employer, and the affairs of the government and country in general.

Original Cartomantic Interpretations

De Mellet (1781): The king.

Court de Gébelin (1773–82): The king.

Lévi (1855): The Hebrew letter *Daleth,* the emperor. The Porte (the Turkish Sultan's court), or government of the East, initiation, power, the Tetragram, the quaternary, the cubic stone.

Christian (1870): Arcanum IV. The Cubic Stone. Realization.

Mathers (1888): The Emperor. Realization, effect, development. *Reversed:* Stoppage, check, immaturity.

Golden Dawn (1888–96): Son of the Morning, chief among the mighty. Emperor. War, victory, strife, ambition.

Grand Orient (Waite, 1889, 1909): Emperor. Logic, experience, wisdom, male power.

Waite (1910): The Emperor. Stability, power, protection, realization, a great person, aid, reason, conviction, authority, and will. *Reversed:* Confusion to enemies, obstruction, immaturity.

Suggested Interpretation

Male political power. Stability. Potency. Protection. *Reversed:* Abuse of male political power. Authoritarianism. Micromanagement.

Trump V, the Pope

Alternate names: *Pontifex Pontificium* (Priest of Priests), the Hierophant, the High Priest, Jupiter, *Le Pape, Il Papa*

"Alas! Must I lead the Dance and be the first in line, I who am the very incarnation of God?" cries the Pope when Death comes to confront him in the *Dance* at Les Innocents.

As successor to the apostle Simon Peter, the pope, whose title means "father," was considered to be the head of the Christian Church in western Europe. Basically, however, he was the bishop of Rome. His titles, aside from *Pontifex* (bridge builder between man and divinity), a title he derived from pagan Rome, included *Romanus Pontifex, Sanctissimus Pater, Sanctissimus Dominus Noster,* and many others. The pope was the "vicar," or substitute, for Jesus, and was frequently depicted as holding the symbolic keys that Jesus was believed to have granted to Simon Peter to bind and loose men from the spiritual consequences of their sins.

However, by the end of 1378, about the time we find our first mention of playing cards, the papacy was being contended for by two rival popes. Clement VII, who maintained his court in Avignon, was being backed by France, Scotland, Savoy, Castile, Aragon, and Navarre, while Urban VI in Rome was being supported by the Holy Roman Emperors, Bohemia, Poland, Hungary, and northern and central Italy. Indeed, from 1378 until 1417, there were to be two, sometimes even three, rival popes, each with his administration and college of cardinals! There is no reason to suppose that the pope depicted in the tarot trump is any particular one of them—they were all very mortal, and as such they all took part in the

Dance of Death. However, in the painted fifteenth-century Bembo decks, as we have noted, the pope depicted is probably Nicholas V, the reigning pope at the time of their creation. Nicholas began what was later to become the Vatican Library, and indeed was a great patron of the growing flock of humanists—scholars who exalted Greek and Roman culture—keeping hundreds of copyists and scholars in his employ to forward the advance of literacy and learning.

As with the Female Pope card, during the seventeenth century the church encouraged the remaining German-speaking countries of the Holy Roman Empire to find a substitute image for what they considered the inappropriate depiction of the pope, and it is ironic that the image they selected to replace it was that of Jupiter, the Olympian Sky Father. In medieval representations of the classical gods, Jupiter was often portrayed in the robes of a prelate, monk, or even the pope himself.

In medieval and Renaissance iconography, the image of the Pope represents religious, as opposed to secular, authority. Erhard Schön displays him in the ninth house of his horoscope chart, the House of Religion, which generally deals with long journeys, foreign countries, dreams, and visions, as well as religion, philosophy, and higher intellectual pursuits. As the *Pontifex,* the pope is the interpreter of the mysteries of the unseen, whether religious or what today we would call scientific. It may seem counterintuitive to some, but we should really include research scientists under this trump, as they are today's interpreters of the mysteries of the microcosm and the macrocosm.

The card was renamed the High Priest or Hierophant in the late eighteenth century, again by Court de Gébelin to accord with his ancient Egypt theory. Christian, the Golden Dawn, and Waite all followed Court de Gébelin in his nomenclature and Lévi in his interpretation. Etteilla and Mathers struck out on their own, but de Mellet, who was obviously looking at one of the Besançon decks, cannot be said to provide anything of much use to a cartomancer, if, in fact, he ever intended to.

Original Cartomantic Interpretations

De Mellet (1781): Jupiter. The Everlasting mounted on an eagle.

Court de Gébelin (1773–82): The high priest or chief hierophant.

Lévi (1855): The Hebrew letter *Heh,* the pope. Indication, demonstration, instruction, law, symbolism, philosophy, religion.

Christian (1870): Arcanum V. The Master of the Arcana or Sacred Mysteries, the hierophant or occult inspiration. In the divine world, the universal law; in the intellectual world, religion, the relationship of the absolute to the relative being; in the physical world, inspiration.

Mathers (1888): The Hierophant, or Pope. Mercy, beneficence, kindness, goodness. *Reversed:* Overkindness, weakness, foolish generosity.

Golden Dawn (1888–96): Magus of the eternal gods. Hierophant. Divine wisdom. Manifestation, explanation, teaching. Differing from, though resembling in many aspects, the meaning of the Magician, the Prophet (Hermit), and the Lovers. Occult wisdom.

Grand Orient (Waite, 1889, 1909): Pope, or Hierophant. Aspiration, power of the keys, the outward show of spiritual authority, the temporal power of official religion; on the evil side, sacerdotal tyranny and interference.

Waite (1910): The Hierophant. Marriage, alliance, servitude; by another account [Mathers], mercy and goodness; inspiration; the man to whom the inquirer has recourse. *Reversed:* Overkindness, weakness.

Suggested Interpretation

Religion. Science. Orthodoxy. *Reversed:* Dogmatism. Hypocrisy. Sanctimony.

TRUMP VI, THE LOVERS

ALTERNATE NAMES: LOVE, MARRIAGE. *L'AMOUREUX, L'AMORE,*
GLI AMANTI, GLI INAMORATI

The power that ties the bond
Of nature's laws is Love;
Love rules land and sea alike,
Love regulates the heavens above.

So proclaimed the *Consolation of Philosophy* to the medieval world, and it was a theme that Dante used in the last line of his epic poem *The Divine Comedy*. The Platonic belief that divine love is the motivating power of the cosmos was widely entertained by Renaissance humanists, thereby tying Christianity into pagan philosophy.

Like the Bembo painted decks, the earliest woodcut tarots simply depict a pair of lovers. These could be any lovers, Dante and Beatrice, Petrarch and Laura, Tristan and Isolde, or a Visconti noble and bride; but always overhead flies the mischievous boy-god Eros, classical symbol of all-conquering love. Well, almost all-conquering. Remember, the Lovers as Youth and Maiden also appear in the *Dance of Death,* although they don't think about such matters now.

Later tarots depict a young man apparently torn in his choice between two figures, presumably female, although the seventeenth-century Tarot of Jacques Viéville does show them with peculiarly short hair. The trump here seems to display the archetypal love triangle: one of the supplicating figures will surely lose out, because overhead flies mischievous Eros again, his bow bent, arrow aimed.

Court de Gébelin provided the caption "Marriage," while the Comte de Mellet interpreted the image as that of Hercules choosing between Vice and Virtue, a subject popular among painters of the high Renaissance, although de Mellet hedged his bets by adding the word *love*, too. His interpretation of the card as "a trial of moral strength" was adopted by many later cartomancers, as we shall see. However, an examination of early tarots reveals that Eros—love purely and simply—and not moral choice is the subject of the card.

Eros, or Cupid, as the Romans knew him, possessed a golden bow and quiver full of arrows, some tipped with gold, some with lead. Those beings, mortal or immortal, struck by Eros' golden arrows became infatuated with the being they had their eyes set on, while those pierced by the lead-tipped arrows fled in loathing. In this way Eros, who like Justice and Fortune was frequently depicted blindfolded, played many quite devastating pranks, one of which resulted in the destruction of Troy. He was accordingly treated with deference by even the most powerful gods and goddesses.

Erhard Schön uses an image strikingly similar to the trump to illustrate the seventh astrological house, the House of Marriage and Partnership. A robed pastor stands between a man and a woman, presumably marrying them. If Erhard Schön has anything to tell us, the meanings ascribed to this

trump should therefore be: any type of union, marriage, contract, lawsuit, an open enemy, and dealings with the public generally. All partnerships, sexual or otherwise, emotional or financial, are represented.

Original Cartomantic Interpretations

Pratesi's Cartomancer (1750): Love.

De Mellet (1781): Love. A man hesitating between Vice and Virtue.

Court de Gébelin (1773–82): Marriage.

Lévi (1855): The Hebrew letter *Vau*, Vice, and Virtue. Interlacement, lingam (the Hindu term for phallus, which Lévi introduces in his *Doctrine of Transcendental Magic* as a kabbalistic symbol of Venus), entanglement, union, combination, equilibrium.

Christian (1870): Arcanum VI. The Two Roads. The Ordeal. A man standing motionless at a crossroads. Two women stand each with a hand on his shoulder, indicating one of the two roads. The woman on the right personifies virtue, the one on the left, vice. Above and behind, the genius of Justice, borne on a nimbus of blazing light, is drawing his bow and directs the arrow of punishment at Vice. The whole scene expresses the struggle between the passions and conscience.

Mathers (1888): The Lovers. Trials surmounted. *Reversed:* Unwise plans, failure when put to the test.

Golden Dawn (1888–96): Children of the Voice Divine, Oracles of the Mighty Gods. The Lovers. Inspiration, motive power, impulse.

Grand Orient (Waite, 1889, 1909): Lovers. Material union, affection, desire, natural love, harmony, equilibrium.

Waite (1910): The Lovers. Attraction, love, beauty, trials overcome. *Reversed:* Failure, foolish designs. Another account [Etteilla] speaks of marriage frustrated.

Suggested Interpretation

Union. Marriage. Partnership. *Reversed:* Destructive partnership. End of relationship or partnership.

TRUMP VII, THE CHARIOT

ALTERNATE NAMES: *VICTORIAE PREMIUM* (THE REWARD OF VICTORY),
THE TRIUMPHAL CAR, *LE CHARIOT, IL CARRO, LA CARROZZA*

Trump VII may display one of the pageant wagons on which medieval plays were frequently mounted, or it may display a war chariot. The figure inside it also varies from deck to deck, and with it the meaning. The first printed trumps probably intended the figure to represent the King in the Dance of Death. "You have been riding your high horse with great haughtiness, therefore you mourn all the more so now," says Death to the King in the Lübeck play, "So step right down in front, you too, Mister King!"

In later cards, the figure in the chariot is sometimes the female allegorical figure of Fame from Petrarch's *Trionfi,* but more often it is a male figure in armor, usually crowned, sometimes helmeted, often carrying a scepter or sword. The Charles VI cards show the rider carrying a battle-ax. The fifteenth-century Mantegna engravings suggest that this figure may be Mars, the Roman god of war (see the figure on page 12). This might make a certain amount of sense if we consider the province of the previous card, which dealt with matters of love. *The Consolation of Philosophy* has this to say about the relationship between love and war:

> *Should Love loosen its tight bond*
> *And abrogate its rule of law,*
> *The mutual love which all things share*
> *Would in an instant turn to war.*

Alternatively, if we consider one of the card's other titles, Reward of Victory, then the chariot may be said to represent fame or victory in general. The fifteenth-century Rosenwald deck depicts the figure in the chariot crowned and carrying orb and sword, maybe also inspired by the image of Fame described in Petrarch's famous 1374 poem, *I trionfi:*

> *When, turning round, I saw the*
> *Power advance*
> *That breaks the gloomy grave's eternal trance,*
> *And bids the disembodied spirit claim*
> *The glorious guerdon of immortal Fame.*

Original Cartomantic Interpretations

Pratesi's Cartomancer (1750): Journey.

De Mellet (1781): Chariot of War. Crimes of the Iron Age.

Court de Gébelin (1773–82): Osiris Triumphant.

Lévi (1855): The Hebrew letter *Zayin,* the Cubic Chariot. Weapon, sword, cherubic sword of fire, the sacred septenary, triumph, royalty, priesthood.

Christian (1870): Arcanum VII. The Chariot of Osiris: Victory. A war chariot, square in shape, surmounted by a starred baldaquin upheld by four columns. An armed conqueror advances carrying a scepter and a sword in his hands. He is crowned with a fillet of gold ornamented at five points by three pentagrams or golden stars. The square chariot symbolizes the work accomplished by the will, which

has overcome all obstacles, the four columns supporting the starry canopy, the four conquered elements. The lifted sword is the sign of victory. The two sphinxes, one white, the other black, symbolize Good and Evil—the one conquered, the other vanquished—both having become the servants of the Magus who has triumphed over his ordeals.

Mathers (1888): The Chariot. Triumph, victory, overcoming obstacles. *Reversed:* Overthrown, conquered by obstacles at the last moment.

Golden Dawn (1888–96): Child of the Power of the Waters, Lord of the Triumph of Light. The Chariot. Triumph, victory, health, success, though sometimes not enduring.

Grand Orient (Waite, 1889, 1909): Chariot. Triumph of reason. Success, the right prevailing, conquest.

Waite (1910): The Chariot. Providence, war, triumph, presumption, vengeance. *Reversed:* Riot, dispute, litigation, defeat.

Suggested Interpretation

Heroism. Success. Fame. *Reversed:* Victory delayed. Defeat.

TRUMP VIII, JUSTICE

ALTERNATE NAMES: *LA JUSTICE, LA GIUSTIZIA*

Plato believed in the existence of a primary world of pure forms or archetypes, underlying yet distinct from their dim manifestations in the world of here and now. Justice, Fortitude, Temperance, and Prudence—concepts borrowed from the Persians—were considered by Plato to be such archetypes; later they became known as the Four Cardinal, or Natural, Virtues appropriated by Christian theologians Ambrose, Augustine, and Aquinas. The word *cardinal* implied that the virtue was a principal one, on which other, lesser virtues were hinged (the Latin word *cardo* means "hinge," something on which a thing pivots). The Roman orator Cicero considered them to be the four great cornerstones of all virtue, which he defined in a typical Stoic manner as "a mental habit harmonious with reason and the natural order of things." Three more virtues were added later by the church, the "theological" virtues of the Apostle Paul—Faith, Hope, and Charity. Together, the cardinal and theological virtues made up the heptad of the Seven Virtues. Their absence in a person was considered to give rise to their opposites, the Seven Deadly Sins—Pride, Avarice, Lust, Envy, Gluttony, Wrath, and Sloth, which were deadly because they lay at the root of every other sin.

Virtues and vices turn up personified in medieval morality plays, which is undoubtedly the original reason Justice is depicted as a tarot trump here. She also happened to form one of the cornerstones of *Rerum memorandarum libri* (Things to be Remembered), a book about the

Cardinal Virtues that Petrarch began but never completed. She was a very familiar figure by the fourteenth and fifteenth centuries.

Unlike the other three virtues, the Justice displayed in tarot decks is always female. Like the other Virtues, however, she is often portrayed  with the polygonal or hexagonal halo reserved in Christian iconography for allegorical, as opposed to sanctified, figures. In her hands she carried the scales of logic, and, most important, the sword of Justice, which is one of four suit signs of the Minor Arcana; she appears like this in the Rosenwald and the Charles VI cards.

Christian and Mathers believed that the figure of Justice was the Greek goddess Themis, but actually the figure is believed by art historians to be Astraea, the daughter of Zeus and Themis. Classical mythology tells us that Astraea was born before the Great Flood during the Golden Age, when all of humanity lived in harmony together in an earthly paradise. As wickedness among humans increased, she withdrew from the world and made her home in the heavens, where she may be seen today as the constellation Virgo.

Original Cartomantic Interpretations

De Mellet (1781): Justice.

Court de Gébelin (1773–82): Justice.

Lévi (1855): The Hebrew letter *Cheth,* Justice. Balance, attraction and repulsion, life, terror, promise and threat.

Christian (1870): Arcanum VIII. Themis: Equilibrium. The ancient symbol of Justice weighs in the balance the deeds of men, and as a counterweight, opposing evil with the sword of expiation. The eyes of Justice are covered with a bandage to show that she weighs and strikes without taking into account the conventional differences established by men.

Mathers (1888): Themis, or Justice. Equilibrium, balance, justice.
Reversed: Bigotry, want of balance, abuse of justice, overseverity, bias.

Golden Dawn (1888–96): Daughter of the Lord of Truth, Holder of the Balances. Justice. Strength arrested in the act of judgment. Legal proceedings, a court of law, a trial by law.

Grand Orient (Waite, 1889, 1909): Justice. Equilibrium on the mental side rather than the sensuous; under certain circumstances, law and its decisions; also occult science.

Waite (1910): Justice. Equity, probity, vindication. *Reversed:* Law in all departments, legal complications, bigotry, bias, excessive severity.

Suggested Interpretation

Impartiality. Law. Due process. *Reversed:* Bad laws. Injustice. Corruption.

Trump IX, the Hermit

ALTERNATE NAMES: *Rerum Edax* (Devourer of Things),
the Old Man, *L'Eremite, Le Vieillard, Capuchin,
Le Prêtre, L'Eremita, Il Gobbo, L'Ermita, Il Vecchio*

Hermits are not exempted from the Dance of Death, and indeed are frequently depicted in Death's clutches in medieval art. "To die, that is not difficult for me, were I inwardly prepared and my conscience well cleansed," declares the Hermit in the 1489 Lübeck play. However, the tarot Hermit's other titles also indicate that we're not dealing with your common or garden variety hermit here, at least not in Renaissance tarot decks, which include the painted Visconti cards. The Leber cards' caption, *Devourer of Things,* and the *Old Man* caption in the minchiate indicate that the Hermit has been reinterpreted by these later decks as Time, portrayed as the classical Roman god Saturn.

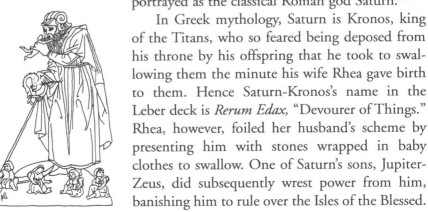

In Greek mythology, Saturn is Kronos, king of the Titans, who so feared being deposed from his throne by his offspring that he took to swallowing them the minute his wife Rhea gave birth to them. Hence Saturn-Kronos's name in the Leber deck is *Rerum Edax,* "Devourer of Things." Rhea, however, foiled her husband's scheme by presenting him with stones wrapped in baby clothes to swallow. One of Saturn's sons, Jupiter-Zeus, did subsequently wrest power from him, banishing him to rule over the Isles of the Blessed.

In this manner Saturn-Kronos came to be looked on as representative of tyrannous, all-devouring Time. As Father Time, he is often portrayed in art carrying Saturn's sickle and an hourglass. In Renaissance tarot trumps the hourglass often takes the place of the original lantern carried by the Hermit. Time is also frequently shown hobbling along on a staff or two crutches, as the artist Giuseppi Maria Mitelli portrayed him in the illusrations of Bolognese tarocchi he engraved in 1664.

Perhaps the most important identification of this card for our purposes may be one that harks back to the *Fulgentius metaforalis,* a fourteenth-century memory manual written by a Franciscan friar, John Ridvall, which identifies Saturn with the virtue Prudence even though in early medieval iconography Prudence was usually portrayed as female (hence my note in the introduction that Prudence may indeed be present in the trumps, albeit in heavy disguise). She also generally holds up a mirror (the Coin suit of the Minor Arcana) in which she sees reflected the image of herself and, behind her, the serpent that she holds in her other hand. The mirror is considered to signify, among other things, that wise people have the power to see themselves as they really are. The serpent may derive from the New Testament, Matthew 10:16: "Be ye as wise [*prudentes*] as serpents," or it may be a rendering of the Ouroboros serpent or dragon consuming its tail, a Gnostic symbol for endless time. This image appears in the Mantegna tarocchi Saturn's hand along with his scythe. The stag that appears in some versions of this Hermit trump was considered to be a creature prudent in its ability to elude pursuers.

To the medieval moralist, a prudent act was one that was neither unpremeditated nor transient in its effect. According to Cicero, the Cardinal Virtue Prudence consists of the knowledge of what is good, what is bad, and what is neither good nor bad, but whose parts consist of memory of the past, intelligence about the present, and foresight concerning the future.

Original Cartomantic Interpretations

Pratesi's Cartomancer (1750): The Old Man.

De Mellet (1781): The Hermit. The sage in search of justice.

Court de Gébelin (1773–82): The Sage, or seeker after truth.

Lévi (1855): The Hebrew letter *Teth,* the Hermit or Capuchin monk. Goodness, revulsion from evil, morality, wisdom.

Christian (1870): Arcanum IX. The Veiled Lamp: Prudence. Arcanum IX is represented by an old man who walks leaning on a stick, holding in front of him a lighted lantern half hidden by his cloak. He personifies experience acquired in the labors of life. The lighted lantern signifies the light of the mind, which should illuminate the past, the present, and the future. The cloak that half conceals it signifies discretion. The stick symbolizes the support given by Prudence to the man who does not reveal his purpose.

Mathers (1888): The Hermit. Prudence, caution, deliberation. *Reversed:* Overprudence, timorousness, fear.

Golden Dawn (1888–96): The Magus of the Voice of Light, the Prophet of the Gods. The Hermit, or Prophet. Wisdom sought for and obtained from above. In the mystical titles, this with the Hierophant and the Magician are the three Magi.

Grand Orient (Waite, 1889, 1909): Hermit. Caution, safety, protection, detachment, Prudence, sagacity, search after truth.

Waite (1910): The Hermit. Prudence, circumspection. Also treason, roguery, corruption. *Reversed:* Concealment, disguise, fear, unreasoned caution.

Suggested Interpretation

Prudence. Contemplation. Caution. *Reversed:* Delay. Obstacle. Apathy.

TRUMP X, THE WHEEL OF FORTUNE

ALTERNATE NAMES: *OMNIUM DOMINATRIX* (MISTRESS OF
EVERYTHING), THE WHEEL, *LA ROUE DE FORTUNE, LA RUOTA,
ROTA DI FORTUNA, RUOTA DELLA FORTUNA, LA FORTUNA*

O Fortuna,
Velut Luna
Statu variabilis,
Semper crescis
Aut decrescis . . .

"O Fortuna, like the moon ever-changing, always waxing or waning." So begins the manuscript of thirteenth-century Latin and German poetry that German composer Carl Orff drew on to compose his dramatic and evocative piece of choral music, *Carmina Burana,* in 1936.

The Roman goddess Fortuna, renamed Dame Fortune, strongly fixated the medieval mind. She continued to be feared and propitiated, possibly even more than the Divinity, on account of her well-known fickleness, right through the Middle Ages. The gifts presented at the turn of the year by subjects to their rulers or servants to their masters (later vice versa) were a direct continuation of this pagan tradition, and her will was made known by the drawing of lots, *sortes,* a term that appears frequently in accounts of her. But by far the greatest contributor to the fame of Fortune's Wheel, indeed the probable reason for its presence in the tarot deck, seems to be the popular work touched on earlier, Boethius's *Consolation of Philosophy.*

The *Consolation* is shaped as a dialog between the unjustly imprisoned and despairing Boethius and the consoling female figure of Philosophy. In book 2, she reminds him that Fortune is a blind goddess, and that the threat of her well-known practice of changing from a bestower of good things to a bestower of bad should elicit in Boethius, as a philosopher, no fear, even as he should feel no desire for her smiles. Rather, he should employ the virtue of prudence to help him size up what things lie ahead, particularly because it's useless for him to try to stop the turning of Fortune's Wheel by force. It can't be done. And what you cannot change should not be dwelt on. Dame Fortune tramples down the mighty king, even while she is raising up the defeated man from his prone position on the ground, declaring: "Ascende, si placet, sed ea lege, uti ne, cum ludicri mei ratio poscet, descendere injuriam putes!" (Ascend, if you want, but on this condition, that when the rule of my game requires it, you will descend without taking offense!)

Clocklike, the Wheel of Fortune's rim is divided into four sections, each showing a different phase in time's passage: the immediate future usually ascends on the left, the present stands at the zenith, what is moving into the past descends on the right, and what is definitely in the past lies at the nadir.

Some wheels, like the one painted in the Visconti-Sforza deck, depict scrolls inscribed with words fluttering out of the mouths of the crowned king at the top and the three other figures clinging to the rim: "Regnabo, regno, regnavi, sum sine regno" (I will reign, I reign, I have reigned, I am without reign)—which tell their own story. Dame Fortune

herself sometimes sits at the center of the turning wheel, blindfolded to demonstrate just how arbitrary she is.

The *Mort le roi Artu,* a thirteenth-century Arthurian text on which Malory drew for his *Morte d'Arthur,* tells us that on the eve of King Arthur's disastrous battle with Mordred, the king dreamed presciently that he was riding the Wheel of Fortune, only to be cast down from its highest peak.

The Wheel of Fortune would appear to be one of the most significant tarot trumps: it was a major symbol in the medieval and fifteenth-century oracle books whose purpose was to provide insight into the fickle whims of the Lady herself. The Marseille-pattern tarot displays three strange-looking creatures riding the wheel in place of kings (see figure on page 107). One of them, an ape- or doglike animal, is said by cartomancers to represent the composite Greco-Egyptian god Hermanubis; a second, a horse or wolf-headed man is said to

be Typhon-Set, Egyptian god of chaos and destruction; the third, on top, a man-headed lion, is the Sphinx. A simpler and probably more accurate identification of the figures is that they represent ordinary animals or theriomorphic humans—the type varies with the deck—the card's comment on people who place their reliance on Fortune's Wheel, a concept provided by Boethius himself.

Erhard Schön gives us a clue to the Wheel's original divinatory import by using it as an emblem for the eleventh astrological house, the House of Friends and Benefactors, considered by astrologers today to represent the subject of the chart's public image, his or her friends and associates, or the financial condition of his or her employer.

Literary historian Howard Rollin Patch defined what he termed the *formula of four* as the essential message delivered by Fortune and the four figures clinging to the Wheel:

> Fortuna: I am that Fortuna who has made and unmade kings and emperors. It is of no avail to worship me. Let him beware who sits on top of the wheel. Let each hold fast to his treasure.

> Regno: I reign at the top of the wheel, as Fortune has destined me. But if the wheel turns I may be deprived of power. Be moderate, ye who are in power, lest you fall to earth. Behold the honor I am paid because I sit at the top of the wheel.

> Regnavi: I reigned for a while, then Fortune put me down and deprived me of everything good. Her friendship avails not. No friend remains when a man falls. Do not be confident when you are rising; Fortune makes you fall with deadly blows. Hearken to my case, how I gained and lost this honor.

> Regnabo: I shall reign if Fortune pleases and the wheel turns to the fourth place. I shall be above and rule all the world. How great is

my pleasure then! Virtue moves me to speak such words, because I plan to do justice and punish those who have maliciously robbed men of good estate. What joy I shall have to be able to punish them!

Sum Sine Regno: I am, as you see, without reign, down low in wretchedness. Fortune has disclaimed me. If I should mount on this wheel, every man would be friendly to me. Let each take warning who considers me.

Original Cartomantic Interpretations

De Mellet (1781): The Wheel of Fortune. The injustice of the fickle goddess.

Court de Gébelin (1773–82): The Wheel of Fortune.

Lévi (1855): The Hebrew letter *Yod,* the Wheel of Fortune. Principle, manifestation, praise, manly honor, phallus, virile fecundity, paternal scepter.

Christian (1870): Arcanum X. The Sphinx: Fortune. A wheel suspended by its axle between two columns. On the right Hermanubis [the Greco-Egyptian god composed of Hermes and dog-headed Anubis], the Spirit of Good, strives to climb to the top of the wheel. On the left Typhon [the Greco-Egyptian Set], the Spirit of Evil, is cast down. The Sphinx, balanced on the top of this wheel, holds a sword in its lion's paws, personifying Destiny ever ready to strike left or right. According to the direction in which it turns the wheel, the humblest rises and the highest is cast down.

Mathers (1888): The Wheel of Fortune. Good fortune, success, unexpected luck. *Reversed:* Failure, unexpected ill luck.

Golden Dawn (1888–96): The Lord of the Forces of Life. Wheel of Fortune. Good fortune and qualified happiness.

Grand Orient (Waite, 1889, 1909): Wheel of Fortune. Mutation, revolution, the external side of fortune.

Waite (1910): Wheel of Fortune. Fortune, success, elevation, luck, happiness. *Reversed:* Increase, abundance, superfluity.

Suggested Interpretation

Meditate on the *formula of four.* Good times may be coming. Well disposed friends and benefactors. *Reversed:* Meditate on the *formula of four.* Bad times may lie ahead. Hollow friends.

TRUMP XI, FORTITUDE

ALTERNATE NAMES: STRENGTH, FORCE, *LA FORCE,*
LA FORTEZZA, LA FORZA

Fortitude is the second of the Four Cardinal Virtues openly portrayed in the tarot trumps. The Marseille pattern exemplifies one of the most popular depictions of this Virtue, as a female figure either wrenching open, or forcing shut, the jaws of a lion.

From the point of view of a Renaissance intellectual, this figure could be the nymph Cyrene, whom Apollo took a fancy to one day when he spotted her wrestling unarmed with such a beast.

There are other Fortitude images, however, and they introduce us to the third group of symbols shared by the Major and Minor Arcanas: the Column, Baton, Wand, or Cudgel. The Rosenwald Tarot, for example, shows Fortitude clasping a Corinthian column, and the Charles VI card shows the figure breaking the column in two.

Although the tarot Fortitude has become a female over time, the prototype was probably male: Samson, breaking one of the pillars of the temple to which he was bound after being betrayed by his faithless

 Delilah. The Visconti-Sforza painted deck, on the other hand, shows a cudgel-wielding man about to take a swing at a lion that crouches at his feet. In this instance Hercules is probably the inspiration, and the beast is the Nemean lion, one of the creatures Hercules encountered during the strenuous labors imposed on him by the goddess Juno-Hera.

Thomas Aquinas considered Fortitude to be the Virtue responsible for all impulses that help us to resist fear. Unlike the Lovers, the Fortitude trump does represent moral trials of strength.

Original Cartomantic Interpretations

Pratesi's Cartomancer (1750): Violence.

De Mellet (1781): Fortitude, who comes to the aid of Prudence by vanquishing the lion, the wild, uncultivated land.

Court de Gébelin (1773–82): Force or Strength.

Lévi (1855): The Hebrew letter *Kaph,* Strength. The hand in the act of grasping and holding.

Christian (1870): Arcanum XI. The Tamed Lion: Strength. In the divine world, the Principle of all strength, spiritual or material; in the intellectual world moral Force; in the physical world organic Force.

Mathers (1888): Strength, or Fortitude. Power, might, force. *Reversed:* Abuse of power, overbearingness, want of Fortitude.

Golden Dawn (1888–96): Daughter of the Flaming Sword, Leader of the Lion. Fortitude, courage, strength, power not arrested in the act of judgment, but passing on to further action, sometimes obstinacy.

Grand Orient (Waite, 1889, 1909): Fortitude, or Strength. Courage, vitality, tenacity of things, high endurance.

Waite (1910): Fortitude. Power, energy, action, courage, magnanimity, success and honors. *Reversed:* Despotism, abuse of power, weakness, discord or disgrace.

Suggested Interpretation

Moral trial of strength. Firm resolve. Take courage. *Reversed:* Foolhardy audacity. Overkill.

TRUMP XII, THE HANGED MAN

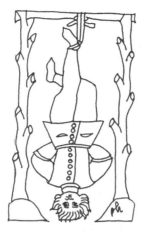

ALTERNATE NAMES: THE HANGING MAN, THE TRAITOR, *LE PENDU,*
IL PENDUTO, L'APPESO, IL TRADITORE, L'IMPICCATO

The figure hanging by one foot in the earliest Hanged Man trumps has generally been considered by playing-card historians to represent an unspecified traitor. Indeed, one of the Italian names for this card is just that, *Il Traditore,* the Traitor, clearly depicted caught in the act in the seventeenth-century tarocchino illustration engraved by Mitelli.

Some have speculated that the original figure of the hanging man may be Judas Iscariot. The fifteenth-century Rosenwald deck shows the upside-down figure clutching a small bag in each hand, which presumably may contain money. The Charles VI Hanged Man certainly shows what seem to be coins stuffed inside the bags.

However, such would not have been the case if the card were adhering strictly to the gospel account. Before Judas hanged himself, he was said to have returned the thirty pieces of silver that were his fee for betraying Jesus. "That which you paid me," says Judas to Pontius Pilate in one mystery play, "divide it as you will, and claim it, clean, for yourself."

Furthermore, there remains yet another annoying hole in the Judas theory. Judas took his own life by hanging himself by the neck, but the Hanged Man is typically depicted "baffled," as the practice was named, hanged by the heels upside down as a traitor. Edmund Spencer, the sixteenth-century poet, describes an instance of "baffling" performed by Prince Arthur on the villainous and still living knight, Sir Turpine, in his chivalric Elizabethan romance *The Faerie Queen:*

> *He by the heels him hung upon a tree,*
> *And baffl'd so, that all which passed by*
> *the picture of his punishment might see.*

Gertrude Moakley makes a convincing argument that Bembo's painted fifteenth-century Hanged Man represents Francesco Sforza's father, Muzio Attendolo, who, after being ennobled by the pope, had subsequently taken sides against him. As a consequence, the offended pope ordered pictures of Attendolo hanging upside down and suspended by one foot—"shame painting" it was called—to be displayed on all the gates and bridges of Rome. However, other explanations for the card certainly exist. Sandro Botticelli, for example, depicted on the wall of the Bargello the inglorious end of the Pazzi family—a banking family that perished in an attempt to oust their rivals the Medicis from Florence in a murderous coup in 1478. All figures are shown with ropes around their necks, except a certain Napoleone Francese, whose guilt was uncertain and who escaped death. Botticelli depicted him hanging by one ankle, but this position is thought to indicate his escape rather than his treachery.

So which character is most likely to be the inspiration for our Hanged Man? Is it to be Muzio Attendolo, or Judas, or someone else entirely? The gospels certainly regarded Judas's betrayal of Jesus as a sin of avarice, which would logically lead one directly to the next card, Death, which the Bible clearly identifies as the wages of sin. However, the Renaissance interpretation of the trump may have had nothing to do with Judas, or even treason, despite the various card titles. There is a source that has not been explored sufficiently, I believe, perhaps because it does not specifically refer to a man hanging upside down. If we consider the words closely, however, this is surely the image they convey.

The source is once again Boethius's *Consolation of Philosophy,* where we find the following lines of verse, referring to the necessity for a man to remember at all times the Neoplatonic doctrine that his individual mind has access to the Divine Mind. This means that he can access Wisdom directly, by recollection, as well as through the senses; and that therefore he should at all times hold his head high and aspire to the divine understanding:

Alone the human race lifts high its head,
And stands with body upright;
With head held high and upturned face, you seek the sky:
So must you let your thoughts rise up.
Unless, earthbound, you lose your wits, this picture warns,
Let not your mind sink downward, lower than your
body poised above.

Does the last line evoke the image of a man hanging upside down or does it not? Plato himself in his *Timaeus* describes the embodied human soul enmeshed by worldliness as *anatrope* (upside down): "as you might imagine a person upside down, his head leaning upon the ground and his feet up against something in the air," an image that may be the source of Boethius's concept.

Court de Gébelin and de Mellet both made the mistake of reversing the image on this card and viewing it as somebody treading on a serpent. Hence their misnomer "Prudence." Lévi at least got the card the right way up.

Erhard Schön depicts a man imprisoned in the stocks, possibly a comparable, if less lethal, punishment than hanging by the heels, and places the image in the twelfth astrological house, the House of Mystery and Uncertainty. This house is interpreted by astrologers as relating to unseen or unexpected troubles, restraints, exile, seclusion, hospitals, and secret enemies, so perhaps this is the divinatory interpretation we should accept.

Original Cartomantic Interpretations

Pratesi's Cartomancer (1750): The Traitor, betrayal.

De Mellet (1781): The Hanged Man. Prudence.

Court de Gébelin (1773–82): Prudence.

Lévi (1855): The Hebrew letter *Lamed,* a man hanging by one foot. Example, instruction, public teaching.

Christian (1870): Arcanum XII. The Sacrifice: Violent Death. Arcanum XII expresses in the divine world the revelation of the law; in the intellectual world the teaching of duty; in the physical world sacrifice.

Mathers (1888): The Hanged Man. Self-sacrifice, sacrifice, devotion, that which is bound. *Reversed:* Selfishness, that which is unbound, partial sacrifice.

Golden Dawn (1888–96): The Spirit of the Mighty Waters. Hanged Man or Drowned Man. Enforced sacrifice, punishment, loss, suffering.

Grand Orient (Waite, 1889, 1909): Hanged Man. Renunciation, for whatever cause and whatever motive.

Waite (1910): The Hanged Man. Wisdom, circumspection, discernment, trials, sacrifice, intuition, divination, prophecy. *Reversed:* Selfishness, the crowd, the body politic.

Suggested Interpretation

Reevaluation. Reversal of values. New insights. *Reversed:* Treachery. Restraints. Seclusion.

TRUMP XIII, DEATH

ALTERNATE NAMES: *LA MORT, IL MORTE, LA MORTE*

I am Death, that dreads no man,
That catches every man and spares no one;
For God's commandment is
That all to me must be obedient . . .
I heed neither gold, silver nor riches,
Nor Pope, Emperor, King, Duke, nor Princes,
For if I were to receive great gifts,
I might gain the world . . .

So speaks Death in the sixteenth-century English morality play *Everyman*. Moreover, he cheerfully informs his victims in his fifteenth-century *Dance* at Les Innocents: "You who live: it is certain that, however long delayed, you will dance."

However, Death appeared in his dance not just as a destroyer but also as the Angel of Death, God's messenger, who summoned people to the world of the hereafter. The setting of the actual *Dance of Death* play was usually a churchyard, although the interiors of churches were also used. According to the oldest known text (which appears in the woodcuts of Guyot Marchant that once adorned the walls of the Cimetière des Innocents and illustrated the Dance of Death) the priest would first pick on one of the spectators and address him with the words:

Oh Thou,
Rational Creature!
Who desires eternal life,
You have here a lesson worthy of your attention,
For the best conclusion of your mortal life
It is called the Dance of Death;
Everyone learns to dance it.

Then figures clad in the traditional guise of Death—tight-fitting yellowish linen suits painted with bones to look like skeletons—would appear from the charnel house, a room or vault attached to the church where cadavers or bones were interred. One of these figures would address the first victim, generally someone portraying the emperor or the pope, and invite him to accompany him to the next world. The invitation would inevitably be protested and declined for one reason or

another, and just as inevitably insisted upon. The pope or emperor would be led away, as a second fatal messenger would grab the hand of the next victim, somebody lower down the social scale, and the performance would be repeated.

The number of classes in society was usually reckoned to be twenty-four, so the Dance would in effect involve twenty-four episodes. The Mantegna engravings portray only ten out of the total number of available ranks.

In the earliest tarot decks, Death is depicted as a corpse, later as a skeleton, wielding his scythe on horseback or on foot. All of humanity falls before the sweep of his blade, all classes high and low, popes, prelates, emperors, paupers. The painted trumps, the fifteenth-century Rosenwald Collection, and the Metropolitan Museum of Art cards all depict him thus, as indeed do all the old printed decks.

While many decks designed specifically for cartomancy have kept this card in the traditionally unlucky thirteenth position in the trump sequence and, also in line with tradition, tactfully omitted the caption "Death," some have begun to depict the figure with its face hidden discreetly within the fold of a hooded garment. The Rider-Waite deck shows a robed skeleton carrying a standard emblazoned with what Waite calls a "mystic" white rose that symbolizes life.

Erhard Schön in his 1515 horoscope chart placed the image in the eighth house, the House of Death, which does not necessarily indicate death itself, but can also refer to legacies or to the financial affairs of one's partner.

Original Cartomantic Interpretations

Pratesi's Cartomancer (1750): Death.

De Mellet (1781): Death.

Court de Gébelin (1773–82): Death.

Lévi (1855): The Hebrew letter *Mem*. Death. The Heaven of Jupiter and Mars [this non sequitur is a prime example of the stultification produced by Lévi's forced marriage of Kircher's table of correspondences with the cards], domination and force, new birth, creation and destruction.

Christian (1870): Arcanum XIII. The Scythe: Transformation. In the divine world, the perpetual movement of creation, destruction and renewal; in the intellectual world the ascent of the Spirit into the divine spheres; in the physical world death, that is, the transformation of human nature on reaching the end of its organic period.

Mathers (1888): Death, change, transformation, alteration for the worse. *Reversed:* Death just escaped, partial change, alteration for the better.

Golden Dawn (1888–96): The Child of the Great Transformers, Lord of the Gates of Death. Death, time, transformation, change, sometimes destruction, but only if borne out by the cards with it.

Grand Orient (Waite, 1889, 1909): Death, transforming force, destruction.

Waite (1910): Death. End, mortality, destruction, corruption. Also, for a man, the loss of a benefactor, for a woman, many obstacles; for an unmarried woman, failure of marriage projects. *Reversed:* Inertia, sleep, lethargy, petrification, hope destroyed.

Suggested Interpretation

Legacy. Shadow of mortality. Major change. *Reversed:* Cancellation. Annulment. Death.

Trump XIV, Temperance

Alternate names: *Atrempance, La Temperance, La Temperanza*

The Temperance trump represents the third, and last, of the Four Cardinal Virtues openly depicted in the tarot, the vessels she carries being versions of the fourth Minor Arcana suit sign, the Cup.

In his *Republic,* Plato considered that the carnal lusts of the working class in his ideal city-state would, for some reason, be greater than those of other classes; he therefore believed that Temperance would be the Virtue most needed by them. The renowned Roman orator and statesman Cicero, on the other hand, thought Temperance, which he considered to mean general self-restraint in foregoing any pleasures, a good habit for everyone to cultivate, as did the Dominican theologian Thomas Aquinas. Temperance was said to fulfill the condition of being "restrained within measure." Temperance was also considered to be the virtue that defeated the deadly sin of Wrath. The dictionary today simply defines it as "moderation" or "self-restraint."

Three of the early printed tarot decks—the Cary Milanese, the Rosenwald, and the Metropolitan Museum—portray Temperance as a woman pouring liquid from one vessel into another, diluting wine with water. This is her standard iconographical form in Western art. Various theories have been advanced as to who the figure pouring the liquid originally was. Most likely it once represented Ganymede, a young Trojan

prince whom Zeus fell in love with and abducted to become his cup-bearer. In modern decks, Temperance is winged like an angel and sports in her hair an astrological solar symbol, which was bestowed on her by Etteilla and later embraced by Lévi as "the sign of the sun on her forehead."

Actually, the solar symbol began life as a simple little flower in the old Marseille design—another instance of imaginative rectification.

Etteilla also placed one of Temperance's feet on a solid triangular block, the other on a sphere, something that Waite translates in his deck as one foot on land (the element earth, perhaps) and the other in water. Waite also includes Etteilla's "priest" reference in his interpretation. I shall include Etteilla's input on this trump card, as it seems to have been so influential.

Original Cartomantic Interpretations

Pratesi's Cartomancer (1750): Time.

De Mellet (1781): Temperance. An angel instructs Man on the avoidance of Death.

Court de Gébelin (1773–82): Temperance.

Etteilla (1785–1807): Temperance. The Angel of the Apocalypse. *Reversed:* Convictions. The services of a priest, for whatever sacramental reasons determined by the other cards.

Lévi (1855): The Hebrew letter *Nun*. Temperance: the Heaven of the Sun, climates, seasons, motion, changes of life, which is ever new yet ever the same.

Christian (1870): Arcanum XIV. The Solar Spirit: Initiative. In the divine world, the perpetual motion of life; in the intellectual world, the combination of ideas that create morality; in the physical world, the combination of natural forces.

Mathers (1888): Temperance. Combination, conformation, uniting. *Reversed:* Ill-advised combinations, clashing interests.

Golden Dawn (1888–96): Daughter of the Reconcilers, the Bringer Forth of Life. Temperance. Combination.

Grand Orient (Waite, 1889, 1909): Temperance. New blood, combination, admixture.

Waite (1910): Temperance. Household economy, moderation, frugality, management, accommodation. *Reversed:* Things connected with churches, religions, sects, the priesthood, sometimes even the priest who will marry the inquirer. Also disunion, unfortunate combinations, competing interests.

Suggested Interpretation

Self-restraint. Moderation. Good combination. *Reversed:* Excessive self-restraint. Anorexia. Bad combination.

TRUMP XV, THE DEVIL

ALTERNATE NAMES: *PERDITORUM RAPTOR* (CAPTOR OF THE LOST),
LE DIABLE, IL DIAVOLO

*Thus from infernal Dis do we ascend
To view the subjects of our monarchy,
Those souls which sin seals the black sons of Hell,
'Mong which as chief, Faustus, we come to thee,
Bringing with us lasting damnation . . .*

So speaks Lucifer in the last act of Christopher Marlowe's *Dr. Faustus,*
one of the last great morality plays. He might just as well have been
speaking of the soul of Judas, whom in some tarot trumps the Devil has
come to carry off and devour.

In medieval drama, Satan was always played as a monstrous ogre
rather than a fallen angel, and indeed that is also how he is depicted in the

old printed tarots. The actor who played him was frequently dressed in shaggy wolf or calfskin pants to simulate satyr's legs, with cloven hooves or bird of prey claws attached to them, and horns on his head, of course.

Sometimes he wore bat's wings and a scorpion's tail, and sometimes he carried a besom broom. He could be dressed in red, black, blue, or, according to the theater historian Karl Mantzius, green like a reptile. His costume could be embellished with facelike ornaments on his knees and elbows and a mask on his belly, as you can see depicted in the seventeenth-century Tarot of Paris and the Tarot of Jacques Viéville (see figure at the bottom of page 34). This may be an allusion to the response of Satan to Jesus in the New Testament story of the Gaderene swine: "My name is legion."

The eighteenth-century Marseille decks, however, show a slightly different image. Here the Devil is presented on a pedestal. He has oddly oriental-looking eyes, bat's wings, and eagle's claws; wields a blazing torch rather than a pitchfork or besom; and wears what looks like a helmet with stag's horns sprouting from either side. He is accompanied by two smaller, captive demons that also appear to be wearing antlered hats and are chained by the necks to a ring on the base of their master's pedestal. It is worth noting that in medieval drama, the devil and his cohorts frequently wore chains around their necks and fetters on their hands and legs to symbolize their captivity. They also carried staves filled with combustible explosives, or torches laced with sulfur.

Waite took the Marseille-pattern Devil as a foundation for his own trump, but built on it, obviously inspired by a drawing made by Éliphas Lévi.

Now this is very odd, because Lévi believed the figure of the Devil depicted in the tarot to be far from the Enemy of Man and God, but rather "a pantheistic and magical figure of the Absolute." Furthermore, Waite—who was himself responsible for this English translation of Lévi's text—never lost an opportunity to castigate Lévi's fertile imagination when it came to matters occult, and this surely extended to Lévi's Devil interpretation. Nevertheless, paradoxically, Waite adapted Lévi's own drawing for his Devil trump. To quote Waite's critical remarks in his *Key to the Tarot* about Lévi's Devil image and the interpretation Lévi put on it:

Lévi's Baphometic Goat   *Waite's Devil trump*

With more than his usual derision for the arts which he pretended
to respect and interpret as a master therein, Éliphas Lévi affirms that
"the Baphometic figure [the devil] is occult science and magic. . . ."
What it does signify is the Dweller on the Threshold without the
Mystical Garden when those are driven forth therefrom who have
eaten the forbidden fruit.

Baphomet was the name of an idol that the Roman Catholic
Inquisition accused the crusading monastic order of the Knights Templar
of worshiping in the fourteenth century. Waite's references to a "Mystical
Garden" and "forbidden fruit" probably allude to the *Pardes Rimmonim*,
the poetic name for a paradisiacal state of ecstatic trance entered by traditional kabbalists in quest of divine illumination. Waite therefore seems
to have interpreted this card, not as a symbol for occult science, but
rather as an illustration of the punishment meted out to those who try to
lay hands on it unworthily. If this is the case, then he undoubtedly
derived the idea from Alfred Faucheux, also known as François-Charles
Barlet, a fellow initiate of Papus in the French Rosicrucian group L'Ordre
Kabbalistique de la Rose Croix. Papus quoted Barlet extensively in his *Le
tarot des Bohémiens* (The Gypsies' Tarot), and as already noted, Waite
edited and wrote the preface for the English edition of this book.

In reference to the Devil trump (Arcanum XV, Typhon) Papus, quoting Barlet, wrote:

According to your deserts, you will be enraptured like St. Paul or you will expose yourself to madness, to the spiritualization of evil or sorcery. This is the Sabbat or the Ecstasy. The reader cannot pay too much attention to this solemn monument of practical occultism, so well described in Lytton's "Zanoni" under the name of the "Dragon of the Threshold," it is the formidable danger which necessitates so many secrets. This threshold is reached by many artificial paths: hasheesh, narcotics, hypnotics of every kind, the practices of spiritual mediums, but woe to him who attempts to pass it before he has triumphed in the long and laborious preliminary preparation!

In other words, Waite, Barlet, and Papus are solemnly warning their readers of the heavy price to be paid by the unworthy or unprepared person who tries to meddle with occult powers, which I doubt very much would have been an interpretation of the trump during the fifteenth century. Nor, as is happens, does it seem to have entered the list of suggested card interpretations that Waite gave either as Grand Orient or under his own name!

Original Cartomantic Interpretations

Pratesi's Cartomancer (1750): Anger.

De Mellet (1781): The Devil. Typhon. Human nature defiled and enslaved.

Court de Gébelin (1773–82): Typhon.

Lévi (1855): The Hebrew letter *Samekh*. The Devil. The Heaven of Mercury, occult science, magic, commerce, eloquence, mystery, moral force.

Christian (1870): Arcanum XV. Typhon: Fate. In the divine world predestination; in the intellectual world Mystery; in the physical world the Unforseen, Fatality. Typhon, the spirit of catastrophes, who rises out of a flaming abyss and brandishes a torch above the heads of two men chained at his feet.

Mathers (1888): The Devil. Fatality for good. *Reversed:* Fatality for evil.

Golden Dawn (1888–96): Lord of the Gates of Matter, Child of the Forces of Time. Devil. Material Force. Temptation, obsession, especially with the Lovers.

Grand Orient (Waite, 1889, 1909): The Devil, or Typhon. Fatality, evil, the false spirit; can indicate also the good working through evil.

Waite (1910): The Devil. Violence, vehemence, fatality. What is pre-destined, but not for this reason evil. *Reversed:* Evil fatality, weakness, blindness.

Suggested Interpretation

Tyranny. Major force. Avoidable evil. *Reversed:* Fate at its cruelest. Nature's dark side. Unavoidable evil.

TRUMP XVI, THE TOWER

ALTERNATE NAMES: THE LIGHTNING-STRUCK TOWER,
THE HOUSE OF GOD, THE HOSPITAL, THE ARROW, THE THUNDERBOLT,
THE FIRE, *LA MAISON DIEU, LE FOUDRE, LA TORRE,
IL FUOCO, LA SAETTA, LA SAGITTA*

Trump XVI in modern decks is usually labeled the Tower, which is simply a bald description of the picture shown. The earliest wood-block tarots, such as the uncut sheets in the Cary Collection, the Rosenwald Collection, and the Harris Brisbane Dick Collection at the Metropolitan Museum, all display it as a tower with its battlements ablaze.

In other Tower trumps, like that in the Rothschild Collection or the Marseille-pattern decks, bodies fall from the Tower or collapse on the ground around it.

The inscription *La Maison Dieu,* which appears in the seventeenth century J. P. Meyer Tarot, has led some to speculate that the Tower depicts the temple at Jerusalem, either that of Solomon or the building destroyed centuries later during the Roman occupation. However, the word *Dieu* (God) may be a corruption, as one may see if one consults early decks, where *Diefel*

(devil) can appear instead. So quite the reverse interpretation could apply: the Tower could be "the devil's house." Moreover, a poem written by Giulio Bertoni in an exercise of *Tarocchi appropriati* around 1550 clearly names the Tower as just that, *la Casa del Diavolo.* Court de Gébelin seems to have been on the right track when he dubbed the card the Castle of Plutus.

Other fifteenth-century Italian titles for this trump, *la Sagitta* (the Arrow) and *la Saetta* (the Thunderbolt) refer to the lightning bolt striking the Tower's battlements. And still other trumps, like *il Fuoco* of the Florentine minchiate, show a blazing doorway from which a naked and distraught woman tries to flee.

Where are we to find a reference to this Devil's House struck by lightning, or this blazing doorway, for that matter? Solomon's temples, Sodom and Gomorrah, or the Tower of Babel have all been suggested as sources for the image, but one must question how these fit in with the sequence of other trumps. Solomon's temples were destroyed by the hand of man. Sodom and Gomorrah were destroyed by fire and brimstone, admittedly, but they aren't necessarily associated with towers. Babel was defeated by a proliferation of foreign tongues, not lightning bolts.

Once more, medieval drama seems to provide the most compelling answer to the puzzle. In Trump XVI we see Satan's defeat, the conquest of the power of darkness by the power of light, as dramatized in the mystery play known as *The Harrowing of Hell.*

The Harrowing, which means "pillaging" or "plundering," occurs just before the Last Judgment in the play cycle, and represented Jesus's descent into Hell after his crucifixion, where he breaks down its gates, sometimes with the help of the archangel Michael. Though not mentioned in the Bible, Jesus's journey to Hell is recorded in detail in the *Descensus Christi ad Inferos* (Christ's Descent into Hell), which forms the second part of the apocryphal third-century *Gospel of Nicodemus.* The tradition of the Harrowing was a highly popular one, moreover, and was used extensively by medieval poets and playwrights, forming a vital element in the mystery plays of all European countries.

The play had as its foundation a liturgical ceremony known as the *Tollite Portas* (Lift up your Gates) used at the consecration of medieval churches, which was in effect a form of exorcism. In the usual version of the ritual, the bishop would lead the choir in procession through the churchyard up to the closed church doors, on which he would strike three blows with his pastoral staff. In response to the words of King David's Psalm 24:7–10 sung by the choir, "Principes, portas tollite, et introibit Rex Gloriae!" (Lift up your gates, O ye princes, and the King of Glory shall enter in!), the deacon, who would have taken up his place within the church previously, would reply, "Who is the King of Glory?" The response given would be "Dominus virtutem ipse est Rex Gloriae!" (The Lord strong and mighty, he is the King of Glory!). As the procession entered, the deacon, who symbolized the old spirit of evil conquered by the new spirit of holiness, would then slip quietly away.

Despite its name, *The Harrowing of Hell,* the play's real drama would actually take place not in the torture chambers of Hell itself, but in Limbo, the barred prison where the unbaptized souls of those born before the birth of Jesus awaited release. It is in Limbo that Adam and Eve and the prophets were lodged, a limbo which, until Christ's harrowing, the Devil and his cohorts controlled.

In the mystery play, battlements would be placed along the upper part of the pageant wagon to represent the fortified walls of Hell. The illustration by Hubert Cailleau of the Valenciennes Mystery Play of 1547, which was performed on a fixed stage, depicts Limbo as a tower with unredeemed souls peering through its prison bars, flames blazing from the roof. Fire-breathing demons watch from the battlements of the tower of Hell nearby, and Satan himself is elevated above the entire scene, riding a dragon on top of a pole (see figure at the top of page 34). The Florentine minchiate's fiery doorway seems to represent Adam and Eve's escape from Limbo as the divine thunderbolt cracks hell open.

In eighteenth-century Belgian decks, however, the Tower of Limbo is replaced by a tree above which a huge burst of light appears, and beneath which a startled shepherd stands with his flock of sheep. These are the cards that carry the caption *le Foudre* (the Thunderbolt.) The astonished shepherd and his flock could simply be taking shelter from a storm beneath the tree. On the other hand, we may be seeing here an illustration of *The Play of the Shepherds* that frequently accompanied the *Tres Reges,* or *Play of the Three Wise Kings,* which sometimes forms the subject of the next trump. If this is the case, then the angel has just announced the birth of Jesus to the astonished shepherd, and it is not a lightning bolt, but the glory of the Host of Heaven that has just exploded above with a chorus of hosannas to greet the arrival of the Messiah.

However, these thunderbolt card designs are atypical. The devil's tower would seem to have been the original target of the divine lightning.

Here is the main action of the *Harrowing of Hell* taken from an English mystery play, very much abbreviated and very freely translated by myself from Middle English. It must have been highly popular when performed with all the customary pyrotechnics and stage effects. The characters in this excerpt are Jesus, Satan (also called Lucifer), a demon (in other mystery plays named Ribald), the devil Belsabub, and, among others in limbo (including Adam and Eve), the as yet unredeemed patriarch King David.

Jesus smites for a second time on the gates of Limbo with his cruciform staff:

Jesus:
Principes, portas tollite!
Lift up your gates, ye lords of pride!
Et introibit rex glorie!
The King of Bliss comes in his tide!

Satan:
Alas, alack! What rogue is he
That says his kingdom shall be cryed?

King David:
(calling out from Limbo)
That may thou in my Psalter see
For that very point of prophecy.
I said that he should break
Thy bars and bonds by name,
And on thy works his vengeance take!
Now shalt thou see the same!

Jesus:
This place shall stand no longer fast!
Open up, and let my people past!

He strikes the gates of Limbo again, and this time they burst open with a crash and blaze of gunpowder. The denizens of Hell rush about like chickens in a blind panic.

Demon:
Alas, behold our Tower is broken!
And burst are all our bars of brass!
Tell Lucifer all is unlocked!

Belsabub:
What then, is limbo lost?! Alas!

Even allowing for the fact that they were ignorant of the origins of this trump, it is surprising that all the cartomancers except Court de Gébelin and the Golden Dawn consistently miss the fact that the blasted tower is the Devil's house, so the catastrophic destruction depicted would appear to be a blow directed against evil, not the converse. The Golden Dawn, interestingly, refers to the trump as "Lord of the Hosts of the Mighty," and "Courage," terms that happen to coincide with verbal elements present within the psalm on which the *Tollite Portas* ritual is based.

Original Cartomantic Interpretations

De Mellet (1781): The Tower. The House of God. The earthly paradise from which man and woman are expelled by a comet and hailstorm, or a fiery sword.

Court de Gébelin (1773–82): House of God, or the Castle of Plutus.

Etteilla (1785–1807): The Lightning-Struck Temple. The Capitol. Poverty. *Reversed:* Prison. Unjust calumny.

Lévi (1855): The Hebrew letter *Ayin.* Tower: The Heaven of the Moon, alterations, subversions, changes, failings.

Christian (1870): Arcanum XVI. The Lightning-Struck Tower: Ruin. In the divine world, the punishment of pride; in the intellectual world, the downfall of the Spirit that attempts to discover the mystery of God; in the physical world, reversals of fortune. Material forces that can crush great and small alike. Rivalries which only end in ruin for all concerned. Frustrated plans, hopes that fade away, ruined ambitions and catastrophic deaths.

Mathers (1888): The Lightning-Struck Tower. Ruin, disruption, loss, bankruptcy. *Reversed:* These in a partial degree.

Golden Dawn (1888–96): Lord of the Hosts of the Mighty. Tower. Ambition, fighting, courage. In certain combinations (or reversed), destruction, danger, fall.

Grand Orient (Waite, 1889, 1909): Ruined Tower. Destruction, confusion, judgment; also the idea of divine wrath.

Waite (1910): The Tower. Misery, indigence, adversity, calamity, disgrace, deception, unforeseen catastrophe. *Reversed:* According to one account [Mathers again], the same in a lesser degree. Also imprisonment, tyranny.

Suggested Interpretation

Downfall of tyranny. Release. End of bondage. *Reversed:* Release, to a lesser degree.

TRUMP XVII, THE STAR

ALTERNATE NAMES: *INCLITUM SYDUS* (RENOWNED STAR, STAR OF WONDER), *L'ETOILE, LA STELLA, LE STELLE, THE STARS.*

Several different sets of imagery are used to portray the Star trump. Some decks depict astrologers observing a large star. Others, which I shall concentrate on here, as I believe they carry clues to the trump's identity, depict it as the morning star, or star of Bethlehem.

The fifteenth-century Milanese deck in the Cary Collection, and indeed all subsequent Marseille-pattern decks, shows an androgynous-looking nude figure with flowing hair (in modern decks a female) kneeling and emptying jars of liquid, water perhaps, into a stream or pond (see bottom center figure on page 13). One jar is tucked under the figure's right arm, the other supported on the left shoulder. Above it shines an enormous scintillating star surrounded by four lesser stars. A fifth star nestles on the figure's right shoulder, maybe implying that this is the image of a constellation.

The figure's most obvious identification would be Aquarius, the water carrier, the eleventh sign of the zodiac, and there are various medieval and later woodcuts and engravings illustrating the water carrier emptying two containers in just such a manner. However, there seems no obvious reason why this particular astrological sign should be associated with this trump other than by happenstance.

The only clue I can find to the source of this puzzling image lies in a reference in the sixteenth-century book of allegorical images called *Iconologia,* compiled by Cesare Ripa, a Perugian student of medieval and

Renaissance iconography. Here, we find an illustration entitled *Crepuscolo della Mattina* (Twilight of the Morning), depicting a winged, androgynous-looking youth flying over a landscape. Above his head shines a large star, and a small bird, a swallow, dips in flight beside his shoulder. In his right hand he holds an inverted torch, in his left an upended jar from which drops of water fall.

The swallow was used as a symbol of resurrection in Renaissance painting, as may be seen in Crivelli's *Madonna* of 1490–1492. The bird was also considered to be sacred to Venus. The star itself is stated by Ripa to be definitely male. Quoting Petrarch's *Triumph of Fame,* he names it the Morning Star, Lucifer the light-bearer—that is to say, the planet Venus, herald of the coming day.

On the other hand, the tarot collection of Edmond de Rothschild at the Louvre introduces us to the second significant type of tarot star imagery. Here, the uncut sheet of six trumps displays the star of Bethlehem and the three wise kings. Once more, we must look to the medieval mystery plays for the source.

The second-largest unit of these plays was made up of those that arose around the feast of Epiphany on January 6. Among them evolved a small but popular drama, again taken from the New Testament, that concerned the three wise men or magi from the east who followed the miraculous star of Bethlehem that led them to the newborn Jesus.

The belief that they were kings arose during the sixth century, and that their names were Jasper or Casper, Melchior, and Balthasar, during the twelfth. The play was known variously as the *Tres Reges, Magi,* or the *Stella,* "Star," and it was per-formed by three of the clergy, who donned crowns and regal robes to play the kings. In the Rouen version of the play, the kings would approach from the west, north, and south ends of the church. They would meet and identify themselves and their mission, displaying their gifts in gilt chalices: gold from Tharsis to honor Jesus's kingship, frankincense from Arabia to pay homage to his divinity, and myrrh used for embalming (foreshadowing Jesus's death) from Saba or Sheba, today's Yemen, famous then for its myrrh, aloes, and cassia. Then the kings would follow the star to the high altar in the east. The star itself, frequently lit by candles, would be drawn along a wire strung high above the worshipers' heads.

Both sets of trump imagery use the star as a symbol of hope, expec-tation, and advent; the first for the advent of daylight, the second for the advent of the Messiah.

It's interesting to note that Pratesi's cartomancer focuses on the gift aspect of the card. Christian actually identifies the card as the Star of the Magi. As "Grand Orient," Waite begins by following Christian, Mathers, and the Golden Dawn in interpreting the Star as a sign of hope. Eleven years later, writing under his own name now, he includes an inter-pretation of the trump as a star of ill omen, something that was started by Etteilla with his addled rearrangement and "rectification" of the trumps.

Original Cartomantic Interpretations

Pratesi's Cartomancer (1750): Gift.
De Mellet (1781): The Star. The creation of the stars and fishes.
Court de Gébelin (1773–82): Sirius the Dog Star with Isis.

Lévi (1855): The Hebrew letter *Peh*. The Blazing Star. Heaven of the soul, outpouring of thought, moral influence of idea on form, immortality.

Christian (1870): Arcanum XVII. The Star of the Magi: Hope. In the divine world, Immortality; in the intellectual world, the Inner Light that illuminates the Spirit; in the physical world, Hope.

Mathers (1888): The Star. Hope, expectation, bright promises. *Reversed:* Hopes not fulfilled, or only in a minor degree.

Golden Dawn (1888–96): Daughter of the Firmament, Dweller between the Waters. Star. Hope, faith, unexpected help. *Reversed:* Deceived hope.

Grand Orient (Waite, 1889, 1909): Star. Light descending, hope; the symbol of immortality.

Waite (1910): The Star. Loss, theft, abandonment; another reading says hope and bright prospects. *Reversed:* Arrogance, haughtiness, impotence.

Suggested Interpretation

Birth of hope. Rebirth. Healing. *Reversed:* Lessened hope, but not an annulment.

TRUMP XVIII, THE MOON

ALTERNATE NAMES: *LA LUNE, LA LUNA*

The painted Visconti-Sforza decks of the Renaissance depict the classical goddess Phoebe or Diana in this trump.

However, the more common version is exemplified by the Marseille pattern. This displays the moon alone, letting fall drops of dew into a dew pond, out of which rises a crayfish or crab, the symbol for the zodiacal sign Cancer, which the moon rules. This trump design also appears in the prototypical fifteenth-century Milanese Cary Collection sheet. All that is absent from the Milanese trump are the two howling canines featured by later decks, including Waite's.

The fifteenth-century Florentine Rosenwald wood-block deck simply shows the moon's disk. Seventeenth-century decks like the French Viéville deck and the cards made in Rouen by Adam de Hautot and copied a hundred years later by Belgian card makers Vandenborre and Jean Galler show a female figure spinning yarn from a distaff, possibly tying in with a folklore belief in the moon as a goddess of destiny. In iconography, the distaff

is also frequently used as an image denoting feminine domesticity.

The Moon's position in the trump sequence may be indicative of the imminent arrival of the Last Judgment, the final mystery play in the cycle. The prophet Isaiah alludes to this moment: "The moon shall shine with a brightness like the sun's . . . on the day when the Lord binds up the broken limbs of his people and heals their wounds." As Kaplan observes, both the moon and the sun appear in the sky at the same time in illustrations of Petrarch's *Triumph of Eternity*.

As you will note, most of the old cartomantic interpretations are fairly negative, in line with traditional associations of the moon with lunacy, foolishness, and inconstancy. However, the moon was also considered by Renaissance magicians as the archetype responsible for the phenomenon of flux and reflux, as exhibited by the ocean's tides, the red tide of the human bloodstream, a woman's menstrual cycle, and ultimately anything in nature—like the moon itself—that waxes and wanes and is periodically cyclic. This was one interpretation, among others, promoted by the Golden Dawn Tarot.

Original Cartomantic Interpretations

Pratesi's Cartomancer (1750): Night.

De Mellet (1781): The Moon. Creation of the Moon and terrestrial animals. The wolf and the dog represent wild and domesticated animals.

Court de Gébelin (1773–82): The Moon.

Lévi (1855): The Hebrew letter *Tzaddi*. The Moon. The elements, the visible world, reflected light, material forms, symbolism.

Christian (1870): Arcanum XVIII. Twilight: Deceptions. In the divine world, the abysses of the Infinite; in the intellectual world, the darkness that cloaks the Spirit when it submits itself to the power of the instincts; in the physical world, deceptions and hidden enemies.

Mathers (1888): The Moon. Twilight, deception, error. *Reversed:* Slight deceptions, trifling mistakes.

Golden Dawn (1888–96): Ruler of Flux and Reflux, Child of the Sons of the Mighty. Moon. Dissatisfaction, voluntary change (as opposed to XIII, Death). *Reversed:* Error, lying, falsity, deception.

Grand Orient (Waite, 1889, 1909): Moon. Half-light, mutation, intellectual uncertainty, region of illusion; false-seeming.

Waite (1910): The Moon. Hidden enemies, danger, calumny, darkness, terror, deception, occult forces, error. *Reversed:* Instability, inconstancy, silence, lesser degrees of deception and error.

Suggested Interpretation

Period of increase. Flood tide. Waxing moon. Illusion. *Reversed:* Period of decline. Ebb tide. Waning moon. Delusion.

Trump XIX, the Sun

ALTERNATE NAMES: *Le Soleil, Il Sole*

Whereas the moon rules the night, the sun rules the day. This image forms a natural pair with the previous one, and together they corroborate the arrival of the Day of Judgment in the mystery play cycle. "The sun [shall shine] with seven times his wonted brightness, seven days' light in one," predicts Isaiah.

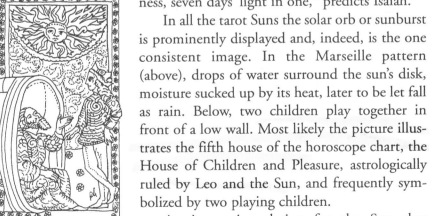

In all the tarot Suns the solar orb or sunburst is prominently displayed and, indeed, is the one consistent image. In the Marseille pattern (above), drops of water surround the sun's disk, moisture sucked up by its heat, later to be let fall as rain. Below, two children play together in front of a low wall. Most likely the picture illustrates the fifth house of the horoscope chart, the House of Children and Pleasure, astrologically ruled by Leo and the Sun, and frequently symbolized by two playing children.

An interesting design for the Sun that appears on seventeenth- and eighteenth-century tarots of the Belgian pattern depicts a single boy, sometimes naked, riding a horse and carrying a banner.

Éliphas Lévi describes this image as "a naked child mounted on a

white horse and displaying a scarlet standard," and Waite used it for his deck, feeling it conveyed what he perceived to be the spiritual import of the card better than the two playing children.

Waite was also undoubtedly influenced by a verse from a work popular among Golden Dawn initiates, the *Chaldean Oracles of Julianus,* a book of fairly inscrutable writings attributed to one Julian the Theurgist, a Neoplatonist of the second century C.E.: "But these things I revolve in the reclusive temples of my mind . . . to see a horse more glittering than light, or a boy riding on the back of the horse, fiery or clad in gold, or naked."

Using Erhard Schön's astrological fifth house as a guide, we can interpret this trump as good health, a heightening of creative powers, organizational abilities, abundant joy, the realization of the Star's hope, and maybe quite literally, children.

Original Cartomantic Interpretations

Pratesi's Cartomancer (1750): Day.

De Mellet (1781): The Sun. The Creation of the Sun and the union of man and woman.

Court de Gébelin (1773–82): The Sun.

Lévi (1855): The Hebrew letter *Kaph*. A radiant Sun: composites, the head, apex, prince of heaven.

Christian (1870): Arcanum XIX. The Blazing Light: earthly happiness. In the divine world, the supreme Heaven; in the intellectual world, sacred Truth; in the physical world, peaceful Happiness.

Mathers (1888): The Sun. Happiness, contentment, joy. *Reversed:* These in minor degree.

Golden Dawn (1888–96): Lord of the Fire of the World. Sun. Glory, gain, riches, sometimes also arrogance. *Reversed* or when with evil cards: Display, vanity.

Grand Orient (Waite, 1889, 1909): Sun. Full light, intellectual and material, earthly happiness, but not attained individually.

Waite (1910): The Sun. Material happiness, fortunate marriage, contentment. *Reversed:* The same in a lesser sense.

Suggested Interpretation

Good health. Creativity. Joy. Children. *Reversed:* The same.

TRUMP XX, THE JUDGMENT

The so-called *Judicium,* Last Judgment, constituted the group of mystery
plays performed at the end of the pageant cycle. This event, based in large
part on Jesus's account of the final cosmic reckoning in the gospel according to Matthew, brought the play cycle to a spectacular climax. Humanity
was judged and the world and time itself brought to an end.

In the play that was performed in York, England, the World was built
on the lower deck of the pageant wagon. There were probably trapdoors
through which the dead could rise. Heaven was built on the upper level
of the wagon, where angels performed, and where Jesus could return with
his saved souls at the end of the play. All this appears in the last two
trumps of the tarot deck.

The Marseille pattern for Judgment depicts an angel hovering in the
heavens and sounding a trumpet. Below, tombs and graves open and the
naked bodies of the dead rise in answer to the summons, hands prayer-
fully clasped in front of them. The Italian decks, however, are not so consistent. One of Bembo's painted Visconti Judgment cards depicts a
paternal Deity flanked by two angels as the central tableau; the other, in
the Cary-Yale Collection, depicts two angels by themselves. The
Florentine minchiate offers yet another version, giving a solitary angel
two trumpets to blow, deleting the rising dead altogether, and replacing
them with a town that probably represents the city of Florence itself.

Most modern decks, including Waite's, follow the Marseille pattern

and feature a single trumpeting angel. In view of the action being performed, this could be the archangel Gabriel, but a cross-emblazoned banner floating from the trumpet identifies it as Michael.

At the top of the Cary-Yale Bembo Judgment card seen above, the
words the angel is uttering, "Surgite ad Judicium," may be seen painted
in gold. If the angel's message is anything like the words declaimed in the
York play, it goes something like this:

Surgite! All men arise!
Venite ad judicium! Come you to Judgment!
For now is set the high justice,
And the day of doom!
Come you quickly to this assize,
All great and small,
And of your answer now take care,
What you say when that you come,
Your answer for to tell.
For when God shall examine, beware!
The truth alone He will hear,
And send you to Heaven or to Hell!"

Original Cartomantic Interpretations

Pratesi's Cartomancer (1750): Angel, wedding, and settlement.

De Mellet (1781): The Angel. The creation of man. Men and women formed from the earth, summoned by Osiris.

Court de Gébelin (1773–82): Creation, or the Last Judgment.

Lévi (1855): The Hebrew letter *Resh*. The Judgment. Vegetative principle, generative virtue of the earth, eternal life.

Christian (1870): Arcanum XX. The Awakening of the Dead: Renewal. Represents the passage from life on earth to the life of the future. The sign of the change that is the end of all things, of Good as well as of Evil.

Mathers (1888): The Last Judgment. Renewal, result, determination of a matter. *Reversed:* Postponement of result, delay, matter reopened later.

Golden Dawn (1888–96): The Spirit of the Primal Fire. Judgment. Final decision. Sentence. *Reversed:* Determination of matter without appeal on its plane.

Grand Orient (Waite, 1889, 1909): The Last Judgment. Resurrection, summons to new things, a change in the face of everything.

Waite (1910): The Last Judgment. Change of position, renewal, outcome. Another account specifies total loss through a lawsuit. *Reversed:* Weakness, cowardice, simplicity; also deliberation, decision, sentence.

Suggested Interpretation

Final determination. Resolution. Day of Reckoning. *Reversed:* Hesitation. Delay. Postponement. Sentence.

TRUMP XXI, THE WORLD

ALTERNATE NAMES: LE MONDE, IL MONDO

Of the many designs for the final trump card, I propose to examine the two most prevalent today. Probably the best-known depiction of the World trump is that adapted from the Marseille pattern by Pamela Colman Smith for Waite's 1909 deck and 1910 book: a naked female figure draped in a wafting stole and carrying a rod in each hand, floating aloft and surrounded by what looks like a laurel wreath bound in places by ribbons. At each corner of the card is positioned one of the heads of the four Holy Living Creatures of Ezekiel—lion, bull, man, and eagle. In 1910, Waite believed that this design represented "the perfection of the cosmos, and the state of the soul become conscious of the divine vision," that is, the beatific vision of Christian theology, the state of consciousness enjoyed eternally by the sanctified souls of the saved, and briefly by Dante at the end of his *Divine Comedy*.

However, it becomes quite apparent, judging by the mid-seventeenth-century World card designed by Jacques Viéville and a similar printed World card discovered at the Sforza castle in Milan that the central figure of the original decks was not female but male.

The four animal heads, the Holy Living Creatures of Ezekiel, also happen to be the standard representations in liturgical art of the four gospel makers, Matthew, Mark, Luke, and John. It seems reasonable to suppose that the central figure might be that of Jesus, wearing a cloak and halo and carrying a scepter, depicted appearing in glory to judge the living and the dead, the final tableau of the mystery play cycle.

Indeed, according to an English mercer's indenture of 1433, a document describing the technical requirements for the stage setting of *The Last Judgment* at the York cycle of mystery plays, the area of the stage designated to represent the World was the actual pageant wagon floor, and thrones of judgment would be erected there for Jesus and his apostles—and the four evangelists. The oval wreath surrounding the figure in the tarot trump would seem then to have been formed out of his almond-shaped mandorla. This is the first and most common type of World card design.

The tarocchi of fifteenth-century Italy introduce us to the second type of World trump. Two painted Visconti decks and the wood-block printed Rosenwald and Metropolitan Museum decks exemplify the type, presenting the World, not as Christ in glory, but as a landscape with buildings. As the material world, in fact.

In three of the decks, the landscape is depicted within a globe; in the fourth, it lies beneath an overarching firmament. In the Visconti-Sforza card, two *putti,* cherubic angels, support this globe from below.

In the Metropolitan Museum's wood-block cards, the World's globe is presided over by a winged angel, as indeed it is in the Rosenwald Collection, but in the latter case the perimeter of the globe is composed of a wreath of leaves that looks suggestively like the wreath that shows up later in the French Marseille pattern.

The globe and angel motifs are also to be found in one form or another in the seventeenth-century Paris Tarot, the Belgian tarot of Jean Galler, the Florentine minchiate, the tarocchi of Bologna, and in the Charles VI cards preserved in the Bibliothèque Nationale. In this last deck, the angelic figure is crowned, perhaps significantly, with the polygonal halo meant to designate an allegorical figure—in this case, possibly the missing virtue Prudence.

Why, one may wonder, this wide divergence of symbolism? The simplest way to account for it is as follows: Recalling that early Italian painted tarocchi are unnumbered, let us suppose that the card we call the World was in fact meant originally to be placed not at the end but as the penultimate card in the sequence. In that position it would have represented just one more celestial sphere following the Star, the Moon, and the Sun, thereby rounding out the cosmos being depicted and representing the planet Earth itself.

In this sequence, the ultimate card, quite fittingly, would have been the one that showed the end of time and the beginning of eternity—the trump depicting the Last Judgment. However, other card makers might have felt that the trump that ended the sequence should reflect not just the archangel Michael summoning the dead from their graves (the

Judgment trump) but the final tableau of the last mystery play—Christ in his glory. Ironically, and confusingly, this is in fact exactly what the Marseille-pattern World trump depicts, even as it retains the misleading caption of "the World."

As to the trump's interpretation, Pratesi's Bolognese cartomancer continues to surprise us to the very end, but there's little doubt about the general cartomantic consensus: the card is a symbol of completion. Interestingly, Waite backs up Pratesi's manuscript with an allusion to a long journey, physical or maybe metaphysical, as in a quest. Notions of eternity are also embodied in this card. Boethius defined eternity as "the total and perfect possession at once of endless life," which certainly resonates with Waite's interpretation. We are dealing here with the divine world of mystics, of the beatific vision, of Dante's final glimpse of heaven, of which he wrote in his *Commedia,* "Nothing shall be to come, and nothing past, but an eternal Now shall ever last."

What better note to end on?

Original Cartomantic Interpretations

Pratesi's Cartomancer (1750): Long journey.

De Mellet (1781): The World. The universe, represented by Isis and the four seasons.

Court de Gébelin (1773–82): Time, or the World.

Lévi (1855): The Hebrew letter *Tau.* Kether or the kabbalistic Crown: in the middle of the Crown is Truth holding a rod in each hand. The microcosm, the sum of all in all.

Christian (1870): Arcanum XXI. The Crown of the Magi: the Reward. This, the supreme Arcanum of Magism, is represented by a garland of golden roses surrounding a star and placed in a circle around which are set at equal distances the heads of a man, a bull, a lion, and an eagle. This is the sign with which the Magus decorates himself when he has reached the highest degree of initiation and has thus acquired a power limited only by his own intelligence and wisdom.

Mathers (1888): The Universe. Completion, good reward. *Reversed:* Evil reward, or recompense.

Golden Dawn (1888–96): The Great One of the Night of Time. Universe. The matter itself. Synthesis. World. Kingdom. Usually denotes the actual subject of the question, and it therefore depends entirely on the accompanying cards.

Grand Orient (Waite, 1889, 1909): The World. The glory thereof under the powers of the highest providence, the sum of manifest things; conclusion on any subject.

Waite (1910): The World. One of the worst explanations concerning it is that the figure symbolizes the Magus when he has reached the highest degree of initiation. [!] Assured success, recompense, voyage, route, emigration, flight, change of place. *Reversed:* Inertia, fixity, stagnation, permanence.

Suggested Interpretation

Prize. Reward. Achievement. Long journey. *Reversed:* Permanence.

5

THE MEANINGS OF THE
SUIT CARDS:
THE MINOR ARCANA

In this chapter we shall take a close look at the legendary associations of the suit cards, as well as their cartomantic interpretations. For convenience, I shall arrange them in a Pythagorean progression from earth to water to air to fire, starting from what might be considered the most material, the Ace of Coins, and progressing to the highest or most ethereal, the King of Batons.

The authorities cited here, whom I believe to be the primary ones, are some of those we encountered in the last chapter, namely Pratesi's cartomancer (when he or she has something to say), Etteilla, Mathers, the Golden Dawn, and Waite, incorporating the interpretations listed in the various editions of his *Key to the Tarot*.

The Golden Dawn's source for its decan interpretations of the suit cards two through ten appears to be *Picatrix*. Israel Regardie's volumes of the *Golden Dawn* published between 1937 and 1940 were until fairly recently the only published source of Golden Dawn documents. However, the material they contained was an edited and expurgated Stella Matutina version of the original Golden Dawn material. One of the highly significant papers that had been dropped at some point by the Stella Matutina was one entitled *The Magical Images of the Decans*, which on examination proves to be essentially a word-for-word English translation from the Latin of *Picatrix*. By comparing the Golden Dawn suit card interpretations with this material, it becomes immediately apparent where their tarot suit interpretations are drawn from.

Regardie later made good for the Stella Matutina omission by including the paper in his *Complete Golden Dawn System of Magic* (1984), which was based on a considerably earlier set of Golden Dawn documents dating from between 1894 and 1896 that had originally belonged to Golden Dawn initiate F. L. Gardner. Generally, as we shall see, this decan material is very much at variance with Etteilla's cartomantic interpretations.

As for the Golden Dawn court cards, the order's total and utter disregard of the traditional court sequence of King, Queen, Knight, and Knave remains problematic. Its kabbalistic reformulation of the Knights as Kings, Kings as Princes, and Knaves as Princesses seems to me not only at odds with the historical tarot but as addled in its own way as Etteilla's "rectified" trump scheme was. For the sake of completeness, however, confusing as they may be to some, I shall include the Golden Dawn courts and interpretations if only to reveal their debt to Etteilla or Mathers.

The two images with which I've chosen to illustrate each of the suit cards are based on the eighteenth-century Marseille-pattern deck of Nicholas Conver and Pamela Colman Smith's 1910 cards designed for A. E. Waite, which generally provide the inspiration for the suits of most contemporary tarot decks. The Conver card images appear on the left after each card heading, the images from Waite's deck on the right. Note that Waite characterized his Coin suit as "Pentacles" and his Baton suit as "Wands," English suit names that first appear as alternatives to Coins and "Sceptres" in Mathers' book *The Tarot* in 1888. Waite also chose to entitle his Knave court cards "Page," a perfectly valid translation of the French *Valet*.

The importance of Etteilla's interpretations of the Minor Arcana cards cannot be overstated. Aside from providing the prototype for each card's interpretation, the list of synonyms and associated words for each meaning that Etteilla and d'Odoucet provided are helpful for constructing the character of a card in one's memory. One may find similar, though modern, versions of the list in contemporary tarot books, but I believe it correct to say that the list given here is the prototype of all others, whether the cartomancer happens to know it or not.

The lists may seem repetitious to some, with quaint and out-of-date references that can be safely ignored. However, if you truly wish to learn to divine with the tarot in the traditional manner, it pays to take the time to read and reflect on Etteilla's, maybe traditional, interpretations, which all in some way represent different facets of each Minor card.

THE SUIT OF COINS OR PENTACLES

The Coin and Mirror are symbols pertaining to the Cardinal Virtue Prudence and, as I see it, to the ancient Persian class of *Rúzistar,* workers. Many cartomancers believe the Coin, also referred to today as a Pentacle, represents the Pythagorean element earth. Be that as it may, the virtue Prudence connotes, in addition to the idea of caution, notions of reflection, memory, foresight, communication, and exchange, whether financial or informational. Coins are considered a "feminine" suit in some card games, and for divination purposes may be associated with things to do with money, materiality, economics and financial matters: the more limited meanings of Prudence in fact.

As already noted, Etteilla equated the Coin, not with the Diamond as you might expect, but with the French cloverleaf suit sign *trèfle,* and Mathers followed him in this. If you compare the design inside a Marseille-pattern Coin with the conventional Club suit sign, the equation will not seem so far-fetched.

Mathers was also responsible for introducing the term, *Pentacle,* as we have also noted. In this he was, inaccurately, following Lévi's example— inaccurately because in 1855, in chapter 10 of his *Doctrine of Transcendental Magic,* Lévi had actually referred to the tarot Coin as a "Pantacle." This was a variation of the word *pentacle* he had invented to distinguish it from its common dictionary meaning as a five-pointed star or pentagram.

The five-pointed pentagram was originally a very ancient symbol used in Mesopotamia and India, later adopted by the school of Pythagoras as an emblem signifying good health, and therefore highly suitable for inscription on amulets and talismans. It was subsequently adopted by early Christians to represent the five wounds of Christ and, like the sign of the cross, Christianity itself; later Christian kabbalists used it to represent spirit or the quintessence, the fifth element believed by alchemists to rule the other four envisaged by Pythagoras and Aristotle—earth, water, air, and fire.

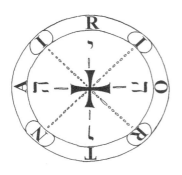

Waite also copied Lévi's illustration of a Pantacle of Ezechiel from The Doctrine of Transcendental Magic *to use as the center of his new Wheel of Fortune trump card.*

However, this was not Lévi's intended usage of the word, even though his rationale for his neologism was rooted in medieval magic. Here the word *pentacle* is also often used to refer to a talisman rather than a pentagram, and it was in this sense that Lévi was employing it. As Lévi defined it, a "Pantacle" (read "talisman") was "a synthetic character resuming the entire magical doctrine in one of its special conceptions," that is, an all-embracing design that represented the magical system you were working with at the time, in this case, the system of transcendental magic according to Éliphas Lévi.

However, Waite obviously instructed Pamela Colman–Smith to display pentagrams on his Coin suit, and in this manner we arrive at the disks decorated with five-pointed stars, Pentacles, which so frequently replace Coins in modern Tarot decks.

♦ Ace of Coins or Pentacles ♦

The Mamlûk deck represents the Ace as a golden *dînâr*. Lévi thought it was a Hebrew shekel. Most cartomancers concur that the card augurs wealth.

That Pratesi's Bolognese cartomancer chose to interpret this card as "table" is interesting. Etteilla, who, as we shall see later, ascribed the interpretation "table" not to the Ace of Coins but to the Ace of Cups, has other ideas. Furthermore, Mathers, the Golden Dawn, and Waite all concur with him. The color red and the "medicines" Etteilla mentions derive from his alchemical interests and refer to the red and final stage of the philosophers' stone, in which it changes base metals into gold.

Original Cartomantic Interpretations

Pratesi's cartomancer (1750): Table.

Etteilla (1785–1807): Perfect contentment, felicity, happiness, ravishment, enchantment, ecstasy, marvel, entire satisfaction, complete joy, inexpressible pleasure, the color red, the perfect medicine, the solar medicine, pure, accomplished. *Reversed:* Sum, capital, principal, treasure, riches, opulence, rare, dear, precious, inestimable.

Mathers (1888): Perfect contentment, felicity, prosperity, triumph. *Reversed:* Purse of gold, money, help, profit, riches.

Golden Dawn (1888–96): The Root of the Powers of Earth. It represents materiality in all senses, good and evil, and is therefore in a sense illusionary. It shows material gain, labor, power, wealth, etc.

Waite (1910): Perfect contentment, ecstasy, speedy intelligence, gold. *Reversed:* The evil side of wealth, bad intelligence, great riches.

Suggested Interpretation

Financial security. *Reversed:* The price of security.

♦ Two of Coins or Pentacles ♦

ALTERNATE NAMES THE DEUCE OF COINS OR PENTACLES

Decan: Capricorn, degree 1 to degree 10, ruled by Jupiter.
Picatrix (c. 1256): It is a decan of wandering travail, labor and joy, alternate gain and loss, weakness and necessity.

Here we begin to see the Golden Dawn's introduction of *Picatrix* material as a source of interpretation. In this instance it serves to reinforce what I take to be the traditional readings of Etteilla. Perhaps we can say that the figure-of-eight symbol so frequently to be found enclosing the two coins on this card suggested an omen of instability and fluctuation, calling for flexibility and some juggling on the part of the inquirer, a concept Pamela Colman Smith introduced into her design for Waite's deck.

Original Cartomantic Interpretations

Etteilla (1785–1807): Embarrassment, obstacle, engagement, obstruction, hang-up, hitch, trouble, concern, emotion, embroilment, confusion, difficulty, prevention, entwinement, obscurity, agitation, disquiet, perplexity, solicitude. *Reversed:* Note, writing, handwriting, text, literature, doctrine, erudition, works, book, production, composition, dispatch, epistle, missive, character, literal sense, alphabet, elements, principles, letter of exchange.

Mathers (1888): Embarrassment, worry, difficulties. *Reversed:* Letter, missive, epistle, message.

Golden Dawn (1888–96): Lord of Harmonious Change. Harmony of change. Alternation of gain and loss, weakness and strength, ever-varying occupation, wandering, discontented with any fixed condition of things; now elated, now melancholy; industrious yet unreliable; fortunate through prudence of management, yet sometimes unaccountably foolish. Alternately talkative and suspicious. Kind yet wavering and inconsistent. Fortunate in journeying. Argumentative.

Waite (1910): A card of gaiety, recreation and its connections. Also news and messages in writing, as obstacles, agitation, trouble, embroilment. Another reading indicates that troubles are more imaginary than real. *Reversed:* Enforced gaiety, simulated enjoyment, literal sense, handwriting, composition, letters of exchange. Also bad omen, ignorance, injustice.

Suggested Interpretation

Juggling, maybe financial. Embarrassing news. *Reversed:* Obstacles, maybe financial. An important communication.

♦ Three of Coins or Pentacles ♦

ALTERNATE NAME: THE TREY OF COINS OR PENTACLES

Decan: Capricorn, degree 11 to degree 20, ruled by Mars.
Picatrix (c. 1256): It is a decan of ever seeking what cannot be known and of what cannot be attained to.

Although Etteilla and d'Odoucet include a wealth of detail ignored by other cartomancers, we can see a thread of esteem being carried through all the interpretations, whether it's the unearned esteem derived from a noble or wealthy birth or the earned esteem derived from excellence of a job well done. If you accept the validity of *Picatrix's* decan input, then you have to include an element of unrealistic idealism.

Original Cartomantic Interpretations

Etteilla (1785–1807): Noble, of consequence, celebrated, important, large, major, extended, vast, sublime, renowned, famous, powerful, elevated, illustrious, illustration, consideration, greatness of soul, noble deeds, generous deeds, magnificently, splendidly. *Reversed:* Puerility, childhood, childishness, frivolity, enfeeblement, abasement, diminution, politeness, paucity, mediocrity, pettiness, trifle, frivolity, baseness, cowardice, faint-heartedness, reject, little girl, puerile, feeble, low, groveling, worthless, abject, humble, abjection, humility, humiliation.

Mathers (1888): Nobility, elevation, dignity, rank, power. *Reversed:* Children, sons, daughters, youths, commencement.

Golden Dawn (1888–96): The Lord of Material Works. Working and constructive force, building up, erection, creation, realization, and increase of material things, gain in commercial transactions, rank, increase of substance, influence, cleverness in business, selfishness, commencement of matter to be established later. Narrow and prejudiced, keen in matter or gain. Modified by dignity (that is, whether upright or reversed, and including the influence of neighboring cards). Sometimes given to seeking after the impossible.

Waite (1910): Vocation, trade, skilled labor. A card of nobility, aristocracy, renown, glory. If for a man, celebrity for his eldest son. *Reversed:* Mediocrity, in work and otherwise. Puerility, pettiness, weakness. Interpretation depends on neighboring cards.

Suggested Interpretation

Skill, earned esteem, celebrity. *Reversed:* Failing grade. Mediocrity.

♦ Four of Coins or Pentacles ♦

Decan: Capricorn, degree 21 to degree 30, ruled by the Sun.

Picatrix (c. 1256): It is a decan of covetousness, suspicion, careful ordering of matters, but with discontent.

Picatrix is unequivocal about the meaning of this decan, but Etteilla's interpretation is the polar opposite. Mathers follows Etteilla; Waite and the Golden Dawn follow *Picatrix*. Etteilla's "lunar medicine" and "white stone" refer to the alchemist's philosopher's stone in its early, white stage, when it can turn base metals into silver only.

Original Cartomantic Interpretations

Etteilla (1785–1807): Present, gift, generosity, benefit, liberality, New Year's gift, grace, offering, donation, gratuity, tip, the color white, the lunar medicine, the white stone. *Reversed:* Pregnant, circuit, circumvolution, circumscription, circumference, circle, circulation, intercept, obstruction, engorgement, monopolization, cloister, monastery, convent, arrested, fixed, determined, definitive, extremity, boundaries, limits, terms, end, barrier, compartment, rampart, hedge, partition, obstacles, bars, prevention, suspension, slowing down, opposition.

Mathers (1888): Pleasure, gaiety, enjoyment, satisfaction. *Reversed:* Obstacles, hindrances.

Golden Dawn (1888–96): The Lord of Earthly Power. Assured material gain, success, rank, dominion, earthly power completed, but leading to nothing beyond. Prejudiced, covetous, suspicious, careful and orderly, but discontented. Little enterprise or originality.

Waite (1910): The surety of possessions, cleaving to that which one has, gift, legacy, inheritance. For a bachelor, pleasant news from a lady. *Reversed:* Delay, opposition.

Suggested Interpretation

A gift, or assured material gain. *Reversed:* Hard times, or avarice.

✦ Five of Coins or Pentacles ✦

Decan: Taurus, degree 1 to degree 10, ruled by Mercury.
Picatrix (c. 1256): It is a decan of plowing, sowing, building, and earthly wisdom ("est arandi et laborandi terram, scienciarum, geometrie, et seminandi et fabricandi").

As Waite dryly notes, the various meanings attributed to this card cannot be harmonized. Which direction you follow is entirely up to you. Of course, if you're using the Rider-Waite deck or any of its derivatives, the image of Victorian destitution Waite provides will guide your interpretation toward Waite's rather dismal view.

Original Cartomantic Interpretations

Etteilla (1785–1807): Lover, loving, gallant, husband, wife, spouse, boyfriend, girlfriend, fan, mistress, to love, to cherish, to adore, affinity, concord, convenience, appropriateness, suitability. *Reversed:* Disordered, muddle, misconduct, disorder, trouble, confusion, chaos, damage, ravage, ruin, dissipation, consumption.

Mathers (1888): Lover or mistress, love, sweetness, affection, pure and chaste love. *Reversed:* Disgraceful love, imprudence, license, profligacy.

Golden Dawn (1888–96): The Lord of Material Trouble. Loss of money or position. Toil, labor, land cultivation, building, knowledge and acuteness of earthly things, poverty, carefulness. Kindness, sometimes money regained after severe toil and labor. Unimaginative, harsh, stern, determined, obstinate.

Waite (1910): Material trouble, destitution or otherwise. For some, a card of love and lovers, wife, husband, friend, mistress, also concordance, affinities. Conquest of fortune by reason. These alternatives cannot be harmonized. *Reversed:* Disorder, chaos, ruin, discord, profligacy, troubles in love.

Suggested Interpretation

Love. Material loss. Financial difficulties. *Reversed:* Trouble in love. Chaos.

✦ Six of Coins or Pentacles ✦

Decan: Taurus, degree 11 to degree 20, ruled by the Moon.
Picatrix (c. 1256): It is a decan of power, nobility, rule over the people.

Again, the Coins theme of materiality reasserts itself in this card. Mathers makes a translation error that, oddly, Waite reproduces, suggesting that he might have taken Mathers's little book on the tarot more seriously than he cared to admit. The Golden Dawn adheres closely to *Picatrix*.

Original Cartomantic Interpretations

Etteilla (1785–1807): The present. Actually, immediately, now, on the spot, suddenly, instantly, at this moment, today, assistant, witness, contemporary, attentive, caring, vigilant. *Reversed:* Desire, wish, ardor, zeal, passion, pursuit, cupidity, longing, jealousy, illusion.

Mathers (1888): Presents, gifts, gratification. [Note that Mathers mistranslates Etteilla's "*le présent*" as "gifts" or "presents," and many cartomancers perpetuate this interpretation.] *Reversed:* Ambition, desire, passion, aim, longing.

Golden Dawn (1888–96): Lord of Material Success. Success and gain in material undertakings, power, influence, rank, nobility, rule over the people. Fortunate, successful, just and liberal. If ill-dignified, may be purse proud, insolent from success, or prodigal.

Waite (1910): Presents, gifts, gratification. Another account says attention, vigilance. Now is the accepted time, present prosperity. The present must not be relied on. *Reversed:* Desire, cupidity, envy, jealousy, illusion. A check on the querent's ambition.

Suggested Interpretation

Present prosperity. No time like the present. *Reversed:* Zeal.

◆ Seven of Coins or Pentacles ◆

Decan: Taurus, degree 21 to degree 30, ruled by Saturn.

Picatrix (c.1256): It is a decan of misery, slavery, necessity, madness, and baseness.

None of the cartomancers except the Golden Dawn agrees with *Picatrix* on this card.

Original Cartomantic Interpretations

Etteilla (1785–1807): Money, riches, sum, coinage, silverware, whiteness, parity, candor, innocence, ingenuousness, the moon. *Reversed:* Disquiet, spiritual torment, impatience, affliction, chagrin, concern, solicitude, care, attention, diligence, application, apprehension, fear, diffidence, mistrust, suspicion.

Mathers (1888): Money, finance, treasure, gain, profit. *Reversed:* Disturbance, worry, anxiety, melancholy.

Golden Dawn (1888–96): Lord of Success Unfulfilled. Loss of an apparently promising fortune. Hopes deceived and crushed. Disappointment. Misery, necessity, slavery, and baseness. A cultivator of land, and yet is loser thereby. Sometimes it denotes slight and isolated gains with no fruits resulting therefrom, and of no further account, though seeming to promise well. According to dignity (the attitude of the card and the influence of the other cards around it).

Waite (1910): A card of money, business, barter, but one reading gives altercation, quarrel, and another innocence, ingenuity [sic: Waite's mistranslation of *ingénuité,* actually "ingenuousness"], purgation. Also an improved position for a lady's future husband. *Reversed:* Impatience, apprehension, suspicion, cause for anxiety regarding money that it may be proposed to lend.

Suggested Interpretation

Steady growth through work. Exchange. *Reversed:* Small returns for much labor.

♦ Eight of Coins or Pentacles ♦

Decan: Virgo, degree 1 to degree 10, ruled by the Sun.
Picatrix (c. 1256): A decan of sowing, plowing, planting herbs, colonization, and of storing money and food.

Two aspects of Virgo, femininity and prudence, seem to be demonstrated in the interpretations of this card. Etteilla and Mathers emphasize an interpretation that involves a brunette or dark girl, while the Golden Dawn and Waite, owing to the more Hermetic orientation of their systems, opt for *Picatrix*'s decan allusions to prudence and industriousness. Etteilla's "*grande nuit*" remains a mystery to me, unless it refers to some anticipated great event or big occasion.

Original Cartomantic Interpretations

Etteilla (1785-1807): A dark-haired girl, passive, *grande nuit. Reversed:* Siphoning, avarice, usury.

Mathers (1888): A dark girl, beauty, candor, chastity, innocence, modesty. *Reversed:* Flattery, usury, hypocrisy, shifty.

Golden Dawn (1888–96): Lord of Prudence. Over-careful in small things at the expense of the great. "Penny-wise and pound-foolish." Gain of ready money in small sums. Mean, avariciousness. Industrious, cultivation of land, hoarding, lacking in enterprise.

Waite (1910): Work, employment, commission, craftsmanship, skill in craft and business, perhaps in the preparatory stage. A young man in business who has relations with the inquirer. A dark girl.

Reversed: Voided ambition, vanity, exaction, usury. May also signify the possession of skill, in the sense of the ingenious mind turned to cunning and intrigue. The inquirer will be compromised in a matter of moneylending.

Suggested Interpretation
Dark-haired girl or young woman. Manual or commercial ability. *Reversed:* Beware of greed or extortion.

◆ Nine of Coins or Pentacles ◆

Decan: Virgo, degree 11 to degree 20, ruled by Venus.
Picatrix (c. 1256): It is a decan of gain, covetousness, taking of goods, and rising by care and treasuring up.

Virgo again indicates prudence in this card. Etteilla's students felt that it indicated a sort of guarantee of result.

Original Cartomantic Interpretations
Etteilla (1785–1807): Effect, realization, positive, accomplishment, success. *Reversed:* Flimflam, swindling, deception, promises without result, vain hopes, aborted projects.

Mathers (1888): Discretion, circumspection, prudence, discernment. *Reversed:* Deceit, bad faith, artifices, deception.

Golden Dawn (1888–96): Lord of Material Gain. Complete realization of material gain, inheritance, covetousness, treasuring of goods and sometimes theft, and knavery. All according to dignity.

Waite (1910): Prudence, safety, success, accomplishment, certitude, discernment, prompt fulfillment of what is presaged by neighboring cards. *Reversed:* Roguery, deception, voided project, bad faith, vain hopes.

Suggested Interpretation

Prudence and self-sufficiency. Prompt fulfillment. *Reversed:* Self-sufficiency compromised. Voided project.

♦ Ten of Coins or Pentacles ♦

Decan: Virgo, degree 21 to degree 30, ruled by Mercury.

Picatrix (c. 1256): It is a decan of old age, slothfulness, loss, and depopulation.

There seems to be no doubt about the import of this card for most cartomancers. Financial security and the inquirer's home are predominant themes. *Picatrix's* gloomy signification appears only in the reversal of the card. Waite's acknowledgment of *Picatrix* is registered in the elderly man seated in the left foreground of the Colman Smith card.

Original Cartomantic Interpretations

Pratesi's cartomancer (1750): Money.

Etteilla (1785–1807): House, household, household economy, savings, dwelling, domicile, habitation, manor, lodging, regiment, bastion, vessel, vase, archive, castle, cottage, family, extraction, race, posterity, lair, cavern, den. *Reversed:* Lot, fortune, game, unforeseen occurrence, gamble, ignorance, sortilege, fate, destiny, fatality, happy or unhappy occasion.

Mathers (1888): House, dwelling, habitation, family. *Reversed:* Gambling, dissipation, robbery, loss.

Golden Dawn (1888–96): Lord of Wealth. Completion of material gain and fortune, but nothing beyond, as it were, at the very pinnacle of success. Old age, slothfulness, great wealth, yet sometimes loss in part, and later heaviness, dullness of mind, yet clever and prosperous in money transactions.

Waite (1910): Gain, riches, family matters, archives, extraction, house or dwelling, the abode of a family. Derives its value from other cards. *Reversed:* Chance, fatality, loss, robbery, games of hazard, sometimes gift, dowry, pension, an occasion which may be fortunate or otherwise.

Suggested Interpretation:

The home. Security. Family. *Reversed:* Loss, maybe through a gamble.

✦ Knave or Page of Coins or Pentacles ✦

The most common identification for the French-suit version of this card was Lancelot, the handsomest knight of all. Indeed, the *Valet de Trèfle* has been known as Lancelot since the late fifteenth century.

Lancelot was not one of the Nine Worthies, but he was an extremely popular character in medieval romance. Some say he was the son of King Bran of Brittany, but raised from infancy by the Lady of the Lake. As Nimue—possibly a misreading of the manuscript name Ninive, Niniane, or Viviane—this enchantress also plays a large part in Arthurian romance as Merlin's mistress and King Arthur's protector against the mischief of another enchantress, Arthur's half sister, Morgan Le Fay. Lancelot's guilty love for Arthur's wife, Guinevere, was one of the ultimate causes of the downfall of Arthur's kingdom of Logres, although he fathered his son, Galahad, upon the daughter of Pelles the Grail King. Later, after he had knighted Galahad and introduced him to Arthur's court, Lancelot went in quest of the Holy Grail, but because of his

amorous imperfections, he only sighted it twice, whereas Galahad achieved it.

An English deck of the eighteenth century names this card, not inappropriately, "Contradiction."

Pratesi notes that the Page or Knave card named in the manuscript he discovered was the *Fantesca,* the female version of the card, indicating that a pre-1750 tarocco of Bologna was being used by the writer. Obviously, for a female court card, a female interpretation would be appropriate. Etteilla's divinations, however, operated with a male *Valet.* Mathers resorts only to the Coins/Prudence/Earth interpretation, as does Waite, with a little bit of Etteilla thrown in.

Original Cartomantic Interpretations

Pratesi's cartomancer (1750): *Fantesca* of Coins, young lady.

Etteilla (1785–1807): A dark-haired youth, study, instruction, application, meditation, reflection, work, occupation, apprenticeship, schoolboy, disciple, pupil, apprentice, amateur, student, speculator, negotiator. *Reversed:* Profession, superfluity, largesse, luxury, sumptuousness, magnificence, abundance, multiplicity, liberality, benefit, generosity, beneficence, crowd, multitude, degradation, dilapidation, pillage, dissipation.

Mathers (1888): A dark youth, household economy, rule, management. *Reversed:* Prodigality, profusion, waste, dissipation.

Golden Dawn (1888–96): Princess of the Echoing Hills. Rose of the Palace of Earth. She is generous, kind, diligent, benevolent, careful, courageous, preserving, pitiful. If ill-dignified (reversed), she is wasteful and prodigal.

Waite (1910): A dark youth; a young officer or soldier; a child. Application, study, scholarship, reflection, news, messages and the bringer of these. Rule, management. *Reversed:* Prodigality, dissipation, liberality, luxury. Unfavorable news.

Suggested Interpretation

A sensible younger person. Diligence (the postive aspect of Lancelot). Study. *Reversed:* A careless, crass younger person (Lancelot at his worst). Waste.

♦ Knight of Coins or Pentacles ♦

 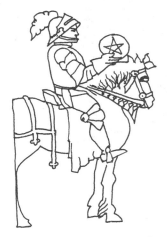

Cartomancers often interpret Knaves (in this instance Knights), representing as they do servants or dependents of the King or Queen of their suits, as their "thoughts," and this is what Pratesi's cartomancer did. A King or Queen is generally considered to represent either the inquirer or a person with whom he or she is having or will have dealings.

Original Cartomantic Interpretations

Pratesi's cartomancer (1750): The thought of the man (the King of Coins).

Etteilla (1785–1807): Usefulness, advantage, gain, profit, interest, profitable, interesting, advantageous, important, necessary, obliging, officious. *Reversed:* Peace, tranquility, repose, sleep, apathy, inertia, stagnation, inactivity, unemployment, free time, pastimes, recreation, carelessness, nonchalance, indolence, laziness, idleness, torpor, discouragement, extermination.

Mathers (1888): A useful man, trustworthy, wisdom, economy, order, regulation. *Reversed:* A brave man, but out of employment, idle, unemployed, negligent.

Golden Dawn (1888–96): Prince of the Chariot of Earth. Increase of matter, increase of good and evil, solidifies, practically applies things, steady, reliable. If ill-dignified, animal, material, stupid. Is slow to anger, but furious if roused.

Waite (1910): Utility, serviceableness, interest, responsibility, rectitude. A useful man, useful discoveries. *Reversed:* Inertia, idleness, repose of that kind. Stagnation, also placidity, discouragement, carelessness, a brave man out of employment.

Suggested Interpretation

A useful person. Propitious occasion. Taking responsibility. *Reversed:* A dull, careless person. Unemployment.

◆ Queen of Coins or Pentacles ◆

The most popular caption for the French-suit version of this card was Argine, thought by many to be an anagram of *Regina* (Queen), representing Mary of Anjou, the wife of the French king Charles VII. Others have said she represents Marie de Médicis, wife to Henry IV. Alternatively, the name is claimed to be a version of Argea, the daughter of Ardrastus, an ancient king of Argos in Greece.

　　Another Argea, however, turns up in the tales of the sixteenth-century Ferrarese poet Torquato Tasso: Argea Queen of the Fays, sister to the  enchantress Filidea and protector of the hero Floridante. Tasso may well have been drawing his inspiration for her character from fourteenth-century Spanish and Portuguese material contained in the popular chivalric romance *Amadis of Gaul,* however. Furthermore, the thirteenth-century English priest and chronicler Layamon introduces another fay with a similar name in his Arthurian chronicle, notably Argante, the "fairest of elves" and queen of Avalon, who takes the wounded King Arthur into her care to heal him after his last battle. If Argine/Argea is indeed Argante, she would seem to be an alter ego of Morgan le Fay. Some old French decks label this card *"Tromperie"* (Faithlessness), which might be an accurate description of Morgan from Arthur's point of view.

　　Pratesi's interpretation is pretty inscrutable, though echoed to some degree by the Golden Dawn.

Original Cartomantic Interpretations

Pratesi's cartomancer (1750): Truth.

Etteilla (1785–1807): A dark-haired woman, wealth, riches, pomp, luxury, sumptuousness, assurance, surety, confidence, certitude, affirmation, security, toughness, liberty, frankness. *Reversed:* Unsure, doubting, uncertain, doubt, indecision, uncertainty, disquiet, fear, terror, timidity, apprehension, vacillation, hesitation, undetermined, irresolute, perplexed, in suspense.

Mathers (1888): A dark woman, a generous woman, liberality, greatness of soul, generosity. *Reversed:* Certain evil, a suspicious woman, a woman justly regarded with suspicion, doubt, mistrust.

Golden Dawn (1888–96): Queen of the Thrones of Earth. She is impetuous, kind, timid, rather charming, greathearted, intelligent, melancholy, truthful, yet of many moods. Ill-dignified, she is undecided, capricious, foolish, changeable.

Waite (1910): Opulence, generosity, magnificence, security, liberty. A dark woman. Presents from a rich relative. Rich and happy marriage for a young man. *Reversed:* Evil, suspicion, suspense, fear, mistrust, illness.

Suggested Interpretation

A mature, affluent, outspoken woman. Generosity. Economic security. *Reversed:* An affluent but untrustworthy woman. Venality.

♦ King of Coins or Pentacles ♦

The most popular caption for the Paris-pattern version of this card was Alexander, who, aside from being great, was also king of Macedon and one of the Nine Worthies.

Alexander's fourth-century B.C.E. reign ushered in the Hellenistic Age, the age of the Greek Empire. Pupil of Aristotle, conqueror of Asia and Egypt, superhero of the ancient world, Alexander also found time

to be the lover of Hephaestion and to marry a variety of princesses from the lands he conquered. He subsequently became a hugely popular figure in French medieval romance. The earliest Alexander tale was supposedly written by one of his early companions, Callisthenes, and was current in Egypt around 200 C.E. Callisthenes tells us that Alexander was fathered by the Egyptian sorcerer-pharaoh Nectanebus on Olympias, wife of King Philip of Macedon during Philip's absence, making sure that the baby was born under favorable astrological aspects. Alexander had hair like a lion's mane, eyes of different colors, and a prodigious strength belied by his short stature. He was adored by his troops, and on his marches of conquest supposedly encountered dog-headed men and centaurs, a magnetic mountain, oracular trees, and lion-sized ants! He visited the depths of the ocean in a prototypical bathysphere, and took to the skies in a chariot drawn by griffins. The twelfth-century French poem the *Romance of Alexander* was composed in twelve-syllable meters, subsequently given the name "alexandrines."

Alexander's story, not unnaturally, was also taken up by the Persians, whom he defeated. They passed it on in turn to the Turks and other Muslims, who entitled Alexander *Dhul-Qarnain,* "the Two-horned One" (as he appears in chapter 18 of the Koran), probably because he had himself depicted on coins wearing the ram's horns of the Egyptian god Amun, whose priests had prophesied his victories. As one of the Nine Worthies, Alexander was famous for his generosity with the spoils of his wars. Largesse was a knightly virtue, and Alexander made his soldiers wealthy with the booty of battle.

Again, Pratesi's cartomancer presents us with one of his (or her) enigmatic oracles. Mathers and Waite seem more focused and on target. The Golden Dawn seems way off the mark.

Original Cartomantic Interpretations

Pratesi's cartomancer (1750): The man.

Etteilla (1785-1807): A dark-haired man, businessman, negotiator, banker, secretary of finance, calculator, stock market speculator, physics, geometry, mathematics, science, master, professor. *Reversed:* Imperfection, defect, weakness, defectiveness, defective construction, malformation, disordering, ugliness, deformity, corruption, fetid.

Mathers (1888): A dark man, victory, bravery, courage, success. *Reversed:* An old and vicious man, a dangerous man, doubt, fear, peril, danger.

Golden Dawn (1888–96): Lord of the Wild and Fertile Land. King of the Spirits of the Earth. Unless very well dignified (by the proximity of positive cards), he is heavy, dull, and material. Laborious, clever and patient in material matters. If ill-dignified he is avaricious, grasping, dull, jealous, not very courageous, unless assisted by other symbols. [This is hardly a portrait of the Alexander of legend!]

Waite (1910): A rather dark man, a merchant, master, professor. Valor, realizing intelligence, business and normal intellectual aptitude, sometimes mathematical gifts and attainments of this kind. *Reversed:* An old and vicious man. Vice, weakness, ugliness, perversity, corruption, peril.

Suggested Interpretation

A wealthy man. Business aptitude. A financial speculator. *Reversed:* A wealthy man. Avarice or corruption.

THE SUIT OF CUPS OR CHALICES

The Cup, Chalice, and Flask are symbols of the Cardinal Virtue Temperance, the ancient Persian class of *Súristár,* cultivators and farmers, and the element water. In card games Cups, like Coins, are also considered a "feminine" suit. In divination, Cup cards are generally interpreted as having to do with love, pleasure, receptivity, comfort, civility, fertility, emotional matters, and female sexuality. Etteilla and Mathers equated Cups with Hearts. Again, a comparison of the bowl of a Marseille-pattern Cup with a conventional Heart will show the similarity.

Éliphas Lévi believed the Cup represented the silver cup of the biblical hero Joseph, by means of which he performed his divinations, presumably by scrying, as in a crystal ball. On the other hand, the tarot Cup, as already noted, is considered by many cartomancers today to refer to the legendary Holy Grail of the Arthurian Cycle, and sometimes to its presumed pagan Celtic forerunner, the inexhaustible cauldron of the Dagda, which could even bring the dead back to life. In both instances, the symbols would connote divine inspiration, nourishment, and fertility.

✦ Ace of Cups or Chalices ✦

Pratesi's Bolognese interpretation of this card as "the house" can probably be equated to Etteilla's "hotel" and "inn." Furthermore, the interpretation of the Ace of Hearts or Cups as the "house of the inquirer" is a fairly widely established cartomantic tradition. So the Bolognese reading may in fact be the correct choice. However, Waite takes a stab at reconciling all the interpretations.

Original Cartomantic Interpretations

Pratesi's cartomancer (1750): The house.

Etteilla (1785–1807): Table, repast, feast, gala, regalement, nourishment, food, nutrition, guests, service, invitation, prayer, supplication, convocation, host, hotel, hostelry, inn, abundance, fertility, production, solidity, stability, fixedness, constancy, perseverance, continuation, duration, following, assiduousness, persistence, firmness, courage, tableau, painting, image, hieroglyph, description, shelves, portfolio, bureau, desk, table of Nature, bronze table, marble table, law, catalog, table of contents, harmonic table, garden table, altar table. *Reversed:* Mutation, permutation, transmutation, alteration, vicissitude, varieties, variation, inconstancy, lightness, exchange, barter, purchase, sale, market, treatise, convention, metamorphosis, diversity, versatility, reversal, upending, revolution, reversion, version, translation, interpretation.

Mathers (1888): Feasting, banquet, good cheer. *Reversed:* Change, novelty, metamorphosis, inconstancy.

Golden Dawn (1888–96): The Root of the Powers of Water. It symbolizes fertility, productiveness, beauty, pleasure, happiness, etc.

Waite (1910): House of the true heart, joy, content, abode, nourishment, abundance, fertility, holy table, felicity hereof. Inflexible will, unalterable law. *Reversed:* House of the false heart, mutation, instability, revolution, unexpected change of position.

Suggested Interpretation

Happy home. Nourishment. Abundance. Inspiration. *Reversed:* Sad home. Emotional letdown. Change. Inconstancy.

◆ Two of Cups or Chalices ◆

ALTERNATE NAME: THE DEUCE OF CUPS OR CHALICES

Decan: Cancer, degree 1 to degree 10, ruled by Venus.

Picatrix (c. 1256): Dominion, science, love, mirth, subtlety, and magistracy.

The traditional dragon, lion, or dolphin heads, sometimes read as a caduceus, that appear on this card are obviously derived from a design to be found in the original Mamlûk deck, a fact noted by tarot historian Jan Bauwens in 1972.

As to the card's interpretation, everybody seems in accord. The harmonious influence of Venus, the planet of peace and love, in the water sign Cancer would appear to be fairly unambiguous, if you accept the decan theory.

Original Cartomantic Interpretations

Etteilla (1785–1807): Love, passion, inclination, sympathy, attractiveness, propensity, friendship, goodwill, affection, attachment, taste, liaison, gallantry, attraction, affinity. *Reversed:* Desire, wish, vows, will, longing, lust, avarice, sensuality, jealousy, passion, illusion, appetite.

Mathers (1888): Love, attachment, friendship, sincerity, affection. *Reversed:* Crossed desires, obstacles, opposition, hindrance.

Golden Dawn (1888–96): Lord of Love. Harmony of masculine and feminine united. Harmony, pleasure, mirth, subtlety, sometimes folly, dissipation, waste, and silly action, according to dignity.

Waite (1910): Love, passion, friendship, affinity, union, concord, sympathy, the interrelation of the sexes, that desire which is not in nature but by which nature is sanctified. Favorable in things of pleasure and business, as well as love, also wealth and honor. *Reversed:* Passion.

Suggested Interpretation

Emotional bonding. Good omen. *Reversed:* Head ruled by heart. Bad omen.

✦ Three of Cups or Chalices ✦

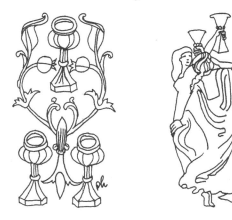

ALTERNATE NAME: THE TREY OF CUPS OR CHALICES

Decan: Cancer, degree 11 to degree 20, ruled by Mercury.
Picatrix (c. 1256): A decan of pleasure, mirth, abundance, and plenty.

Again, we seem to have, if not an exact concurrence of opinion, at least agreement on the general tenor of the card.

Original Cartomantic Interpretations

Etteilla (1785–1807): Success, science, happy issue, happy ending, victory, suppression of illness, cure, relief, accomplishment, perfection. *Reversed:* Expedience, dispatch, enactment, completion, ending, conclusion, termination, accomplishment.

Mathers (1888): Success, triumph, victory, favorable issue. *Reversed:* Expedition of business, quickness, celerity, vigilance.

Golden Dawn (1888–96): Lord of Abundance. Abundance, plenty, success, pleasure, sensuality, passive success, good luck and fortune. Love, gladness, kindness, and bounty. According to dignity.

Waite (1910): The conclusion of any matter in plenty, perfection, and merriment. Happy outcome, victory, fulfillment, solace, healing. *Reversed:* Expedition, dispatch, achievement, end, consolation, cure, excess in physical enjoyment, the pleasures of the senses, the end of the business.

Suggested Interpretation

Happy conclusion. Recovery. Relief. *Reversed:* Expeditious conclusion.

◆ Four of Cups or Chalices ◆

Decan: Cancer, degree 21 to degree 30, ruled by the Moon.
Picatrix (c. 1256): It is a decan of running, hunting, pursuing, acquiring goods by war, and contention among men.

Mathers follows Etteilla here; the Golden Dawn combines Etteilla with *Picatrix;* Waite combines Etteilla with the Golden Dawn.

Original Cartomantic Interpretations

Etteilla (1785–1807): Boredom, displeasure, discontent, disgust, aversion, unfriendliness, hate, horror, disquiet, worry, concern, affliction, difficult, annoying, unpleasing, worrying, afflicting. *Reversed:* New instruction, new light, index, indication, conjecture, augury, prescience, presentiments, prognostication, prediction, novelty.

Mathers (1888): Ennui, displeasure, discontent, dissatisfaction. *Reversed:* New acquaintance, conjecture, sign, presentiment.

Golden Dawn (1888–96): Lord of Blended Pleasure. Success or pleasure approaching its end. A stationary period in happiness that may not continue. It does not show marriage and love so much as the previous symbol. It is too passive a symbol to represent perfectly complete happiness. Swiftness, hunting, and pursuing. Acquisition by contention; injustice sometimes. Some drawbacks to pleasure implied.

Waite (1910): Weariness, disgust, aversion, imaginary vexations, blended pleasure, contrarieties. *Reversed:* Novelty, presage, new instruction, new relations, presentiment.

Suggested Interpretation

Satiation. Boredom. Aversion. *Reversed:* New light on the matter. New beginning.

◆ Five of Cups or Chalices ◆

Decan: Scorpio, degree 1 to degree 10, ruled by Mars.
Picatrix (c. 1256): A decan of strife, sadness, treachery, deceit, destruction, and ill will.

Picatrix presents a mixed bag of disasters of varying degrees. Etteilla seems blithely unaware of any of this. Here his "Kabbala" represents the precise meaning of the word, a doctrine handed down or transmitted. Waite incorporates Mathers's reversed interpretation of the card, "false projects."

Original Cartomantic Interpretations

Etteilla (1785–1807): Inheritance, succession, legacy, gift, donation, dowry, patrimony, transmission, testament, tradition, resolution, Kabbala. *Reversed:* Consanguinity, blood, family, forbears, ancestors, father, mother, brother, sister, uncle, aunt, cousin, line of descent, extraction, race, ancestry, marriage, alliance, acquaintance, rapport, liaisons.

Mathers (1888): Union, junction, marriage, inheritance. *Reversed:* Arrival, return, news, surprise, false projects.

Golden Dawn (1888–96): Lord of Loss in Pleasure. Death or end of pleasures: disappointment, sorrow and loss in those things from which pleasure is expected. Sadness, deceit, treachery, ill will, detraction, charity, and kindness ill requited. All kinds of anxieties and troubles from unexpected and unsuspected sources.

Waite (1910): A card of loss. A card of inheritance, patrimony, legacies, gifts, success in enterprise, transmission, but not according to expectations. With some it is a card of marriage, but not without bitterness or frustration. Other meanings are generally favorable, indicating a happy marriage, for instance. *Reversed:* News, alliances, affinity, consanguinity, ancestry, false projects, return. Return of some relative who has not been seen for long.

Suggested Interpretation

A mixed blessing. Sad inheritance. Legacy. *Reversed:* Renewal of old ties.

♦ Six of Cups or Chalices ♦

Decan: Scorpio, degree 11 to degree 20, ruled by the Sun.

Picatrix (c. 1256): A decan of affronts, detection, strife, stirring up of quarrels, science, and detection.

Etteilla, Mathers, and Waite stick close together in their interpretations here. Only the Golden Dawn appears to have incorporated any of *Picatrix's* ominous decan material.

Original Cartomantic Interpretations

Etteilla (1785–1807): The past, passed away, faded, stale, long ago, previously, since the first instant, long since, in the past, age, decrepitude, antiquity. *Reversed:* That which is to come, future, after, at last, afterward, ultimately, regeneration, resurrection, reproduction, renewal, reiteration.

Mathers (1888): The past, passed by, faded, vanished, disappeared. *Reversed:* The future, that which is to come, shortly, soon.

Golden Dawn (1888–96): Lord of Pleasure. Commencement of steady increase and pleasure, but commencement only. Also affront, detection, knowledge, and in some instances, contention and strife, arising from unwarranted self-assertion and vanity. Sometimes thankless and presumptuous. Sometimes amiable and patient, according to dignity.

Waite (1910): Past and memories, looking back, as for example, on childhood, happiness, enjoyment from the past, things that have vanished, pleasant memories. Another reading reverses this, giving new relations, new knowledge, new environment. *Reversed:* The future, renewal, that which will come to pass presently. Inheritance to fall in quickly.

Suggested Interpretation

Dwelling on the past. Self-analysis may be helpful. *Reversed:* Looking to the future will be helpful.

◆ Seven of Cups or Chalices ◆

Decan: Scorpio, degree 21 to degree 30, ruled by Venus.
Picatrix (c. 1256): A decan of war, drunkenness, fornication, wealth, pride, and of rage and violence against women.

Etteilla presents what seems to be the most popular interpretation of this card, one indicative of the power of the imagination. Waite expands on this. Again, only the Golden Dawn rings warning bells, in fact quoting *Picatrix* practically word for word.

Original Cartomantic Interpretations

Etteilla (1785–1807): Thought, soul, spirit, intelligence, idea, memory, imagination, understanding, conception, meditation, contemplation, reflection, deliberation, view, opinion, sentiment. *Reversed:* Project, design, intention, desire, will, resolution, determination, premeditation.

Mathers (1888): Idea, sentiment, reflection. *Reversed:* Plan, design, resolution, decision.

Golden Dawn (1888–96): Lord of Illusionary Success. Possibly victory, but neutralized by the supineness of the person. Illusionary success. Deception in the moment of apparent victory. Lying, error, promises unfulfilled. Drunkenness, wrath, vanity, lust, fornication, violence against women. Selfish dissipation. Deception in love and friendship. Often success gained, but not followed up. Modified by dignity.

Waite (1910): Fairy favors, images of reflection, sentiment, imagination, things seen in the glass of contemplation. Some attainment in these degrees but nothing permanent is suggested. A fair child, idea, design, resolve, movement. *Reversed:* Will, determination, project.

Suggested Interpretation
Pipe dreams. *Reversed:* Definite plan of action.

♦ Eight of Cups or Chalices ♦

Decan: Pisces, degree 1 to degree 10, ruled by Saturn.
Picatrix (c. 1256): It is a decan of many thoughts, of anxiety, of journeying from place to place, of misery, of seeking riches and food.

Mathers, as so often, sticks close to Etteilla's interpretation of the card. The Golden Dawn relies on *Picatrix*'s quite different input. Waite characteristically tries to harmonize all the interpretations.

Original Cartomantic Interpretations
Etteilla (1785–1807): Blond girl, honest girl, practical girl, honor, discretion, modesty, moderation, timidity, fear, apprehension, sweetness, consent. *Reversed:* Satisfaction, happiness, contentment, gaiety, joy, delight, rejoicing, diversion, feasting, excuse, reparation, exoneration, public rejoicing, spectacle, pomp, decoration, preparation, disposition.

Mathers (1888): A fair girl, friendship, attachment, tenderness. *Reversed:* Gaiety, feasting, joy, pleasure.

Golden Dawn (1888–96): Lord of Abandoned Success. Temporary success, but without further result. Things thrown aside as soon as gained. No lasting even in the matter in hand. Indolence in success. Journeying from place to place. Misery and repining without cause. Seeking after riches. Instability according to dignity.

Waite (1910): Readings are entirely antithetical, giving joy, mildness, timidity, honor, modesty. In practice, it is usually found that the card shows the decline of a matter, or that a matter that has been thought to be important is really of slight consequence. Marriage with a fair woman. *Reversed:* Great joy, happiness, feasting, perfect satisfaction.

Suggested Interpretation

Moderation. The decline of a matter. Moving on. *Reversed:* Great satisfaction. Festivity.

♦ Nine of Cups or Chalices ♦

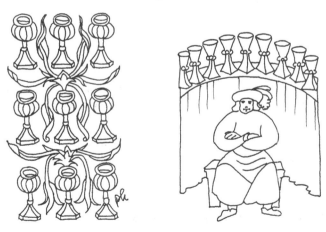

ALTERNATE NAMES: THE WISH CARD, THE GREAT NINE

Decan: Pisces, degree 11 to degree 20, ruled by Jupiter.

Picatrix (c. 1256): It is a decan of self-praise, of high mind, and of seeking after great and high aims.

Mathers and Waite all cling closely to Etteilla's interpretation. Only the Golden Dawn draws on *Picatrix,* too.

Original Cartomantic Interpretations

Etteilla (1785–1807): Victory, success, achievement, advantage, gain, pomp, triumph, trophy, preeminence, superiority, spectacle, trappings, attire. *Reversed:* Sincerity, truth, reality, loyalty, good faith, frankness, ingenuousness, candor, open-heartedness, simplicity, liberty, science, impertinence, familiarity, audacity, ease, disturbance.

Mathers (1888): Victory, advantage, success, triumph, difficulties surmounted. *Reversed:* Faults, errors, mistakes, imperfections.

Golden Dawn (1888–96): Lord of Material Happiness. Complete and perfect realization of pleasure and happiness almost perfect. Self-praise, vanity, conceit, much talking of self, yet kind and loveable, and may be self-denying therewith. High-minded, and not easily satisfied with small and limited ideas. Apt to be maligned through too much self-assumption. A good, generous, but, maybe, foolish nature.

Waite (1910): Concord, contentment, physical well-being, victory, success, advantage, of good augury for military men, satisfaction. *Reversed:* Truth, loyalty, liberty, good business, but the readings vary and include mistakes and imperfections.

Suggested Interpretation

The inquirer will get his or her wish. Satisfaction. Victory. *Reversed:* Good omen. Success, giving rise to vanity.

♦ Ten of Cups or Chalices ♦

Decan: Pisces, degree 21 to degree 30, ruled by Mars.
Picatrix (c. 1256): It is a decan of pleasure, fornication, of quietness, and of peacemaking.

Pratesi's simple Bolognese ascription "roof tiles" is of interest in the light of Etteilla's "town, city, village, dwelling, habitation," etc. As usual, Mathers follows Etteilla; the Golden Dawn, *Picatrix;* Waite tries to reconcile all.

Original Cartomantic Interpretations

Pratesi's cartomancer (1750): Roof tiles.

Etteilla (1785–1807): A town, city, homeland, country, borough, village, place, site, dwelling, habitation, residence, citizen, burghers, townsfolk. *Reversed:* Anger, indignation, agitation, irritation, ravagement, fury, violence.

Mathers (1888): The town wherein one resides, honor, consideration, esteem, virtue, glory, reputation. *Reversed:* Combat, strife, opposition, differences, dispute.

Golden Dawn (1888–96): Lord of Perfected Success. Permanent and lasting success, happiness because inspired from above. Not sensual as Nine of Cups, the Lord of Material Happiness, yet almost more truly happy. Pleasure, dissipation, debauchery. Pity, quietness, peacemaking. Kindness, generosity, wantonness, waste, etc., according to dignity.

Waite (1910): Contentment, repose of the entire heart, the perfection of that state, also the perfection of human love and friendship. If with several picture cards, a person who is taking charge of the querent's interests. Also the town, village, or country inhabited by the inquirer. For a male inquirer, a good marriage and beyond his expectations. *Reversed:* Repose of the false heart, indignation, violence, sorrow.

Suggested Interpretation

The home. Recognition. Emotional contentment. *Reversed:* Domestic or workplace stress. Negativity.

♦ Knave or Page of Cups or Chalices ♦

The most popular titles for the French-suit version of this card were *La Hire* and Paris of Troy. Neither was a member of the Nine Worthies, the first because he was born long after their legend was devised, the second because he was regarded during the Middle Ages as something of a coward, an ill-mannered seducer and immediate cause of the Trojan War.

On the other hand, Etienne de Vignoles (aka La Hire) was a soldier, a close friend and supporter of Joan of Arc, and the rumored inventor of the French suit signs as substitutes for Coins, Cups, Swords, and Batons. He was born about 1390 and died in 1443, but his name may have been added to the Knave of Hearts at a later date.

One of the earliest *Valets de Coeur* is depicted holding a blazing torch or large candle, thought to represent the torch of Hymen, the Greek god of marriage.

Paris of course was the Trojan lover of the beautiful Helen, whom he stole from her husband Menelaus, king of Sparta, thereby bringing about the ten-year Trojan War. The Rouen pattern of this card names it "Siprian Roman," intended perhaps as Cyprian Roman, "Roman favored by Aphrodite."

If Troy is considered the antecedent of Rome, then Paris indeed fulfilled this definition, having bestowed on Aphrodite the golden apple of Eris. In any case, we can imagine the kind of persona being depicted. An English deck of around 1750 simply labels him the "Sly Knave."

Pratesi's cartomancer uses the female version of the Page, so his interpretation probably refers to the thoughts of the Queen of Cups. Waite, however, certainly seems to be referring to the invaluable aid La Hire rendered Joan of Arc. Mathers, Etteilla, and the Golden Dawn join him in agreeing on the reversed values of the card, which all seem to point to the "Paris" persona. Perhaps we can say the Knave represents La Hire when upright, Paris of Troy when reversed—truly someone, as Etteilla remarks, with "a penchant which threatens ruin, and leads to final destruction!"

Original Cartomantic Interpretations

Pratesi's cartomancer (1750): *Fantesca* of Cups, the lady.

Etteilla (1785–1807): A blond youth, studious, study, application, work, reflection, observation, consideration, meditation, contemplation, occupation, work, profession, employment. *Reversed:* Penchant, leaning, propensity, inclination, attraction, taste, sympathy, passion, affection, attachment, friendship, heart, longing, desire, charm, engagement, seduction, invitation, agreement, flattery, cajolery, fawning, adulation, eulogy, praise. A penchant that threatens ruin and leads to final destruction.

Mathers (1888): A fair youth, confidence, probity, discretion, integrity. *Reversed:* A flatterer, deception, artifice.

Golden Dawn (1888–96): Princess of the Waters and Lotus of the Palace of the Floods. Sweetness, poetry, gentleness, and kindness.

Imagination, dreamy, at times indolent, yet courageous if roused. Ill-dignified, she is selfish and luxurious.

Waite (1910): Fair young man, one impelled to render service and with whom the inquirer will be connected. A studious youth. News, message, good augury, application, reflection, meditation. Also these things directed to business. *Reversed:* Taste, inclination, attachment, seduction, deception, artifice, obstacles of all kinds.

Suggested Interpretation

An attractive, helpful younger person. Good news. *Reversed:* An attractive but destructive younger person. Seduction.

♦ Knight of Cups or Chalices ♦

The eighteenth-century interpretation of this card seems to carry the sense of somebody arriving and the repayment or settlement of a loan, quite apart from the Knight's possible identity as the inquirer or another person. Mathers picks up the thread of somebody making a visit, as Waite does, but it remains for the Golden Dawn to delineate the type of personality the Knight portrays. Colman Smith's design for this card borrows elements from the Sola-Busca deck, the unorthodox tarocchi deck designed in Venice for the Sola-Busca family by a Ferrarese artist in the sixteenth century.

Original Cartomantic Interpretations

Pratesi's cartomancer (1750): Settlement.

Etteilla (1785–1807): Arrival, coming, approach, coming aboard, reception, access, reconciliation, conformity, advent, approximation, accession, confluence, comparison. *Reversed:* Crookedness, rascality, deceit, ruse, artifice, slickness, cleverness, suppleness, trickery, subtlety, lawlessness, wickedness.

Mathers (1888): Arrival, approach, advance. *Reversed:* Duplicity, abuse of confidence, fraud, cunning.

Golden Dawn (1888–96): Prince of the Chariot of the Waters. He is subtle, violent, crafty, and artistic. Powerful for good or evil, but more attracted by the evil, if allied with apparent Power or Wisdom. If ill-dignified, he is intensely evil and merciless.

Waite (1910): Arrival, approach, sometimes that of a messenger. A visit from a friend who will bring unexpected money to the inquirer Also advances, proposition, demeanor, invitation, incitement. *Reversed:* Trickery, artifice, subtlety, swindling, duplicity, fraud.

Suggested Interpretation

Arrival. Invitation. Proposition. *Reversed:* A deceiver. Fraud.

♦ Queen of Cups or Chalices ♦

The most popular caption for the Paris-pattern French-suit version of this card was Judith, Old Testament Apocrypha beauty and heroine from the besieged city of Bethulia. The widow of one Manasses, Judith seduced, then beheaded, Nebuchadnezzar's general Holofernes while he slept, in this manner causing the rout of the besieging Assyrian army. The apocryphal book of Judith reports Ozias, the governor of Bethulia, acknowledging her deed with what sounds like oddly faint praise: "All that thou hast spoken hast thou spoken with a good heart, and all the people have known thy understanding, because the disposition of thy heart is good." Presumably, this qualified her for her position as the Queen of Hearts.

However, some old French *Dames de Coeur* carry the words *La foy est perdue* (Faith, or trust, is lost) inscribed on them. So obviously Judith's not all sweetness and light (possibly in view of her deed), a fact that apparently wasn't lost on Etteilla, Mathers, and Waite, either.

Original Cartomantic Interpretations

Pratesi's cartomancer (1750): Married lady.

Etteilla (1785–1807): A blond woman, honest woman, virtue, wisdom, honesty. *Reversed:* A highly placed woman, honest woman, defect, dishonesty, depravity, disorder, corruption, scandal.

Mathers (1888): A fair woman, success, happiness, advantage, pleasure. *Reversed:* A woman in good position, but intermeddling, and to be distrusted. Success, but with some attendant trouble.

Golden Dawn (1888–96): Queen of the Thrones of the Waters. She is imaginative, poetic, kind, yet not willing to take much trouble for another. Coquettish, good-natured, underneath a dreamy appearance. Imagination stronger than feeling. Very much affected by other influences, and therefore more dependent upon good- or ill-dignity [upright or reversed] than upon most other symbols.

Waite (1910): A fair woman, honest, devoted, who will do service to the inquirer. Loving intelligence, and hence the gift of vision. Success, happiness, pleasure. Also wisdom, virtue. Sometimes denotes a woman of equivocal character. *Reversed:* The accounts vary. Good woman, otherwise distinguished woman but one not to be trusted. Perverse woman. Vice, dishonor, depravity. A rich marriage.

Suggested Interpretation

A mature woman friend, wife, or faithful fiancée. Honesty. Devotion. *Reversed:* Untrustworthy woman. Fickleness. Sensuality.

♦ King of Cups or Chalices ♦

The enduring caption for the Paris-pattern version of this card is Charles, that is, Charlemagne, the first Holy Roman Emperor of the West and one of the Nine Worthies. His name first appears on the King of Hearts in about 1480. Initially king of the Franks, Charlemagne was crowned emperor in 799.

Noted as a lawmaker, Charlemagne was also known as a promoter of education and—by reason of his office as Holy Roman Emperor—protector of the Roman Catholic Church. He and his paladin knights became the center of a huge series of medieval chivalric romances.

Legend told that Charlemagne, truly named Charles the Great, was eight feet tall and could bend three horseshoes at once in his hands. He was buried at Aix-la-Chapelle but is said to await the day when, armed and crowned once more, he will appear to save Christendom and do battle with the Antichrist. As one of the Nine Worthies, he was considered to embody the peace and stability that his rule brought to Europe.

Waite's caution to "beware of ill will" and "hypocrisy pretending to help" seems more fitting to the reversal of the card rather than to its upright position.

Original Cartomantic Interpretations

Pratesi's cartomancer (1750): An old man.

Etteilla (1785–1807): A blond man, an honest man, probity, fairness, art, science. *Reversed:* A highly placed man, a distinguished man, an honest man, a dishonest man, usury, extortion, injustice, a bandit, a thief, a crook, corruption, scandal.

Mathers (1888): A fair-haired man, goodness, kindness, liberality, generosity. *Reversed:* A man of good position, but shifty in his dealings. Distrust, doubt, suspicion.

Golden Dawn (1888–96): Lord of the Waves and the Waters. King of the Hosts of the Sea. Graceful, poetic, Venusian, indolent, but enthusiastic if roused. Ill-dignified, he is sensual, idle, and untruthful.

Waite (1910): Fair man, a man of business, law, or divinity. Responsible, disposed to oblige the inquirer. Also equity, art and science, including those who profess science, law, and art. Creative intelligence. Beware of ill will on the part of a man of position, and of hypocrisy pretending to help. *Reversed:* Dishonest, double-dealing man. Roguery, exaction, injustice, vice, scandal, loss.

Suggested Interpretation

A cultured, friendly man. Arts and sciences. Generosity. *Reversed:* A cultured but untrustworthy man. Extortion, loss.

The Suit of Swords

The Sword (and Scales) are symbols of the Cardinal Virtue Justice; maybe the ancient Persian class of *Húristár,* or warriors, who promote equity; and, by some accounts, the element air. The sword symbol obviously suggests cutting and penetration, but also acts of discriminating, discerning, making a judgment. The Sword suit is considered "masculine" in card games. In divination, it's a suit that signifies division, struggle, misfortune, sorrow, and disappointment; today it also connotes matters to do with legalities, mental challenges, or painful issues. Etteilla and Mathers both equated it with Spades. The French *Pique* or "pike" and Italian *Spada* or "sword" evidently share a common ancestor in the Mamlûk scimitar. In Irish Celtic myth, the death-dealing sword of Nuada of the Silver Hand, from whose stroke none recovered, was once considered to be the prototype for the Grail Sword of Authurian legend. The Grail Sword, however, was said to be either the sword of the biblical King David or the blade used to behead John the Baptist. If it's considered to be the sword of King David, then we may be standing on firmer ground.

♦ Ace of Swords ♦

Éliphas Lévi believed the tarot Sword represented the sword of King David, which would seem appropriate, as the French King of Spades is usually considered to depict King David himself. Elsewhere, however, Lévi refers to the tarot Sword as that of Michael, the archangel of Justice. The coronet, laurel branch, and palm frond on the Tarot of Marseille Ace of Swords were identified in 1998 by playing-card historian Ronald Decker as a heraldic device of the Milanese Visconti-Sforzas.

None of the cartomantic interpretations of this card betray the Justice association of Swords, and all save Pratesi's Bolognese cartomancer plump for the obvious phallic connotation. Mathers and Waite are undoubtedly following Etteilla's interpretation of the card, but in true Victorian fashion are being somewhat coy. The Golden Dawn is more concerned about Hermetic issues.

Original Cartomantic Interpretations

Pratesi's cartomancer (1750): Letter.

Etteilla (1785–1807): Extreme, large, excessive, over the top, furious, ravaged by, extremely, passionately, excessively, vehemence, animosity, transport, ravagement, anger, fury, rage, extremity, borders, confine, end, limits, last gasp, last extremity, embroilment. *Reversed:* Pregnancy, germ, seed, sperm, matter, enlargement, engenderment, conception, fructification, childbearing, childbirth, fecundation, production, composition, aggrandizement, augmentation, multiplicity.

Mathers (1888): Triumph, fecundity, fertility, prosperity. *Reversed:* Embarrassment, foolish and hopeless love, obstacle, hindrance.

Golden Dawn (1888–96): The Root of the Powers of Air. It symbolizes invoked as contrasted with natural force. Raised upward, it invokes the Divine Crown of Spiritual Brightness [Kether, the first divine emanation of the kabbalistic sefirothic Tree]. Reversed it is the invocation of demoniac force, and becomes a fearfully evil symbol. It represents therefore very great power for good or evil, but invoked. And it also represents whirling force, and strength through trouble. It is the affirmation of Justice, upholding divine authority; but it may become the Sword of Wrath, Punishment, and Affliction.

Waite (1910): Triumph, the excessive degree in everything, conquest, the triumph of force. A card of great force, in love as well as hatred. It can indicate great prosperity or great misery. The crown [as depicted in the Marseille pattern] may carry a much higher significance than comes usually within the sphere of fortune-telling. [See the Golden Dawn interpretation above.] *Reversed:* The same, but the results are disastrous. Another account says conception, childbirth, augmentation, multiplicity [see Etteilla above]. For a woman, marriage broken off by her own imprudence.

Suggested Interpretation

Authority. Triumph. Vehemence. Conquest. *Reversed:* Excess. Conception. Enlargement.

♦ Two of Swords ♦

ALTERNATE NAME: THE DEUCE OF SWORDS

Decan: Libra, degree 1 to degree 10, ruled by the Moon.
Picatrix (c. 1256): It is a decan of Justice, aid, truth, and helping the poor.

The Golden Dawn is prolix here, where Etteilla is unusually succinct. (The omission mark in the Golden Dawn entry indicates where I have omitted, as unnecessary for our purposes, the Golden Dawn description of the design of its version of the card.)

Original Cartomantic Interpretations

Etteilla (1785–1807): Friendship, attachment, affection, tenderness, goodwill, rapport, relationship, identity, intimacy, conformity, sympathy, affinity, attraction. *Reversed:* False, falsity, lies, imposture, duplicity, bad faith, calculated deceit, dissimulation, swindling, deception, superficial, skin deep, surface.

Mathers (1888): Friendship, valor, firmness, courage. *Reversed:* False friends, treachery, lies.

Golden Dawn (1888–96): Lord of Peace Restored. Contradictory characteristics in the same nature. Strength through suffering. Pleasure after pain. Sacrifice and trouble yet strength arising therefrom. . . . Peace restored, truce, arrangement of differences, justice. Truth and untruth. Sorrow and sympathy for those in trouble, aid to the weak and oppressed, unselfishness. Also an inclination to repetition of affronts if once pardoned, of asking questions of little moment, want of tact, often doing injury when meaning well. Talkative.

Waite (1910): Conformity and the equipoise that it suggests, courage, friendship, concord in a state of arms, affection, intimacy. Gifts for a lady, influential protection for a man in search of help. Another reading gives tenderness, affection, intimacy. Favorable readings must be considered in a qualified manner, as Swords generally are not symbolic of beneficent forces in human affairs. *Reversed:* Imposture, falsehood, duplicity, disloyalty, dealings with rogues.

Suggested Interpretation

Truce. Friendship. Equilibrium. *Reversed:* Duplicity. Disloyalty.

♦ Three of Swords ♦

ALTERNATE NAME: THE TREY OF SWORDS

Decan: Libra, degree 11 to degree 20, ruled by Saturn.
Picatrix (c. 1256): A decan of quietness, ease, plenty, good life, and dance.

This is a problematic card for a number of reasons. To begin, whoever translated the decans' meanings from *Picatrix* and used them to interpret the Golden Dawn tarot suit cards somehow contrived to transpose the images and meanings of the second and third decans of Libra. Both the edition of *Picatrix* that I have consulted for this analysis and Agrippa's *Occult Philosophy* confirm this. So to find what the Golden Dawn *thought* the decan interpretation of this card should be, we must read the decan associated with the next card, the Four of Swords, and vice versa.

Where Mathers got his "nun" from, one cannot tell.

Waite's design for this card, however, the heart pierced by three swords, was undoubtedly based upon the fifteenth-century Sola-Busca deck, which displays an almost identical symbol.

Whether the Sola-Busca design was a fanciful one or based on a tradition is hard to tell. A heart pierced by seven swords, however, was a recognized Christian liturgical symbol of the "Seven Sorrows of Mary," which were: Simeon's grim temple prophecy of the fate of the infant Jesus, the family's flight into Egypt, Mary's temporary loss of the youthful Jesus while he was disputing the rabbis in the temple, the terrible road to Calvary, the crucifixion itself, the removal of Jesus's dead body from the cross, and the body's entombment. The Festival of Mary's Seven Sorrows was inaugurated as a church observance in 1423, so undoubtedly the symbol of a heart pierced by swords would have conveyed something of the sort when depicted on a fifteenth-century playing card, which may explain what seems to be its widespread divinatory interpretation as described by Etteilla.

Original Cartomantic Interpretations

Etteilla (1785–1807): Distance, departure, absence, removal, dispersion, distant, delay, disdain, repugnance, aversion, horror, incompatibility, contrariness, opposition, unsociability, misanthropy, incivility, separation, division, rupture, antipathy, section, severance. *Reversed:* Confusion, dementia, meandering, mental alienation, distraction, mad conduct, error, miscalculation, loss, detour, diversion, dispersion.

Mathers (1888): A nun, separation, removal, rupture, quarrel. *Reversed:* Error, confusion, misrule, disorder.

Golden Dawn (1888–96): Lord of Sorrow. Disruption, interruption, separation, quarreling, sowing of discord and strife, mischief making, sorrow, tears, yet mirth in evil pleasures, singing, faithfulness in promises, honesty in money transactions, selfish and dissipated, yet sometimes generous, deceitful in words and repetition, the whole according to dignity.

Waite (1910): Removal, absence, delay, division, rupture, dispersion, for a woman the flight of her lover. *Reversed:* Mental alienation, error, loss, distraction, disorder, confusion, a meeting with one whom the inquirer has compromised.

Suggested Interpretation

Absence. Loss. Separation. *Reversed:* Distraction. Confusion.

♦ Four of Swords ♦

Decan: Libra, degree 21 to degree 30, ruled by Jupiter.
Picatrix (c. 1256): It is a face (decan) of ill deeds yet of singing and mirth and gluttony, sodomy and following of evil pleasures.

Remember, this *Picatrix* decan interpretation was misapplied by the Golden Dawn to the previous card, the Three of Swords, although even then, its interpretation seems a far cry from *Picatrix*'s singing, mirth, gluttony, and sodomy. For the Four of Swords the Golden Dawn introduced the "quietness, ease, plenty, good life, and dance" of the second decan of Libra. Maybe because of this confusion, Waite follows Etteilla only.

Original Cartomantic Interpretations

Etteilla (1785–1807): Solitude, desert, retreat, hermitage, exile, banishment, proscription, uninhabited, isolated, abandoned, derelict, tomb, sepulcher, sarcophagus. *Reversed:* Economy, good conduct, wise administration, prudence, direction, housekeeping, savings, avarice, order, arrangement, rapport, convenience, concert, accord, concordance, harmony, music, disposition, testament, reserve, restriction, exception, circumspection, circumscription, moderation, wisdom, sympathy, management, precaution.

Mathers (1888): Solitude, retreat, abandonment, solitary, hermit. *Reversed:* Economy, precaution, regulation of expenditure.

Golden Dawn (1888–96): Lord of Rest from Strife. Rest from sorrow, yet after and through it. Peace from and after war. Relaxation of anxiety. Quietness, rest, ease and plenty, yet after struggle. Goods of this life, abundance. Modified by the dignity as in the other cases.

Waite (1910): Vigilance, retreat, solitude, hermit's repose, exile, tomb and coffin. A bad card, but if reversed a qualified success may be expected by wise administration of affairs. *Reversed:* Wise administration, circumspection, economy, avarice, precaution, testament.

Suggested Interpretation

Retirement. Loneliness. Meditation. *Reversed:* Fixed income. Economy measures.

♦ Five of Swords ♦

Decan: Aquarius, degree 1 to degree 10, ruled by Venus.

Picatrix (c. 1256): It is a decan of poverty, anxiety, grieving after gain, and never resting from labor, loss, and violence.

Etteilla and the Golden Dawn seem closest to *Picatrix,* but of course we have to remember that *Picatrix* is describing decans with a view to using their images on astrological talismans, not tarot cards. However, all the cartomancers seem to concur on this card's general sense, and it isn't a particularly good one to draw.

Original Cartomantic Interpretations

Etteilla (1785–1807): Loss, alteration, shrinkage, degradation, attrition, fading, destruction, deterioration, detriment, diminution, damages, reverses, prejudice, defect, tort, avarice, decadence, destruction, disadvantage, devastation, dilapidation, dissipation, misfortune, griefs, setback, reversal of fortune, ruin, defect, rout, debauch, shame, defamation, dishonor, infamy, ignominy, affront, ugliness, deformity, humiliation, thief, robber, rape, plagiarism, seizure, hideous, horrible, opprobrious, corruption, disarray, seduction, lawlessness. *Reversed:* Grief, enfeeblement, affection, chagrin, dolor, spiritual torment, funeral pomp, interment, obsequies, funerals, burial, entombment.

Mathers (1888): Mourning, sadness, affliction. *Reversed:* Losses, trouble [same signification, whether reversed or not].

Golden Dawn (1888–96): Lord of Defeat. Contest finished, and decided against the person, failure, defeat, anxiety, trouble, poverty, avarice, grieving after gain, laborious, unresting, loss and vileness of nature. Malicious, slandering, lying, spiteful and tale bearing. A busybody and separator of friends, hating to see peace and love between others. Feelings of pity easily roused but unenduring. As dignity.

Waite (1910): Degradation, destruction, revocation, infamy, dishonor, loss, with the variants and analogs of these. An attack on the fortune of the inquirer. *Reversed:* The same. Burial and obsequies. A sign of sorrow and mourning.

Suggested Interpretation

Loss. Degradation. Lost hopes. *Reversed:* The same.

◆ Six of Swords ◆

Decan: Aquarius, degree 11 to degree 20, ruled by Mercury.
Picatrix (c. 1256): It is a decan of beauty, dominance, conceit, good
manners and self-esteem, yet not withstanding modest.

Etteilla has nothing in common with *Picatrix,* which is drawn on by only
the Golden Dawn here. Mathers and Waite concur with Etteilla's impres-
sion of journeys and some kind of declaration. Waite introduces the specific notion of a journey by water, Mathers the notion that the
"declaration" in the card's reversal can be a declaration of love.

Original Cartomantic Interpretations

Etteilla (1785–1807): Route, alley, road, course, passage, path, way,
march, tract, voyage, kind attention, conduct, means, manner, fashion, expedient, course, racetrack, promenade, example, trace, ves-
tige, envoy, messenger. *Reversed:* Declaration, declarative action,
unfolding, explanation, interpretation, charter, constitution,
diploma, legal manifesto, ordinance, publication, proclamation,
ostensibility, poster, publicity, authenticity, notoriety, denunciation,
census, enumeration, knowledge, discovery, unveiling, vision, revelation, apparition, appearance, avowal, confession, protestation,
approbation, authorization.
Mathers (1888): Envoy, messenger, voyage, travel. *Reversed:* Declaration,
love proposed, revelation, surprise.

Golden Dawn (1888–96): Lord of Earned Success. Success after anxiety and trouble. Selfishness, beauty, conceit, but sometimes modesty therewith, dominion, patience, labor, etc., according to dignity.

Waite (1910): Journey by water, route, way, envoy, commissionary, expedient, the voyage will be pleasant. *Reversed:* Declaration, confession, publicity. Unfavorable issue of a lawsuit. One account [Mathers] says that it is a proposal of love.

Suggested Interpretation

Travel. A route to success. Messenger. *Reversed:* Revelation. Declaration. Explanation.

♦ Seven of Swords ♦

Decan: Aquarius, degree 21 to degree 30, ruled by the Moon.
Picatrix (c. 1256): It is a decan of abundance and compliments, detection and affronts.

Etteilla initiates the notion of "hope" here, and the other cartomancers agree for the most part. The Golden Dawn tries to integrate this with *Picatrix*'s "affronts."

Interestingly, Waite may have had more than just the Golden Dawn decan attribution to draw on here. Although he states that "the design is uncertain in its import, because the significations are widely at variance with each other," he appears to have gone to the Sola-Busca deck again for the card's design. The Sola-Busca deck depicts a young man stealing off with four swords, already carrying three in a container strapped to his back.

Now, the origin of this Sola-Busca image may derive, in turn, from the "sequel" to a popular medieval *chanson de geste* that we shall encounter shortly, the story of Renaut de Montaubon. One of the characters who make an appearance in Renaut's tale is a sorcerer-knight named Maugis d'Aigremont, whose subsequent popularity gave birth to the sequel, a new *chanson* all of his own, written during the early thirteenth century. As a foster child of the fay Oriande, d'Aigremont was instructed in the magical arts, and notably cast a sleeping spell over Charlemagne and his knights, then made off with their swords.

The incident bears a resemblance to the design on the Sola-Busca card that seems to have been Waite's source, and could conceivably serve to illustrate *Picatrix*'s "detection and affronts." From Waite's interpretations, however, it appears he knew nothing of d'Aigremont.

Original Cartomantic Interpretations

Etteilla (1785–1807): Hope, intention, expectation, aspiration, to rely upon, to overvalue oneself, groundwork, scheme, will, wish, desire, vow, longing, taste, fantasy. *Reversed:* Wise advice, good counsel, salutary warnings, instruction, lesson, observation, reflection, note, warning, thought, reprimand, reproach, tidings, annunciation, poster, consultation, admonition.

Mathers (1888): Hope, confidence, desire, attempt, wish. *Reversed:* Wise advice, good counsel, wisdom, prudence, circumspection.

Golden Dawn (1888–96): Lord of Unstable Effort. Partial success, yielding when victory is within grasp, as if the last reserves of strength were used up. Inclination to lose when on the point of gaining through not continuing the effort. Love of abundance; fascinated by display; given to compliment, affronts, and insolences, and to detect and spy on another. Inclined to betray confidences, not always intentional. Rather vacillating and unreliable, according to dignity as usual.

Waite (1910): A dark girl, design, attempt, wish, hope, confidence, quarreling, a plan that may fail, annoyance. A good card, it promises country life after a competence has been secured. *Reversed:* Good advice probably neglected, counsel, instruction, slander, babbling.

Suggested Interpretation

Hope. Confidence. Attempt. Plan. *Reversed:* Get reliable advice from a reliable source. Be prudent.

◆ Eight of Swords ◆

Decan: Gemini, degree 1 to degree 10, ruled by Jupiter.
Picatrix (c. 1256): It is a decan of writing, calculations, giving and receiving money, and of wisdom in unprofitable things.

The Golden Dawn mixes this "wisdom in unprofitable things" with what is obviously the traditional cartomantic interpretation of the card, criticism or blame, to come up with something more like nit-picking.

Original Cartomantic Interpretations

Etteilla (1785–1807): Criticism, difficult position, critical moment, critical time, decisive instant, unhappy situation, delicate circumstance, crisis, examination, discussion, inquiries, blame, censure, carping, epilog, control, disapprobation, condemnation, annulment, judgment, scorn. *Reversed:* Incident, difficulty, particular circumstance, conjunction, event, accessory, unaware, obstacle, delay, hindrance, abjectness, contestation, contradiction, opposition, resistance, quibbling, unthought of, unforeseen, fortuitous case, adventure, occurrence, destiny, fatality, accident, unhappiness, disgrace, misfortune, symptom.

Mathers (1888): Sickness, calumny, criticism, blame. *Reversed:* Treachery in the past, event, accident, remarkable incident.

Golden Dawn (1888–96): Lord of Shortened Force. Too much force applied to small things, too much attention to detail, at expense of principle and more important points. Ill-dignified [badly placed], these qualities produce malice, pettiness, and domineering qualities. Patience in detail of study, great ease in some things, counterbalanced by equal disorder in others. Impulsive, equally fond of giving and receiving money, or presents. Generous, clever, acute, selfish, and without strong feeling of affection. Admires wisdom, yet applies it to small and unworthy objects.

Waite (1910): Bad news, violent chagrin, crisis, censure, power in trammels, conflict, calumny, sickness. For a woman, scandal spread in her respect. *Reversed:* Disquiet, difficulty, opposition, accident, treachery, fatality, what is unforeseen, departure of a relative.

Suggested Interpretation

Criticism. Opposition. Illness. Bad news. Crisis. *Reversed:* Unforeseen Incident. Treachery. Accident.

◆ Nine of Swords ◆

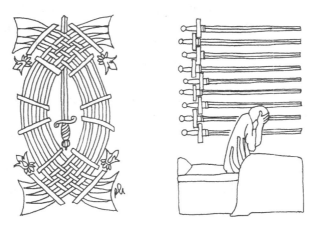

Decan: Gemini, degree 11 to degree 20, ruled by Mars.
Picatrix (c. 1256): It is a decan of burden, pressure, labor, subtlety, dishonesty.

Mars and Gemini are not a happy combination here. However, except in its reversed position, the card traditionally does not seem to deserve the extremely negative spin placed on it by the Golden Dawn. Etteilla, on the other hand, draws on his private sources of, maybe Piedmontese, information and notes that, among other things, the Nine of Swords signifies religious matters or somebody involved with them, an interpretation reflected by Mathers and Waite also.

Original Cartomantic Interpretations

Etteilla: (1785–1807): Bachelor, celibate, virginity, abbot, priest, monk, hermit, friar, nun, temple, church, monastery, convent, hermitage, sanctuary, cult, religion, piety, devotion, rite, ceremony, ritual, recluse, anchorite, vestal. *Reversed:* Justifiable distrust, well-founded suspicion, legitimate fear, mistrust, doubt, conjecture, scruple, timorous conscience, fear, timidity, bashfulness, disgrace, shame.

Mathers (1888): An ecclesiastic, priest, conscience, probity, good faith, integrity. *Reversed:* Wise distrust, suspicion, fear, doubt, shady character.

Golden Dawn (1888–96): Lord of Despair and Cruelty. Despair, cruelty, pitilessness, malice, suffering, want, loss, misery. Burden oppres-

sion, labor, subtlety and craft, lying, dishonesty, slander. Yet also obe-
dience, faithfulness, patience, unselfishness, etc., according to dignity.

Waite (1910): An ecclesiastic, a priest, generally a card of bad omen, pre-
dicting death, failure, miscarriage, delay, deception, disappointment,
despair. *Reversed:* Imprisonment, suspicion, doubt, reasonable fear,
shame. Good ground for suspicion against a doubtful person.

Suggested Interpretation

Integrity. Good faith. Patience. *Reversed:* Well-founded mistrust. Disgrace.

♦ Ten of Swords ♦

 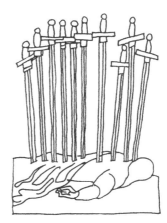

Decan: Gemini, degree 21 to degree 30, ruled by the Sun.

Picatrix (c. 1256): It is a decan of disdain, mirth, and jollity and of
many unprofitable words.

According to Etteilla, when this card is found upright, it may be regarded
as one of the worst cards in the deck. All the other cartomancers follow
him in this, even the Golden Dawn, although it integrates *Picatrix* material as well.

Original Cartomantic Interpretations

Pratesi's cartomancer (1750): Tears.

Etteilla (1785–1807): Weeping, tears, sobs, groans, sighs, wails, lamen-
tations, grievances, affections, chagrins, sadness, dolor, jeremiad,

ballad, desolation. *Reversed:* Advantage, gain, profit, success, grace, favor, benefit, ascendant, ability, empire, authority, power, usurpation.

Mathers (1888): Tears, affliction, grief, sorrow. *Reversed:* Passing success, momentary advantage.

Golden Dawn (1888–96): Lord of Ruin. (Almost a worse symbol than Nine of Swords.) Undisciplined warring force, complete disruption and failure. Ruin of all plans and projects. Disdain, insolence, and impertinence, yet mirth and jolly therewith. A marplot [malicious meddler], loving to overthrow the happiness of others, a repeater of things, given to much unprofitable speech, and of many words, yet clever, acute, and eloquent, etc., depending on dignity.

Waite (1910): Pain, affliction, tears, sadness, desolation. It is not especially a card of violent death. *Reversed:* Advantage, profit, success, favor, but none of these are permanent. Also power and authority. Victory and consequent fortune for a soldier in war.

Suggested Interpretation

Affliction. Sadness. Exhaustion. Pain. *Reversed:* Ray of hope. With good cards, leading to better things.

♦ Knave or Page of Swords ♦

The most frequent titles for the Paris-pattern French-suited version of this card were the medieval Worthies Ogier and Renaut. Although Ogier, or Hogier, was reputed to be a Dane, indeed a son of King Geoffrey of

Denmark, his title "of Dannemarche" should more likely be translated "of the Ardennes marches," or "L'Ardennois."

Ogier's own son was killed by Charlot, the emperor Charlemagne's son, so out of revenge Ogier killed Charlemagne's nephew. Ogier subsequently made peace with the emperor, however, and became one of Charlemagne's twelve paladins. He slew the giant Brehus and came to be regarded as the patron of hunting (a title he shared with the *Valet de Carreau*), and is frequently depicted in cards with his dog at his heels. Fays or enchantresses were said to have attended his birth, among them Morgan le Fay, who finally took him to live with her in Avalon, where, like King Arthur, he dwells immortally until such a time as he shall be summoned back to defend France against its enemies. Significantly, Ogier owned two Spanish swords of legendary excellence named Sauvagine and Cortante.

Alternatively, the *Valet de Pique* is said to represent one of the other great Worthies of medieval romance, Renaut, or Renault, of Montaubon, also a paladin of Charlemagne and one of the four sons of Aymon.

Renaut first appears in a *chanson de geste* of the thirteenth century, and later in Dutch, German, Old Norse, Spanish, English, and Italian texts. During the sixteenth century, Ariosto introduces him in his *Orlando furioso* as Rinaldo, Lord of Monte Albano, rival to his cousin Orlando. In legend, Renaut and his three brothers are represented mounted on their magical horse Bayart, a steed powerful enough to carry all four of them together. After many adventures, frequently at odds with his liege lord Charlemagne, Renaut performed the superhuman feat of building St. Peter's Cathedral in Cologne, but was murdered by envious fellow workers. His remains were interred at Dortmund, another of his family's holdings. Miracles soon began to occur about his tomb, ensuring the eventual canonization of the fallen hero as Saint Reinoldus.

Original Cartomantic Interpretations

Etteilla (1785–1807): A spy, a curiosity seeker, an observer, an examiner, an amateur, a watcher, a supervisor, an examination, note, remark, observation, annotation, speculation, account, calculation, deduction, a learned man, an artist. *Reversed:* Unforeseen, sudden, suddenly, out of the blue, astonishing, surprising, unexpected, the necessity to speak without preparation, to compose and recite on the spot.

Mathers (1888): A spy, overlooking, authority. *Reversed:* That which is unforeseen, vigilance, support.

Golden Dawn (1888–96): Princess of the Rushing Winds. Lotus of the Palace of Air. Wisdom, strength, acuteness, subtleness in material things, grace and dexterity. If ill-dignified, she is frivolous and cunning.

Waite (1910): Authority, overseeing, secret service, vigilance, spying, examination, and the qualities belonging to these activities. An indiscreet person will pry into the Querent's secrets. *Reversed:* More-evil side of these qualities. What is unforeseen, unprepared state. Sickness is also intimated.

Suggested Interpretation

Spy. Secrecy. Vigilance. Examination. *Reversed:* Unexpected occurrence.

♦ Knight of Swords ♦

The Knight of Swords is undoubtedly a man of iron in character, and maybe by profession too. I'm afraid the Golden Dawn's reference to "Alpha and Omega" (of the book of Revelation?) in connection with this card, like so much else created by their juggling of court cards, remains a mystery to me.

Original Cartomantic Interpretations

Etteilla (1785–1807): A military man, a swordsman, an armed man, a master at fencing, a duelist, a soldier of all regiments and all arms, combatant, enemy, dispute, war, combat, battle, duel, attack, defense, opposition, resistance, destruction, ruin, collapse, dislike, hate, anger, resentment, courage, valor, intrepidity, bodyguard, mercenary. *Reversed:* Incompetence, ineptitude, foolishness, stupidity, imprudence, impertinence, extravagance, ridiculousness, trifling, swindle, larceny, crookedness, industriousness.

Mathers (1888): A soldier, a man whose profession is arms, skillfulness, capacity, address, promptitude. *Reversed:* A conceited fool, ingenuousness, simplicity.

Golden Dawn (1888–96): Prince of the Chariots of the Winds. Full of ideas and thoughts and designs, distrustful, suspicious, firm in friendship and enmity, careful, slow, overcautious. Symbolizes Alpha and Omega, the Giver of Death, who slays as fast as he creates. If ill-dignified: harsh, malicious, plotting, obstinate, yet hesitating and unreliable.

Waite (1910): A soldier, man of arms, satellite, stipendiary. Heroic action predicted for soldier. Skill, bravery, capacity, defense, address, enmity, wrath, war, destruction, opposition, resistance, ruin. There is a sense in which the card signifies death, but only in its proximity to other cards of fatality. *Reversed:* Imprudence, incapacity, extravagance. Dispute with an imbecile person. For a woman, struggle with a rival, who will be conquered.

Suggested Interpretation

An assertive person. Heroism. *Reversed:* A hasty person. Intemperance. Imprudence. Mistakes.

♦ Queen of Swords ♦

Pallas was the Paris-pattern name of the Queen of Spades as early as 1493, maybe earlier. In Greek mythology, Pallas, also known as Athene, sprang full-grown from the head of Zeus, the ruling god of Olympus. As the virgin goddess of wisdom, she championed the Greeks during the Trojan War,

 whereas the god of war, Ares, the Greek Mars, championed the Trojans. The poet Homer in his *Iliad* describes both deities battling it out together on the plain in front of Troy, Pallas triumphing over Ares, illustrating the power of intellect over brute force.

In her day, the chaste Pallas was referred to by poets as *la Pucelle* (the Maiden). This also happened to be the nickname given to Joan of Arc, whom the Queen of Spades is also sometimes said to represent.

Original Cartomantic Interpretations

Etteilla (1785–1807): Widowhood, emptiness, privation, absence, penury, sterility, indigence, poverty, empty, vacant, unoccupied, unemployed, daring, free. *Reversed:* A bad woman, malignity, malice, crookery, finesse, artifice, deviousness, bigotry, prudery, hypocrisy.

Mathers (1888): Widowhood, loss, privation, absence, separation. *Reversed:* A bad woman, ill-tempered and bigoted. Riches and Discord. Abundance together with worry, joy with grief.

Golden Dawn (1888–96): Queen of the Thrones of Air. Intensely perceptive, keen observation, subtle, quick, confident, often perseveringly accurate in superficial things, graceful, fond of dancing and balancing. If ill-dignified: cruel, sly, deceitful, unreliable, though with a good exterior.

Waite (1910): Widowhood, female sadness and embarrassment, absence, sterility, mourning, privation, separation. *Reversed:* A bad woman. Malice, bigotry, artifice, prudery, deceit.

Suggested Interpretation

A mature, widowed, unmarried, or solitary woman. Independence. Separation. *Reversed:* A difficult woman. Malice. Misfortune. Sorrow.

✦ King of Swords ✦

The caption for the French-suit version of this card was most frequently David, Old Testament king of Israel, poet and prophet, harpist, conqueror of the giant Goliath and the Philistines, and one of the Nine Worthies.

David was the youngest son of Jesse of Bethlehem-Judah, and tamed the fits of madness suffered by Saul, the first king of Israel, with his skill as a harpist. He was loved deeply by both Jonathan and Michel, Saul's son and daughter; he subsequently married Michel and eventually became king himself.

The sword and harp are David's emblems: After using a slingshot to fell the giant Goliath, the hero of the Philistines, David cut off Goliath's head with the giant's own sword. David hung the huge sword in the tabernacle, the portable sanctu-ary initially used by the Jews in the wilderness, but because he had spilled human blood, he was for-bidden to build the temple itself. The task was left to his son Solomon, who, after he had completed the temple, hung the sword in it, where it remained as a famous talisman.

David has lost his sword in most French suit sign cards, but still appears with his harp, remind-ing us of his authorship of the biblical psalms. King David's name appears as the King of Spades in the Paris pattern from the late fifteenth century onward, and as one of the Nine Worthies, he was considered, by his elevation from shepherd boy to king, to embody the working of divine justice in its recognition of true nobility.

Original Cartomantic Interpretations

Pratesi's cartomancer (1750): Evil tongue.

Etteilla (1785–1807): A man of the judiciary, a man of law, a judge, an attorney, an assessor, a senator, a businessman, a practitioner, an advocate, an agent, a doctor, a physician, a jurist, jurisprudence, a plaintiff, a legal consultant. *Reversed:* Ill-intentioned, wickedness, perversity, perfidy, crime, cruelty, atrocity, inhumanity.

Mathers (1888): A lawyer, man of law, power, command, superior-ity, authority. *Reversed:* A wicked man, chagrin, worry, grief, fear, disturbance.

Golden Dawn (1888–96): Lord of the Winds and Breezes. King of the Spirits of Air. He is active, clever, subtle, fierce, delicate, courageous, skillful, but inclined to domineer. Also to overvalue small things, unless well-dignified. If ill-dignified: deceitful, tyrannical, and crafty.

Waite (1910): Whatever arises out of the idea of judgment and all its connections. Power, command, authority, militant intelligence, law, offices of the crown, and so on. Hence also a lawyer, senator, doctor. *Reversed:* A bad man. Cruelty, perversity, barbarity, perfidy, evil intention.

Suggested Interpretation

Authority figure. Legal matters. Justice put to good ends. *Reversed:* Despot. Perverted justice. Legal troubles.

THE SUIT OF BATONS OR WANDS

The Baton, Cudgel, Wand, and Pillar are symbols of the Cardinal Virtue Fortitude, the ancient Persian class of learned men who maintain the faith known as Magians, or *Húristár,* and by some accounts the element fire. In medieval and Renaissance Europe, the symbols implied support, strength, and courage. Mamlûk polo sticks may have represented the Absolute's ability to bat the destiny of the human soul around; the Persian Magians certainly considered that their rods signified service to the holy fire of Ahuramazda. In card games the Batons are considered a "masculine" suit, and in divination the suit sign is interpreted as an emblem of energy, support, willpower, and matters to do with enterprise and creativity.

Both Etteilla and Mathers equate Batons with Diamonds, the French suit sign *Carreau,* or Paving Tiles. If this is an accurate identification, which I believe it is, then the Paving Tile possibly derives its identity from the lozenge-shaped holes in the lattice made by the Mamlûk polo sticks and subsequently by the Italian Batons (see the figure on the left on page 237, for example). In English this is rendered as "diamond," according to the *Oxford English Dictionary* a jewelers' term used since the fifteenth century to describe the shape made by a plane section of an octahedral crystal when its diagonals are arranged in a vertical and horizontal position.

In Celtic lore the Baton is seen to correspond to the terrible lance of the Irish sun god Lugh, which was thought to be the prototype for the miraculous spear of Longinus that Sir Balin used to inflict the Dolorous Stroke on the Grail King in later Arthurian romance.

♦ Ace of Batons or Wands ♦

Lévi stated that the Wand represented the miraculously flowering rod of Moses' brother Aaron, a concept borrowed in part from Court de Gébelin, who identified it as the rod of Moses himself. As we noted earlier, Aaron's flowering rod was one of the well-known theatrical effects of the mystery plays.

Pratesi's Bolognese interpretation seems to be at odds with everyone here, unless his manuscript was actually indicating the reversed meaning of the card, which would in fact tie in with Etteilla's. Of great interest, Waite seems to have tapped into this Bolognese tradition, or one similar to it, which he mentions in an afterthought as "another reading."

Original Cartomantic Interpretations

Pratesi's cartomancer (1750): Annoyances.

Etteilla (1785–1807): Birth, commencement, nativity, origin, creation, source, principle, supremacy, first fruits, extraction, race, family, rank, house, line, posterity, occasion, cause, reason, first, premises. *Reversed:* Downfall, cascade, decadence, decline, fading, lessening, dissipation, failure, bankruptcy, ruin, destruction, demolition, damage, devastation, fault, error, mistake, weakness, dejection, discouragement, perdition, abyss, gulf, precipice, to perish, to fall, to sink, to derogate, profundity.

Mathers (1888): Birth, commencement, beginning, origin, source. *Reversed:* Persecution, pursuit, violence, vexation, cruelty, tyranny.

Golden Dawn (1888–96): Root of the Powers of Fire. Force, strength, rush, vigor, energy, and it governs according to its nature various works and questions. It implies natural, as opposed to invoked, force.

Waite (1910): Creation, invention, enterprise, the powers that result in these, principle, beginning, source, birth, family, origin, the virility that is behind them, the beginning of enterprises. According to another account, money, fortune, inheritance. Another reading predicts calamities of all kinds. *Reversed:* Fall, decadence, ruin, perdition, to perish, also a certain clouded joy. A sign of birth.

Suggested Interpretation

New beginning. Creativity and enterprise. *Reversed:* A difficult start. Problematic enterprise.

♦ Two of Batons or Wands ♦

ALTERNATE NAME: DEUCE OF BATONS OR WANDS

Decan: Aries, degree 1 to degree 10, ruled by Mars.

Picatrix (c. 1256): It is a decan of boldness, fierceness, resolution, and shamelessness.

Nobody seems to agree about this card. Etteilla considered it a bad one when presented upright, but Mathers and the Golden Dawn preferred to follow the lead of *Picatrix,* emphasizing the decan's beneficent energizing power of Mars in Aries. Waite duly noted that there is really no way to reconcile the contradictory interpretations as good fortune on the one hand, sadness and affliction on the other, although he makes an attempt at it in his card design. This is one of those cards where final judgment is truly left up to the intuition of whoever is interpreting it.

Original Cartomantic Interpretations

Etteilla (1785–1807): Chagrin, sadness, melancholy, affliction, displeasure, dolor, desolation, mortification, temper, disagreement, the vapors, dark thoughts, sourness, anger, spite. *Reversed:* Surprise, enchantment, thrilling, trouble, unforeseen event, unexpected happening, fright, emotion, fear, terror, dread, consternation, astonishment, domination, ravishment, alarms, marvel, phenomenon, miracle.

Mathers (1888): Riches, fortune, opulence, magnificence, grandeur. *Reversed:* Surprise, astonishment, event, extraordinary occurrence.

Golden Dawn (1888–96): Lord of Dominion. Strength, dominion, harmony of rule and justice. Boldness, courage, fierceness, shamelessness, revenge, resolution, generous, proud, sensitive, ambitious, refined, restless, turbulent, sagacious withal, yet unforgiving and obstinate, according to dignity.

Waite (1910): Between the alternative readings there is no marriage possible, on the one hand, riches, fortune, magnificence, on the other, physical suffering, disease, chagrin, sadness, mortification. A young lady may expect trivial disappointments. *Reversed:* Surprise, wonder, enchantment, emotion, trouble, fear.

Suggested Interpretation

Negative thoughts. *Reversed:* Extraordinary surprise.

♦ Three of Batons or Wands ♦

ALTERNATE NAME: THE TREY OF BATONS OR WANDS

Decan: Aries, degree 11 to degree 20, ruled by the Sun.
Picatrix (c. 1256): This is a decan of pride, nobility, wealth, and rule.

All our cartomancers emphasize Etteilla's interpretation of this card as one of hope and enterprise.

Original Cartomantic Interpretations

Etteilla (1785–1807): Enterprise, to undertake, to commence, to encroach, to take possession of, audacity, temerity, boldness, imprudence, enterprising, bold, rash, audacious, undertaken, encumbered, disconcerted, crippled, effort, try, temptation. *Reversed:* Interruption of misfortunes, of torments, of suffering, of travail, end, cessation, discontinuation, discontinuance, repose, influence, intermediary, intermission.

Mathers (1888): Enterprise, undertaking, commerce, trade, negotiation. *Reversed:* Hope, desire, attempt, wish.

Golden Dawn (1888–96): Lord of Established Strength. Established force and strength. Realization of hope. Completion of labor, success of the struggle. Pride, nobility, wealth, power, conceit. Rude self-assumption and insolence. Generosity, obstinacy, according to dignity.

Waite (1910): Established strength, enterprise, effort, trade, commerce, discovery. A very good card, collaboration will favor enterprise. *Reversed:* The end of troubles, suspension or end of adversity, toil, and disappointment.

Suggested Interpretation

Initiative. Enterprise. Cooperation. *Reversed:* End of adversity.

✦ Four of Batons or Wands ✦

Decan: Aries, degree 21 to degree 30, ruled by Venus.
Picatrix (c. 1256): It is a decan of subtlety, beauty, etc.

My own preferred translation of *Picatrix* here, as opposed to the Golden Dawn's rather perfunctory version, would be "This is a decan of subtlety and subtle guidance and of new things and new equipment and so on."

According to Etteilla's cartomantic tradition, however, this card promises well for a social life and a sense of security. Waite adds one of his personal intuitions involving a country getaway.

Original Cartomantic Interpretations

Etteilla (1785–1807): Society, association, assembly, liaison, federation, alliance, assembly, reunion, circle, community, mob, multitude, crowd, rout, crew, band, company, cohort, army, convocation, accompaniment, mixture, medley, alloy, amalgam, covenant, convention, pact, treaty. *Reversed:* Prosperity, augmentation, increase, advancement, success, thriving, good luck, flourishing, happiness, beauty, embellishment.

Mathers (1888): Society, union, association, concord, harmony. *Reversed:* Prosperity, success, happiness, advantage.

Golden Dawn (1888–96): Lord of Perfected Work. Perfection, a completion of a thing built up with trouble and labor. Rest after labor. Subtlety, cleverness, beauty, mirth, success in completion. Reasoning faculty, conclusions drawn from previous knowledge. Unreadiness, unreliable, and unsteady, through overanxiety and hurriedness of action. Graceful in manners. At times insincere.

Waite (1910): Country life, haven of refuge, harvest home, repose, concord, harmony, prosperity, peace, the perfected work of these, unexpected good fortune. *Reversed:* The meaning remains unaltered, prosperity, increase, felicity, beauty, embellishment. A married woman will have beautiful children.

Suggested Interpretation

Safe haven. Family bond. Circle of friends. *Reversed:* Also a safe haven. Maybe stagnation within it.

♦ Five of Batons or Wands ♦

Decan: Leo, degree 1 to degree 10, ruled by Saturn.

Picatrix (c. 1256): A decan of boldness, liberality, victory, cruelty, lust, and violence.

Mathers sticks close to Etteilla, and the Golden Dawn draws its inspiration from *Picatrix* as usual. Waite's interpretation once again strikes a foreign note that may have sprung from private revelation, namely the idea of "imitation" or "sham" violence. Or maybe this is just his attempt to reconcile the "boldness" and "violence" of *Picatrix* with Etteilla's interpretation.

Original Cartomantic Interpretations

Etteilla (1785–1807): Gold, riches, opulence, magnificence, sumptuousness, brilliance, luxury, abundance, fortune; physical, philosophical, and moral sun. *Reversed:* Trial, litigation, differences, wrangles, contestations, disputes, entreaty, instruction, pursuit, oppositions, discussions, chicanery, bickering, contradiction, inconsistency.

Mathers (1888): Gold, opulence, gain, heritage, riches, fortune, money. *Reversed:* Legal proceedings, judgment, law, lawyer, tribunal.

Golden Dawn (1888–96): Lord of Strife. Violent strife and contest, boldness, rashness, cruelty, violence, lust and desire, prodigality and generosity, depending on well- or ill-dignified.

Waite (1910): Imitation, as for example a sham fight, the strenuous competition and struggle of the search after riches and fortune. Hence some attributions say it is a card of gold, gain, opulence, success in financial speculation. *Reversed:* Litigation, disputes, trickery, contradiction. Quarrels may be turned to advantage.

Suggested Interpretation

Wealth. Luxury. Success. *Reversed:* Conflict. Litigation. Bickering.

♦ Six of Batons or Wands ♦

Decan: Leo, degree 11 to degree 20, ruled by Jupiter.

Picatrix (c. 1256): It is a decan of quarrelling, ignorance, pretended knowledge, wrangling, victory over the low and base, and of drawing swords.

Etteilla's card interpretation "domestic" is a reminder of the time in which he was writing, just before and around the time of the French Revolution, when most of his consultants would have had servants at their beck and call. Mathers draws on only Etteilla's reversed-card interpretations.

The Golden Dawn, on the other hand, proposes an interpretation that can by no stretch of the imagination be allied to the attributes of the *Picatrix* decan. This is because, once again, they have managed to transpose the two decans, assigning the values of the second decan of Leo to the third and vice versa, possibly because each decan's attributes seemed more appropriate to the other's ruling planets, Jupiter and Mars, respectively. This may, of course, have been a correct "rectification" on the Golden Dawn's part, but it doesn't accord with the printed texts of either *Picatrix* or Cornelius Agrippa.

Waite, as usual, valiantly tries to marry the various concepts.

Original Cartomantic Interpretations

Etteilla (1785–1807): Domestic, servant, valet, lackey, attendant, mercenary, inferior, slave, courier, messenger, to manage, interior of the house, housework, family, all the house servants. *Reversed:* Expectation, hope, trust, to lay the groundwork, to rely on, to entrust, to hope, reliance, foresight, fear, apprehension.

Mathers (1888): Attempt, hope, desire, wish, expectation. *Reversed:* Infidelity, treachery, disloyalty, perfidy.

Golden Dawn (1888–96): Lord of Victory. Victory after strife, success through energy and industry, love, pleasure gained by labor, carefulness, sociability and avoiding of strife, yet victory therein. Also insolence, pride of riches, and success. The whole depending on dignity.

Waite (1910): A victor triumphing, but also great news, such as might be carried in state by the king's courier. Expectation crowned with its own desire, the crown of hope, and so forth. Also that servants may lose the confidence of their masters, or that a young lady may be betrayed by a friend. *Reversed:* Apprehension; fear, as of a victorious enemy at the gate; treachery; disloyalty, as of gates being opened to the enemy. Also fulfillment of deferred hope.

Suggested Interpretation

Success. Good news. An assistant. *Reversed:* Agonized waiting.

♦ Seven of Batons or Wands ♦

Decan: Leo, degree 21 to degree 30, ruled by Mars.

Picatrix (c. 1256): It is a decan of love, pleasure, society, and avoiding of quarrels and carefulness in parting with goods.

Remember, we have to view the attributes of the previous, *second,* decan of Leo to understand the Golden Dawn's interpretation of this card.

As a historical side note, Mathers appears to draw on the Golden Dawn for the upright interpretation of this card, which would indicate that he was aware of the Order system of tarot interpretation in 1888 when he wrote his *Tarot* booklet. Etteilla's interpretation of the upright card, moreover, is completely different from the Golden Dawn's. Waite, while drawing on Etteilla and the Golden Dawn, generally softens the impact of the card all around.

Original Cartomantic Interpretations

Etteilla (1785–1807): Parley, discourse, conference, colloquy, conversation, dissertation, deliberation, discussion, speech, pronunciation, language, idiom, patois, negotiation, market, exchange, measure, commerce, traffic, correspondence, to speak, to say, to utter, to confer, to chatter, to chat, to sew discord, to babble, to blab. *Reversed:* Indecision, irresolution, uncertainty, perplexity, inconstancy, thoughtlessness, variation, variety, diversity, to hesitate, hesitation, to totter, to vacillate, versatility.

Mathers (1888): Success, gain, advantage, profit, victory. *Reversed:* Indecision, doubt, hesitation, embarrassment, anxiety.

Golden Dawn (1888–96): Lord of Valor. Possible victory, depending on the energy and courage exercised; valor, opposition, obstacles, difficulties, yet courage to meet them, quarreling, ignorance, pretence, wrangling and threatening, also victory in small and unimportant things, and influence over subordinates. Depending on dignity as usual.

Waite (1910): A card of valor, the vantage position, wordy strife, negotiations, war of trade, barter, competition, success. A dark child. *Reversed:* Perplexity, embarrassments, anxiety, a caution against indecision.

Suggested Interpretation

Negotiations. Commerce. Chatter. Success. *Reversed:* Irresolution. Vacillation.

◆ Eight of Batons or Wands ◆

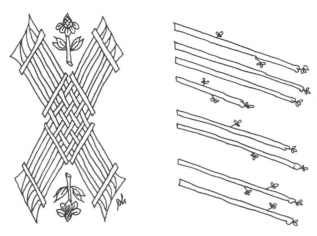

Decan: Sagittarius, degree 1 to degree 10, ruled by Mercury.
Picatrix (c. 1256): It is a decan of boldness, freedom, welfare, liberality, and of fields and gardens.

This is one of the more remarkable coincidences between Etteilla's cartomantic tradition and *Picatrix,* although only the Golden Dawn seems aware of the rural associations of this card.

Original Cartomantic Interpretations

Etteilla (1785–1807): Countryside, field, plain, agriculture, cultivation, tillage, landed property, real estate, farm, farmhouse, garden, orchard, meadow, wood, grove, shade, pleasure, sport, amusement, pastime, merrymaking, peace, calm, tranquility, innocence, rural life, forest, valley, mountain, field of battle. *Reversed:* Interior dispute, examination, argument, misunderstanding, regrets, remorse, to repent, internal agitation, irresolution, uncertainty, indecision, inconceivable, incomprehensible, doubt, qualm, timorous conscience.

Mathers (1888): Understanding, observation, direction. *Reversed:* Quarrels, intestine [internal or domestic] disputes, discord.

Golden Dawn (1888–96): Lord of Swiftness. Too much force applied too suddenly. Very rapid rush, but too quickly passed and expended. Violent but not lasting. Swiftness. Rapidity. Courage, boldness, confidence, freedom, warfare. Violence, love of open air, field sports, garden, meadows. Generous, subtle, eloquent, yet somewhat untrustworthy. Rapacious, insolent, oppressive. Theft and robbery, according to dignity.

Waite (1910): Activity in undertakings, swiftness as that of an express messenger, great haste, great hope, speed toward an end that promises happiness, generally that which is on the move, also the arrows of love. *Reversed:* Internal dispute, stingings of conscience, quarrels, domestic disputes for a married person.

Suggested Interpretation

Swift progress. Country matters. *Reversed:* Internal dispute.

♦ Nine of Batons or Wands ♦

Decan: Sagittarius, degree 11 to degree 20, ruled by the Moon.
Picatrix (c. 1256): It is a decan of fear, lamentation, grief, anxiety, and disturbance.

For once, all the cartomancers seem to ignore *Picatrix* here. What Etteilla interprets as "hindrance," the Golden Dawn interprets as unshakable force, Mathers as "discipline," and Waite as "strength in opposition."

Original Cartomantic Interpretations

Etteilla (1785–1807): Hindrance, intervals, separation, delay, sending back, suspension, lengthening, slowly, slowdown. *Reversed:*

Something that thwarts or crosses, obstacle, preventions, opposition, disadvantage, adversity, toil, misfortune, unhappiness, calamity.

Mathers (1888): Order, discipline, good arrangement, disposition. *Reversed:* Obstacles, crosses, delay, displeasure.

Golden Dawn (1888–96): Lord of Great Strength. Tremendous and steady force that cannot be shaken. Herculean strength, yet sometimes scientifically applied. Great success, but with strife and energy. Victory preceded by apprehension and fear. Health good and recovery, yet doubt. Generous, questioning and curious, fond of external appearances, intractable, obstinate.

Waite (1910): Strength in opposition. If attacked, the person will meet an onslaught boldly. All possible adjuncts, delay, suspension, adjournment. *Reversed:* Obstacles, adversity, calamity.

Suggested Interpretation

Strength in adversity. Delay. *Reversed:* Adversity. Obstacles. Calamity.

♦ Ten of Batons or Wands ♦

Decan: Sagittarius, degree 21 to degree 30, ruled by Saturn.

Picatrix (c. 1256): It is a decan of ill will, levity, envy, obstinacy, and swiftness in all evil things, and of deceitful acts.

Etteilla's interpretations seem to mirror *Picatrix's* decan interpretation very well, as do those of Waite. Mathers, however, seems not only to have given Etteilla's upright interpretation to the reversed card but to have come up with a sunny new upright reading all his own (which Waite dismisses, in characteristic fashion). The Golden Dawn's interpretations are somewhat self-contradictory.

Original Cartomantic Interpretations

Etteilla (1785–1807): Treason, perfidy, swindling, cheating, ruse, surprise, disguise, dissimulation, hypocrisy, prevarication, duplicity, disloyalty, heinousness, falsity, conspiracy, imposture. *Reversed:* Obstacle, zeal, bar, shackle, contrarieties, difficulties, toil, travail, inconvenience, abjectness, quibbling, objection, stumbling block, hedge, entrenchment, redoubt, fortification.

Mathers (1888): Confidence, security, honor, good faith. *Reversed:* Treachery, subterfuge, duplicity, bar.

Golden Dawn (1888–96): Lord of Oppression. Cruel and overbearing force and energy, but applied only to selfish and material ends. Sometimes shows failure in a matter, and the opposition too strong to be controlled arising from the person's too great selfishness at the beginning. Ill will, levity, lying, malice, slander, envy, obstinacy, swiftness in evil, if ill-dignified. Also generosity, self-sacrifice, and disinterestedness when well-dignified.

Waite (1910): Some of the readings cannot be harmonized. I set aside that which connects it with honor and good faith [Mathers's]. The chief meaning is oppression simply, also fortune, gain, any kind of success, and also the oppression of these things. Also a card of false-seeming, disguise, and perfidy. Difficulties and contradictions if near a good card. *Reversed:* Contrarieties, difficulties, intrigues, and their analogies.

Suggested Interpretation

Treachery. Disloyalty. Cheating. *Reversed:* Obstacles. Entrenched attitudes.

✦ Knave or Page of Batons or Wands ✦

The most popular names for the French-suit version of this card were Roland, the legendary nephew and paladin of Charlemagne's and cousin to Renaut, and the equally legendary Trojan hero Hector.

In fifteenth-century Italy Roland became well known as Orlando, who became successively mad with love (*innamorato*), then simply mad (*furioso*), under the penmanship of first Matteo Maria Boiardo, then Ludovico Ariosto, both of whom were favorite poets and tale spinners of the D'Este family.

Roland's exploits are described in *The Song of Roland*, a *chanson de geste* thought to have been written around 1100, although the twelfth-century Anglo-Norman poet and historian Robert Wace tells us that a Norman minstrel entertained William of Normandy's troops with the *Song* on the eve before the battle of Hastings in 1066. Its authorship is ascribed to one Therould or Turoldus, a Norman troubadour. The *Song* tells how, after campaigning six years against the Saracens in Spain, Charlemagne sent Ganelon, Roland's treacherous stepfather, on an embassy to Marsillus, the Saracen king of Saragossa. Owing to Ganelon's treachery, Marsillus learned the route by which Charlemagne's army was planning to return to France and ambushed the rear guard as Roland was conducting it through the mountain pass at Roncevalles. Fighting until only fifty of his men survived, Roland was obliged to try to summon aid by blowing on his enchanted horn, won in an earlier battle with the giant Jutmundus. Charlemagne heard the blast from afar, but the wicked Ganelon persuaded him that Roland was merely hunting deer. Before dying, Roland tried to destroy his sword Durandal to prevent its falling into Saracen hands, but he succeeded only in splitting the rock on which he tried to break it. Durandal lies to this day immersed in a stream, the touch of whose waters brings instant death to anyone who tries to appropriate it.

Noblest and most magnanimous of all the Trojans, Hector was an immensely popular figure of romance during the Middle Ages and early Renaissance. According to Homer, after holding Troy for ten years against the Greeks' siege, Hector was finally slain by the Greek hero Achilles in revenge for Hector's unintentional slaying of Achilles' lover Patroclus, who had put on Achilles' armor to fight. Achilles was generally considered an unworthy knight, whereas Hector embodied the chivalric quality of *prouesse,* prowess. Hector's heroic status throughout Europe guaranteed his inclusion among the Nine Worthies. In fact, he was probably the first of them. Significantly, he appears as such in a 1457 fresco in Augsburg, alongside Emperor Frederick III (the possible Emperor of the trumps sequence) and the Seven Electors, German princes responsible for electing him Holy Roman Emperor.

Pratesi's cartomancer relies on the customary, most basic interpretation of any Knave: the thoughts and feelings of the King or Queen of his suit. Etteilla, Mathers, and Waite all bring out the emissary aspect of Roland or Hector. The Golden Dawn emphasizes the Knave's elemental, fiery qualities.

Original Cartomantic Interpretations

Pratesi's cartomancer (1750): Thought of the lady (the Queen of Batons).

Etteilla (1785–1807): A stranger, an unknown person, something extraordinary, strange, unusual, unaccustomed, unheard of, surprising, admirable, marvelous, prodigious, miracle, episode, digression, anonymous. *Reversed:* Announcement, advice, advertisement, admonition, anecdotes, chronicle, history, stories, fables, notices, instruction.

Mathers (1888): A good stranger, good news, pleasure, satisfaction. *Reversed:* Ill news, displeasure, chagrin, worry.

Golden Dawn (1888–96): Princess of the Shining Flame. The Rose of the Palace of Fire. Brilliance, courage, beauty, force, sudden in anger, or love, desire of power, enthusiasm, revenge. If ill-dignified: superficial, theatrical, cruel, unstable, domineering.

Waite (1910): Dark young man, faithful, a lover, an envoy, a postman. A young man of family in search of a young lady. Beside a man, he will bear favorable testimony concerning him. A dangerous rival, if followed by the Page [Knave] of Cups. He has the chief qualities of his suit. *Reversed:* Anecdotes, announcements, evil news. Also indecision and the instability that accompanies it.

Suggested Interpretation

A reliable young friend. New ideas. Good news. *Reversed:* An unreliable young friend. Bad but valuable news.

✦ Knight of Batons or Wands ✦

Why eighteenth-century Bolognese cartomancers should have considered the Knight of Batons a door knocker is beyond my comprehension, but if he is considered to be slamming the door on his way out, maybe the mystery can be explained. At any rate, all our other cartomancers agree that this is a card signifying a departure, whether from an established mode of living or a literal departure resulting in a separation.

Original Cartomantic Interpretations

Pratesi's cartomancer (1750): Door knocker.

Etteilla (1785–1807): Departure, displacement, separation, absence, abandon, changing, flight, desertion, migration, emigration, transposition, translation, transplantation, transmutation, evasion. *Reversed:* Disunion, discord, rupture, dissension, division, partition, separation, parting, faction, partisan, quarrel, severance, fracture, discontinuation, interruption.

Mathers (1888): Departure, separation, disunion. *Reversed:* Rupture, discord, quarrel.

Golden Dawn (1888–96): The Prince of the Chariot of Fire. Swift, strong, hasty, rather violent, yet just and generous, noble and scorning meanness. If ill-dignified: cruel, intolerant, prejudiced, and ill-natured.

Waite (1910): Departure, absence, flight, emigration. A dark young man, friendly. Change of residence. A bad card, according to some readings. Alienation. *Reversed:* Rupture, division, interruption, discord. For a woman, marriage probably frustrated.

Suggested Interpretation

An enterprising person. A departure into the unknown. Emigration. *Reversed:* A difficult person. Rupture. Divorce.

♦ Queen of Batons or Wands ♦

In very early times Penthesilea, Queen of the Amazons, was a favorite name for the Queen of Diamonds, but her popularity was soon eclipsed by that of Rachel, Old Testament daughter of Laban and the beautiful wife of the patriarch Jacob. Penthesilea's link to the virtue Fortitude is more apparent than Rachel's, but the story of Jacob's love for Rachel was extremely popular in medieval times. Jacob had to toil as a laborer for seven years in Laban's service to win her as his bride, and then a second seven after her wily father foisted Rachel's elder sister Leah off on him first.

Rachel was considered "beautiful and well favored," but also acquisitive and unscrupulous, something one suspects she may have learned from her father. Etteilla appears to be influenced by Père Ménestrier's linkage of Batons and farmers in his interpretation of this card, and Mathers and Waite follow him.

Original Cartomantic Interpretations

Pratesi's cartomancer (1750): Harlot.

Etteilla (1785–1807): Mistress of a country estate, chatelaine, household economy, honesty, civility, sweetness, virtue, honor, chastity. *Reversed:* Good wife, bounty, excellence, obliging, helpful, serviceable, benefit, service, obligation.

Mathers (1888): A woman living in the country. Lady of the manor, love of money, avarice, usury. *Reversed:* A good and virtuous woman, but strict and economical. Obstacles, resistance, opposition.

Golden Dawn (1888–96): Queen of the Thrones of Flame. Adaptability, steady force applied to an object. Steady rule; great attractive power, power of command, yet liked notwithstanding. Kind and generous when not opposed. If ill-dignified: obstinate, revengeful, domineering, tyrannical, and apt to turn suddenly against another without a cause.

Waite (1910): A dark woman, countrywoman, friendly, chaste, loving, honorable. If the card beside her signifies a man, she is well disposed toward him. If a woman, she is interested in the inquirer. Also, love of money. A good harvest, which may be taken in several senses. *Reversed:* Good, economical, obliging, serviceable. Goodwill toward the inquirer, without the opportunity to exercise it. Signifies also—but in certain positions and in the neighborhood of other cards tending in such directions—opposition, jealousy, even deceit and infidelity.

Suggested Interpretation

A mature, friendly, enterprising woman. Love of money. *Reversed:* A manipulative woman. Hidden agendas. Opposition.

◆ King of Batons or Wands ◆

From about 1500 the customary name for the Paris-pattern version of this card has been *Cezar,* Caesar, after the Roman general, consul, and dictator Caius Julius Caesar. Caesar's name was subsequently adopted as a title by all male successors and heirs apparent to the imperial throne of Rome from the time of Augustus to  Hadrian, and it is from this title that we obtain the words *czar, shah,* and *kaiser.*

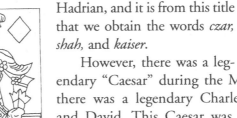

However, there was a legendary "Caesar" during the Middle Ages, just as there was a legendary Charlemagne, Alexander, and David. This Caesar was thought to be not only the first Emperor of Rome but a very pillar of early Christianity, even though he died forty years before the birth of Jesus. One of the earliest extant French Kings of Diamonds dates from 1490 and carries a bundle of rods with an axe in the middle of it, the *fasces* emblem of Imperial Rome (whence our word *fascist*), plainly indicating Caesar's duty as the King of Batons too. As one of the

Nine Worthies, Caesar was considered to be the incarnation of courage and determination, a builder and bringer of civilization.

Again, we can see the influence of Ménestrier at work on the cartomantic interpretations of this card.

Original Cartomantic Interpretations

Pratesi's cartomancer (1750): An unmarried gentleman.

Etteilla (1785–1807): Master of an estate, a good and severe man, a well-intentioned man, an honest man, conscience, probity, a farmer, a worker on the land, a cultivator. *Reversed:* A good and severe man, indulgence, severity, tolerance.

Mathers (1888): Man living in the country, country gentleman. Knowledge, education. *Reversed:* A naturally good but severe man. Counsel, advice, deliberation.

Golden Dawn (1888–96): The Lord of the Flame and the Lightning. King of the Spirits of Fire. He is active, generous, fierce, sudden, and impetuous. If ill-dignified, he is evil-minded, cruel, bigoted, brutal.

Waite (1910): Dark man, friendly, countryman, generally married, honest, and conscientious. The card always signifies honesty, and may mean news concerning an unexpected heritage to fall in before very long. Generally favorable, may signify a good marriage. *Reversed:* Good, but severe. August, yet tolerant. Also advice that should be followed.

Suggested Interpretation

A friendly, mature, reliable man. An austere man. Important advice. *Reversed:* An astute but unscrupulous man. Important advice.

6

READING THE TAROT

Now that you are familiar with the tarot deck, you may want to learn how to read it. Some of my readers will quite obviously be old hands at this, but I hope that even they will find in this chapter some hints that will help them deepen their understanding of the process and sharpen their skills.

There are innumerable techniques for reading the cards, and each reader has his or her own pet methods. They can all produce results, so long as you approach the cards in the right frame of mind. Many are variations of variations that have passed from diviner to diviner down the years. As I have indicated, the oldest cartomantic methods designed for use with tarot cards that I am aware of are those that originated in France or Italy.

Today we suspect that divination works by means of a mental process known to psychologists as projection. Briefly, this process occurs when someone "projects" the inner, unconscious content of his or her mind onto outside events or objects, such as somebody else's actions, an ambiguous visual picture such as an inkblot provided by a psychologist, or the pattern of tea leaves left in a cup. Meaning is then read into these things by the person who is reacting to them.

Projection is also made use of in a psychological assessment tool called a thematic apperception test. In the TAT, examiners present individuals with a set of five to twelve cards displaying pictures of ambiguous situations, mostly featuring people. Respondents construct a story about each picture, describing events that have occurred, are occurring, or will occur, and what the depicted characters are feeling and thinking.

At first glance, this process looks similar to the one you will use with your tarot cards. However, unlike TAT card imagery, tarot card imagery—with its medieval trumps, court cards, coin, cup, sword, and baton symbols—is thought by cartomancers to evoke not just personal fantasy but also primitive patterns of interpretation that are common to all humanity. The patterns are known as archetypes. According to the theories of the influential Swiss psychologist and psychiatrist Carl Gustave Jung, these archetypes are deeply rooted in what he described as our collective unconscious, a sort of group mind that we all share. The unconscious levels of our personal, individual minds grow out of the collective unconscious like trees from a common root.

This common source of symbolic matter gives tarot cards a very special potential. If their imagery is indeed archetypal, they can be used not just to evoke the unconscious content of your own mind into conscious awareness but to reach down to the underlying depths of the collective unconscious, where your own unconscious is one with the unconscious of the person whose cards you are interpreting. The symbols form a psychic bridge between the conscious you and the unconscious mind of the person you are reading for and provides assurance that your interpretation of the cards drawn will be meaningful for both of you.

Now, exactly how the cards predict future events or why we sometimes manage to draw the appropriate cards unseen from the deck time and again in response to the same question remains a mystery. I suspect Neoplatonist magi of the Renaissance would have considered these results to be the work of the world soul (which is pretty close in concept to Jung's collective unconscious). Today's parapsychologists might consider divination the work of psi. You can call it chance if you like. But, then, chance ultimately may turn out to be a rather slipshod concept, regardless of what the laws of statistics seem to imply.

One day we may have to recognize that "coincidence" derives from a principle somehow built into the very nature of reality, a principle that ordains that similar things have no option *but* to flock together, like birds of a feather. This seems to be what Jung was getting at with his theory of synchronicity; it is undoubtedly what the Neoplatonic magi meant by their doctrine of universal sympathy: that everything in the cosmos is connected, we might say "holistically," by the power of meaning.

Naturally, the meaning of "meaning" continues to be a philosophical debate, as do the criteria for similarity and the means by which synchronicity might translate into a quantifiable science. Parapsychologists in a sense have been testing the accuracy of divination techniques for over a century in their quest for answers, although they have had a hard time getting the guardians of scientific orthodoxy to accept their findings.

Oddly enough, today's fundamental physicists may prove allies in the search. Paying little attention to orthodoxy much of the time, these scientists have stumbled across a revolutionary principle derived from quantum theory that they call nonlocality, a concept that Einstein fought bitterly against but that has recently been experimentally proven beyond a shadow of doubt. Essentially, the doctrine of nonlocality states that everything that we have hitherto thought of as separate—people, places, things—is really part of one great thing, which enables these apparently discrete things to be in constant touch from one end of the cosmos to the other. Astonishing as this may seem, all things really are intimately connected, and the speed of light, as once believed, presents no limitation to the instant reaction of one quantum event to another—however far apart they may be, at the other side of the universe even—provided they both arise from the same quantum-event source, among which the Big Bang could surely be counted, and are, as physicists say, "entangled."

As a logical consequence, perhaps the concepts of "far" and "near," or indeed "past" and "future," should now be considered relative viewpoints, limited only to growing organisms with consciousness. All of this, of course, has enormous relevance to the plausibility of divination, which presumes to delve into past, present, and future in addition to other peoples' minds and lives. It also brings me to a pertinent and disturbing philosophical conundrum that parapsychologists have dubbed the intervention paradox.

In the past, divination and prophecy have frequently been regarded by their practitioners as systems for delivering advice and warnings, rather than as statements of set-in-concrete fact about the future. In this way, if the prediction is unwelcome, the inquirer can take steps to prevent its fulfillment. But here lies the paradox. If one can successfully avert the prophesied disaster, that fact alone implies that the prophecy or divination was inaccurate. And if the event does not happen because of the evasive action, what exactly was it that was divined? The event never happened, because of successful intervention.

To account for the future's mutability, what we must discard is belief in a single fate and envisage a universe full of many potential branching futures. Which one becomes real—which pathway the universe takes at any given point in time—would then depend on whether a particular intervention does or doesn't take place. A divination procedure, such as cartomancy, carried out successfully would therefore only predict possible, maybe even probable, futures, of which everyone possesses a multitude to choose from at any instant of his or her life. So cartomancers must be said to read possibilities, not certainties. It is worth repeating that a tarot reading does not describe a destiny written in stone.

It can, however, and often does have a profound psychological effect on the person for whom it's being performed. Diviners should always be aware that the intense atmosphere that may develop during a reading can put the inquirer into a highly suggestible state that increases the chance of a reading's turning into a self-fulfilling prophecy. So, should you, as the cartomancer, see what looks to you like sinister tidings in the cards, be diplomatic. Be more than diplomatic. Find a way to put a positive spin on your interpretation. Remember, if you are reading accurately, you are only seeing one among many possible futures, so always accentuate the positive. Furthermore, always gauge how much your inquirer wants to know before revealing potentially distressing material, such as the possibility that a spouse is straying. And above all, avoid giving destructive suggestions; your authority as cartomancer is simply too powerful to be used carelessly.

SELECTING A TAROT DECK

If you want to begin reading tarot cards, you must obviously obtain a personal deck if you don't already own one. Not only must the deck appeal to you, but the card designs must be striking enough to memorize easily.

With these criteria in mind, aspiring tarot readers frequently pick the deck designed by Colman Smith for Waite or one of its many derivatives. These include, among many others, the Aquarian, Morgan-Greer, and Knapp-Hall decks. All of these illustrate every card in the Minor and Major Arcanas with pictures designed to suggest the meanings that Waite assigned them. If we consider the fifteenth-century Sola-Busca cards and the many wonderful engraved German decks as well as the variety of French and

German fortune-telling decks designed in the eighteenth and nineteenth centuries, Waite's idea to illustrate the suit cards was hardly completely novel. However, maybe because of the accessibility of the cards plus the popular, literate companion book that Waite wrote and Colman Smith illustrated, the Waite–Colman Smith deck has become the most successful tarot pattern in the last century. Although Waite's suit card pictures are nontraditional, they can really help you memorize the cards' traditional meanings.

In selecting your deck, above all be guided by your instincts. People who favor the Kabbala may be drawn to the decks of BOTA (Paul Foster Case's group, "Builders of the Adytum"), Gareth Knight, Golden Dawn, Hermetic, or Thoth, or any of the new decks that continue to be produced by the big playing-card companies. Traditionalists, however, may want to stick with a Marseille pattern or one of the Swiss or many Italian decks. You will find more information about all of these in the appendices at the back of this book.

GETTING IN TOUCH WITH YOUR CARDS

Many of today's tarot books follow the example of Etteilla and his disciple d'Odoucet to provide a wide range of possible meanings for each card to allow the reader the option of selecting one from the manual that makes sense in the situation being inquired about. Using manuals in this manner can be a slow process to begin with, but it can work well. However, unless tarot readers take the time to familiarize themselves with all the meanings, they can become dependent on the manual rather than intuition, which is where the real wisdom flows from.

Dion Fortune, an initiate of the Golden Dawn who later formed her own highly influential group, the Society of the Inner Light, offered this advice to the novice tarot reader: "To use Tarot . . . does not consist merely in a knowledge of the significance of the cards, but in getting in touch with the forces behind the cards." In order to do this, Fortune advised the novice to carry the cards around, sleep with them under the pillow, handle them, and ponder upon the meaning of the pictures in the light of what the book of instructions had to say until the significance of each picture was realized. "As soon as one perceives some sort of significance in the picture on a card," she wrote, "one has made a link with that card, and its appearance in the divination will mean something."

So if you want to read tarot in the traditional manner—and this is really the hardest part of the whole process—memorize the basic meanings of the cards, the interpretations I have provided for the Major Arcana and the principal ones offered by Waite, Mathers, or Etteilla for the Minor. Use these interpretations as mental scaffolding, or starting points, for the file of associations you create for yourself each time you use the cards. Really get to know the basic meanings so they come to you without thinking. This work on the cards you will initiate with the conscious part of your mind, but the unconscious levels should not be neglected either. The easiest way to begin this work is by meditation.

The use of cards from the Major Arcana as guided-meditation symbols for therapeutic group work has become popular over the last thirty years, and it happens to be a very good way of opening up their archetypal potential. However, if you don't have the opportunity to get involved with groups, you can accomplish very similar results through solo meditation. This simply means that you allow your mind to dwell quietly on the image of each card and everything you think it embodies during quiet times in your day, perhaps first thing when you get up in the morning or before going to bed at night. Use the figure, picture, or pattern of symbols on the card as a starting point, and deliberately allow your imagination to wander, observing the mental associations that come up. You may jot them down in a notebook if you like. Gently guide your focus back to the tarot picture if your mind gets too far off track.

After a short while, you may find that each card calls up consistent, personal images for you, in addition to those you memorized at the start. These personal images are your own instinctive insights, and by associating them with particular tarot cards, you start building up your own divination vocabulary in much the same way that born psychics do. Never mind that the images may seem arbitrary or associated for odd reasons. If the tarots are indeed archetypal, they can be trusted to perform autonomously when left to their own devices, making appropriate associations with thoughts and images held in the storehouse of your unconscious mind. These thoughts and images will be among the interpretations available to you when that particular tarot card turns up in a reading. To quote Fortune once again, "When the Great Angel of the Tarot has been contacted, the cards are remarkably revealing."

It is also helpful to start associating the cards with personal experiences. Try connecting people you encounter every day with the court cards; everyday experiences with the Minor Arcana number cards two through ten; major, life-affecting events like births, marriages, and deaths with aces and Major Arcana cards. Start thinking about events in tarot terms. After a particularly bad day at work, for instance, you might say to your-self, "Well, that was a real Ten of Swords day," or when a long-held wish is granted, you can remark to yourself that the Nine of Cups is finally manifesting itself in your life. To get the most out of your tarot deck, each card has to become an expression of some part of your own life experi-ence and have some special relevance for you.

Once you have accomplished this preliminary work of memorizing traditional card meanings and creating personal associations, the cards will begin to act as triggers during readings, prompting your unconscious mind to send up hints to the conscious you about the subject of the div-ination. You will be "in touch" with your cards.

You will undoubtedly find the numbered suit cards of the Minor Arcana the most difficult to deal with initially. Whereas the symbols used by the trumps and court cards are fairly suggestive, the suit cards from two to ten give no hint of their meanings unless you use illustrated cards like those in the Colman Smith–Waite deck. At the beginning, you must sim-ply commit the meanings to memory, and for this reason, cartomancers today frequently attach key words to the number cards to aid in the mem-orization process. If it helps, you can make such a list from the suggested interpretations I have attached to each card description. However, remem-ber that any card can indicate an entire range of meanings, and which you choose should be determined by considering the general trend of the spread and any question that has been asked. It is at this point that your intuition and ability as a cartomancer really begin to come into play.

PREPARING FOR DIVINATION

Now, here are two pieces of advice that you are free to ignore if you wish. They come from my own experience, which may not accord with the experience of others, so you are welcome to consider them my personal dos and don'ts.

I begin with a controversial technical point, but one I believe to be valid: I don't believe it's wise to use the Major Arcana for casual inquiries. In fact, I believe it should only be used for important queries. The trumps are, or should be, too highly charged for ordinary everyday use. Many diviners today disagree, treating the Major Arcana as if it were of the same value as the Minor and assigning it sweetened or watered-down interpretations, generally in order to make it less threatening. I believe this is an enormous mistake. Life does have a dark side to it, whether we like it or not.

This doesn't mean don't practice with the trumps, just use them judiciously when actually divining with them. Take them seriously. By using the Major Arcana you will be opening up the divination to archetypes represented by such cards as the Hanged Man, Death, and the Devil, as well as the reversals of the other trumps. Use the Minor Arcana for all casual readings, retaining the trumps for use as significators, as alternatives to court cards, and of course when the situation demands it. You'll note that several of the layouts I detail later require just that.

Point number two: the secret of successful card reading, as is the case with any form of sortilege, lies in asking the right questions and asking them properly. Don't ask questions that require a date or time as an answer, and don't ask questions that can be answered with a simple yes or no. Some cartomancers do ask these questions, but the methods they use to generate answers strike me as mechanical, and I don't have much use for them. Instead, ask for insight into problems and keep your queries as open-ended as possible, including only the details needed to clarify what you want to find out. When there is a choice to be made between several courses of action, deal with each possibility separately, using a separate spread for each. For example, lay out one spread to answer the question, "How will the inquirer benefit by choosing course A?" and another spread to answer, "How will the inquirer benefit by choosing course B?" and so on.

Now, having considered these points, I recommend trying your first real reading. You can do one for yourself, and I'm sure you will, but your first practical insight into the process will actually come when you do one for someone else. Ask someone to volunteer, but not someone you know well. I have found advice Waite once gave to be true: the less you know of a person, the easier it is to divine for him or her.

GENERAL RULES OF CARTOMANCY

Before actually committing yourself to an interpretation—and this applies to all readings—study the cards that have been drawn to get the overall feel of them. If you are including the Major Arcana in your practice run, check how many trumps there are. This will give you some measure of the gravity of the reading. A good rule of thumb here is the more trumps, the greater the importance. Also notice which suits predominate. These will give an indication of the reading's main thrust: Coins indicate prudence and material or financial matters; Cups, temperance and emotional matters; Swords, justice and matters to do with legalities, mental challenges, or painful issues; Batons, fortitude and matters to do with enterprise and creativity. Remember also—and this is the important part, the notion that Etteilla introduced—that besides being read singly, the cards may also be read as a unit, one card influencing, and often totally changing, the implications of another. If you advance to the stage where you are doing complex readings using what I call card linking, you will find the juxtaposition of several cards produces shades of meaning not seen in the same cards presented singly.

Now here are the steps in the process of doing an actual reading. Most of them come as second nature to the practiced diviner and are slipped through quickly, so I spell them out in detail only for the novice who is coming to tarot for the first time.

Step 1: Creating the Mood

Many, if not most, card readers find that emotional or psychological preparation is an important prerequisite for meaningful divination. Card reading requires a feeling of detachment, an introspective calm, a "wise passivity," as it has been called. This can be achieved with a simple, silent self-affirmation to the effect that you are now no longer your usual rushed, fretful self, but for the time being at least, have taken on the wise, calm, imperturbable form of the virtue Prudence, who is able to see what is past, what is present, and what is to come. You may also find it helpful to devise a simple ritual to help put you in the mood, lighting a candle or a stick of incense maybe, though this is by no means mandatory. Some cartomancers prefer to keep the atmosphere of the session as simple and uncluttered as possible.

Step 2: The Significator

Many cartomancers no longer use significators, but I'm going to teach you the traditional method here so that you will be able to use them if you choose.

Pick up your tarot deck and select the significator, the card that will represent the person who is consulting the cards or, alternatively, will represent the matter that the inquirer is consulting the cards about. It serves as a physical and symbolic focus point for the inquirer and the diviner. When the outcome to some major problem is being sought, the significator should be chosen from among the Major Arcana trumps, selecting one that seems to have an interpretation corresponding to the matter involved. For example, if a love relationship is involved, select the Lovers. Where death or inheritances are involved, select Death. For legal matters use Justice, and so on.

On the other hand, if the inquirer wants a general reading, the significator should be selected from among the court cards to represent the inquirer himself or herself, and there are various ways of assigning these. Waite opts for the Golden Dawn method of allotting Knights to men over forty, Kings to males under forty, Queens to older women, and Knaves to younger females. This counterintuitive juggling of Kings and Knights doesn't appeal to me, however, because I don't subscribe to the Golden Dawn Tarot's kabbalistic court card allocation. I prefer to make things much simpler and more transparent: Kings for mature men, Queens for mature women, Knights for younger people of both sexes, and Knaves for children or adolescents of both sexes. Remember, we're only talking about assigning significators at the moment. The court cards can and do have other meanings when they turn up in a reading. To help resolve this issue, Etteilla introduced a blank card into his decks, which he named the *"Etteilla,"* to act as the significator. He did this to free up the court cards, which until the 1750s, had apparently been used by diviners to represent the inquirer. "If a dark-haired man consulted the cards for himself," Etteilla wrote, "and took the King of Trefoils [Coins], which represents a dark-haired man, to represent himself, he wouldn't be able to discover if [another] dark-haired man intended to help or hinder him." However, the point that Etteilla missed here is that the action of selecting a significator metaphorically, and maybe metaphysically, places the inquirer *within* the deck of cards before him.

If Etteilla's concern doesn't worry you (and it never worried me), then which suit you select the significator from may be determined by the inquirer's physical appearance (the traditional method, which these days can mean very little in view of how easily the appearance may be altered), from his or her temperament, or from his or her astrological birth sign. This last method is the least likely to lead to quibbling, especially if the inquirer knows something about tarot. Alternatively, if you happen to know the inquirer, simply choose a court card whose character you think reflects his or hers. Finally, some cartomancers allow inquirers to choose their own significators. No matter which method you choose, the following box will help you see how court cards can match your inquirer when you are giving general readings.

THE SIXTEEN SIGNIFICATORS AND THEIR CHARACTERS

King, Queen, Knight, and Knave of Coins (Earth)

Very dark hair, with a dark or ethnic complexion; or practical, prudent, laborious, stubborn, gloomy, "melancholic"; or born under the zodiacal sign of Taurus, Virgo, or Capricorn.

King, Queen, Knight, and Knave of Cups (Water)

Blond or very light brown hair, with a medium complexion; or placid, unconcerned, indifferent, undemonstrative, "phlegmatic"; or born under the zodiacal signs of Cancer, Scorpio, or Pisces.

King, Queen, Knight, and Knave of Swords (Air)

Medium-colored hair, with a medium complexion; or confident, opti-mistic, clear-headed, witty, "sanguine"; or born under the zodiacal signs of Gemini, Libra, or Aquarius.

King, Queen, Knight, and Knave of Batons (Fire)

Golden, red, or auburn hair, with a fair, freckled complexion; or pas-sionate, energetic, hot-headed, irascible, sensual, "choleric"; or born under the zodiacal signs of Aries, Leo, or Sagittarius.

Step 3: The Question

Having selected the significator, formulate the question or goal of the divination very specifically on behalf of the inquirer and state it out loud. You can address yourself to the cards or to the room, it makes no difference, just so long as the formulation is made. Some cartomancers write the inquiry down on a piece of paper or in a notebook kept for the purpose at this point. Doing so can certainly help focus the mind and clarify the question (and if you also record the cards and the interpretations you place on them, you can start building up your own tarot thesaurus as Etteilla and his pupils did).

Step 4: The Shuffle

Now shuffle the deck well. If you are performing the divination for yourself, you will be responsible for the shuffle. If you are reading the cards for someone else, both of you should take part in it. Your object is to randomize the cards as much as possible and reverse some of them. Choose any method of doing this that satisfies you. My own preference is to make a pool of the entire deck, cards face down, on the table. The cards should then be stirred around by the inquirer until they are well and truly mixed to the satisfaction of reader and inquirer alike. While doing this the reader should keep his or her mind as blank as possible, while the inquirer should concentrate firmly on the question he or she has come to pose, whether it be general or specific.

Step 5: The Cut

The cards should now be gathered up by the reader and the deck offered, still face down, for the inquirer to cut. Traditionally, the inquirer is asked to cut the cards three times with the left hand toward himself or herself, which I suspect was originally meant to counteract hemispheric dominance in right-handed people's brains. Therefore, I suppose that if you are naturally left-handed, then you should use the right. In my experience, however, it seems to make not one bit of difference which hand is used.

Step 6: The Draw

You are now ready to "draw" the cards, as the old cartomancers would say. Traditionally, cartomancers simply deal from the top of the deck at this point of the operation, which you are absolutely at liberty to do if it feels best for you. However, I follow a radical departure from tradition in this instance, one that has been widely adopted in the last thirty years. My feeling has always been that "chance" is allowed to play a much larger hand if the cartomancer fans out the cards facedown and invites the inquirer to draw the cards from the fan, one after another. The inquirer then hands the cards to the cartomancer.

If you do follow this method, both inquirer and reader should take care to preserve the cards' orientation exactly the way they have been drawn—reversed or upright—while positioning them in the spread.

SIMPLE TAROT SPREADS

The simplest method of reading the cards is by using them in "spreads" or "layouts," both words being used to refer to the same thing. The spread or a layout may be likened to a computer spreadsheet or horoscope chart: each part of the pattern on which a card is placed refers to something different, such as the past, the future, the inquirer's hopes, fears, and so forth. As they are drawn, single cards are laid out on a table by the diviner in these patterns. Effective cartomancers are adept at employing a range of spreads, from the most elementary variety when the response required is a simple one, to more sophisticated ones when a question requires a highly nuanced answer.

Today there are a great many of these patterns to choose from, and every cartomancer has his or her favorites. You will discover which work best for you by trial and error, and much will depend on how well you are able to cope with the cards themselves. The more suggestive the cards are for you—the more in touch you are with your deck—the more complex the spread you can use. If you are new to tarot, begin with the simpler ones with the least number or variables and build to the more complex as you gain confidence.

Restricted Decks

When you're seeking enlightenment on one specific problem, a popular method of narrowing down the range of variables—which I believe was introduced to the public by Papus—is to divine with a restricted deck of the Minor Arcana, using one of the simpler spreads.

A restricted deck simply means using only the suits germane to the problem, either with or without the tarot trumps, depending on how deep the problem is. If the query is a mundane one without deep involvement, as I have already indicated, leave the tarot trumps out entirely. For instance, if you require a specific answer to a question concerning a business transaction, use the combined suits of Coins and Swords and Batons; for a purely financial one, Coins only; an emotional one, Cups, possibly with the addition of the tarot trumps, depending on the seriousness of the question. A problem at work or concerning careers in any form calls for Batons and Cups and may indicate the trumps be included. In short, trust your own intuition to tell you which suits play a part in the question. If you want to make sure you cover all bases, use all four suits.

A Three-Card Method

Aside from simply cutting the deck and reading the card revealed (which may be done), probably the simplest cartomantic method involves three cards: the significator and two others that the inquirer draws at random from the deck. Reputedly a gypsy method, this requires that you first separate the Minor Arcana from the Major, and from the Minor cards select only the suit or suits that best represent the inquirer's question, if there is one. Next, select the significator or have the inquirer select it, placing it upright on the table in front of you. (In every divination you do, the cards should always be placed facing you, for you, the cartomancer, to interpret.) Tell the inquirer to hold his or her question, if any, clearly in mind while mixing and cutting the cards. The first of the cards he or she draws should be placed— oriented exactly as it was drawn, remember—to the right of the significator in front of you. This card is said to represent the inquirer's present predicament. A second card is now drawn and placed to the right of the first. This represents a situation or person the inquirer is about to encounter. This simple spread may be elaborated by drawing a further card. In this instance, the first card drawn (placed to the right of the significator) will act as an indicator of the past, the second (placed to the right of the first) the present, and the third (placed to the right of the second) the future.

Now, if the question is one of greater importance, the inquirer may repeat the operation with the Major Arcana, and place three trump cards above each of the three Minor Arcana cards. The pair of cards on the left are read first, and are said to represent influences operating in the past of the inquirer. Those in the middle represent the influences acting in the present, those on the right, on the future. This method resembles a simplified version of one first introduced by Papus in 1889.

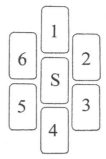

A Hexagram Spread

A spread involving a circle of six cards plus the significator at the center offers a slightly more elaborate version of the three-card method, with more variables. It may be used to answer a question or for a general reading. You can use it with or without the Major Arcana, depending on the importance of the question.

The cards should be dealt clockwise as selected, beginning at the top and concluding at the top left-hand corner. The cards in the ascending triangle should be read as influences working in favor of the inquirer, while those of the descending, inverted triangle are forces working against him or her.

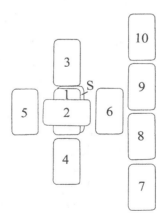

Waite's Celtic Method

Significantly more complex than the simple spreads detailed above, the spread that A. E. Waite introduced to the world as the Celtic method, together with its many variants, is probably the most popular spread used by tarot readers today. It can offer insights into past, present, and future, into the inquirer's drives both conscious and unconscious, into how others

view him or her, as well as into the general outcome to the situation
inquired about. Waite claimed it to be traditional to certain parts of
Britain but believed that the method had not been used with tarot cards
prior to his description of it: "I do not think," he wrote in 1910, "that it
has been published—certainly not in connexion with Tarot cards." I pre-
sume he meant that the spread had only been used with a regular deck of
French-suited cards.

To employ the Celtic method, first decide whether you want to leave
the Major Arcana in or out. The significator, whether it be a court card
or a trump, should then be placed centrally, face up, and an unseen card
drawn by the inquirer from the deck. This card should be turned over
and set on top of the significator, representing the primary matter being
inquired about or the main influence acting on the inquirer at the present, and it is said to "cover" the inquirer.

A second card is drawn and laid crosswise on top of the first, being
said to "cross" the inquirer. It represents any obstacles he or she is con-
fronting at the moment or any secondary factors applying to the matter.
I always use the card's upright meaning as the applicable one here.

The third card is placed above the significator, being said to "crown"
the inquirer. It is an indicator of his or her highest aim or goal in the matter—his or her conscious mind, if you like.

The fourth card is placed below the significator and represents what
is "beneath" the inquirer—namely, the roots of the matter, the basis of
the inquirer's present situation, what the inquirer may have forgotten in
thinking about the matter, or what his or her unconscious mind has to
say about it.

The fifth card represents the past and factors that have passed out of
the question or "that which is behind" the inquirer, and the direction of
the significator's gaze traditionally determines the card's placement on the
table. If the significator's gaze is to the right, then the fifth card is placed
on the left, and vice versa. Should the significator not face in either direction but be presented full face, or have no face at all in the event it's a
trump card, then assume the left-hand side represents the past.

Similarly, the direction in which the gaze of the significator is turned
represents "that which is before" the inquirer—the near future and
approaching influences, and this is where the sixth card must be laid. Should
the significator face front, then the sixth card should be placed to the right.

You have now constructed the basic cross.

Four additional cards are usually selected at this point and placed in a column one above the other on the right-hand side of the cross, beginning at the bottom. Card number seven represents inquirers' present state of mind, as they see themselves at the moment. Card number eight indicates their current social environment and how others see them. Card number nine represents their hopes or fears concerning their situations, or sometimes an unforeseen factor about to rear its head.

Card number ten represents the final, overall outcome and the working out of the influences revealed by all the other cards. This is the card to which you should pay chief attention. If the answer sought during the reading is in any way ambiguous, this card may be taken and used as the significator for another spread, either repeating the Celtic method or using another layout entirely. If it's a court card, it represents a person who will be largely instrumental in determining the outcome of the matter inquired about. In this case, consider using this card as a significator for a new operation to reveal the nature of that person's influence.

When using Waite's spread, study cards one through six carefully, for they represent the present situation. Cartomancer Joan Bunning, whose books and Web site provide good advice on tarot cartomancy for novice and adept alike, suggests also examining cards one through eight in pairs, cards one and two paired to explore the central dynamic of the question, cards three and four to compare the different mental levels on which this question is being hashed out, cards five and six to catch the drift of people and events passing through the inquirer's life, and cards seven and eight to examine how the inquirer is relating to his or her environment. Etteilla thought he had introduced this method of reading paired cards in his early days of divining with French-suited cards, but in fact Marcolino da Forlì was the first to document its use with Italian cards in his *Le ingeniose sorte.*

ADVANCED CARTOMANCY—LINKING THE CARDS

From working with spreads, you may want to progress to working with cards in the advanced manner that Etteilla recommended, by using them to form complex "sentences." This is the manner in which experienced cartomancers work, whether they use tarot or regular French-suited cards. In order to do this effectively, you will of course have to become thoroughly in touch with your deck. You would also be wise to have practiced stringing the cards together by making what I call little "practice runs."

For instance, without formulating any specific question to be answered, simply select several cards unseen from the deck, let's say six or seven, and place them facedown in a row in front of you, left to right or right to left, it doesn't matter at this point. Now, as you read your line of cards beginning from the first one you drew and progressing to the last, let them turn themselves into a story. Remember Etteilla's lists of interpretations—the cards can essentially be used as nouns, verbs, adverbs, or adjectives. Again recalling Etteilla, the cards should be allowed to suggest, rather than be rigidly interpreted. If you have done your homework on them, this won't be difficult.

Sample Readings

Here are four sample readings to illustrate what I mean by a practice run. The first three constitute readings for three entirely different questions, but they are all based on the same cards drawn at random from a deck consisting of only the Minor Arcana, for reasons that I have already explained. This will show you how the same cards can be used to tell three completely different narratives. Which narrative is relevant to your question is, of course, entirely up to you and your intuition. The fourth reading addresses a further, unrelated question concerning a matter of some gravity, so it uses both Major and Minor Arcana.

To begin, I draw six cards from the Minor Arcana only. They turn out to be the Four of Cups, the Seven of Coins, the Three of Batons reversed, the Five of Coins, the Seven of Swords reversed, and the Knave of Cups. You may care to set these cards out on a table in front of you to better follow what I say.

Now, the first question I'm going to ask of these cards is, "What are the prospects for the new relationship I'm getting into?"

First, look up the Four of Cups. You will notice that Etteilla gives seventeen different interpretations, Mathers and Waite far fewer. Of all of these, I am going to select Etteilla's "concern," just because I feel it's the most pertinent.

Now look up the Seven of Coins. Etteilla lists eleven interpretations, Mathers an additional two, Waite three more. Of these, I feel Etteilla's "candor" to be the most appropriate.

Moving on to the Three of Batons reversed; out of the seventeen or so meanings listed by our cartomancers, I'm going to pick Etteilla's "cessation."

The Five of Coins requires a choice between Waite's dismal interpretation "destitution" or Etteilla's and Mathers's focus on love. Under the circumstances, the latter interpretation seems the most suitable, so I'm choosing "lover."

Now we come to the Seven of Swords reversed. All the early cartomancers feel much the same unease about this card, so I'm going to go with the flow and pick "apprehension."

Lastly, we come to the Knave of Cups. He's upright here, so he's in his helpful, "La Hire" aspect. Etteilla describes this card as a him or her (remember, Knaves can represent youngsters of either gender); Mathers, as possessing integrity; and Waite, as one impelled to render service. In any case, it is a good augury.

So my reading in answer to the question "What are the prospects for the new relationship I'm getting into?" would be that there may at first be mutual concerns (Four of Cups) about honesty (Seven of Coins here) implying mutual commitment, but these will cease (Three of Batons, reversed), and that any further apprehensions (Seven of Swords reversed) will be dispelled over time by the recognition of the love and integrity demonstrated in the relationship (Knave of Cups).

Now let's use the same cards to answer the question "What are the prospects for my daughter getting into the college of her choice next year?"

Again, the Four of Cups will yield "concern." The Seven of Coins will now indicate "money;" the Three of Batons reversed, "influence," "intermediary," and "end of troubles;" and the Five of Coins, following Etteilla, "suitability." The Seven of Swords reversed brings "diligence" or "application," and the Knave of Cups, "study" and "application" again, and a good augury.

Therefore, my response to the query, "What are the prospects for my daughter getting into the college of her choice next year?" would be that the worry you have (Four of Cups) about financial aspects of this event (Seven of Coins) will be taken care of through the influence of a helpful intermediary, possibly someone connected with the college (Three of Batons reversed), who will be convinced of your daughter's suitability (Etteilla's Five of Coins). All your daughter need concentrate on is diligence and application (Seven of Swords reversed) in her studies, to bring about a happy outcome (Knave of Cups).

Finally, we'll ask the question, "Shall I be successful in my present undertaking?"

I will take the Four of Cups to indicate "worry" again, the Seven of Coins to mean "ingenuousness" or "innocence," the Three of Batons reversed to mean "cessation of torment," the Five of Coins to indicate "affinity" or "suitability," or maybe even Waite's "destitution." The Seven of Swords reversed yields Waite's "anxiety about money proposed to lend," and the Knave of Cups supplies "the profession" and "one impelled to render service."

My reading would then go something like this: Worry (Four of Cups) about your lack of experience (Seven of Coins) will cease (Three of Batons) when it is seen that you are instantly afflicted neither by disaster nor by your fears of your unsuitability for the task before you (Five of Coins). The only caveat would be that the amount of money you initially invest should be a prudent one (Seven of Swords reversed). Bearing this caution in mind, your business experience should be a happy one, made more so by the presence of a young helpful business associate (Knave of Cups).

Now here is a reading that uses both Arcanas.

I draw seven cards unseen from the well-shuffled pack. They are the Ten of Batons reversed, the Juggler, the Seven of Cups reversed, the Pope, the King of Swords reversed, the Three of Swords reversed, and the Sun. The question I shall ask is, "What is the prognosis for X's mother's illness?"

Note to begin with the comparatively large proportion of trumps that have appeared, indicating the gravity of the question. This may be accentuated by the two Sword cards, which can generally indicate, as you may recall, mental challenges or painful issues.

For the Ten of Batons reversed, I shall select "obstacle" or "inconvenience" from Etteilla's list. For the Juggler, I shall select Mathers's "skill" and Waite's "diplomacy"—interpretations that experience has taught me to approve. For the Seven of Cups reversed I choose Etteilla's "project" and Waite's "definite plan of action"; for the Pope, "orthodox science"— in this case medicine and therapeutic counseling—for the King of Swords reversed, Etteilla's "doctor" and "inhumanity" and Waite's "cruel" or "despotic." Lastly, there's no doubt about the Sun's meaning being "good health" and "abundant joy."

So the reading I would give in response to "What is the prognosis for X's mother's illness?" would be this: The inconvenience she is presently experiencing (Ten of Batons reversed) may be overcome by skillful diplomacy (the Juggler), but what is needed is a determined plan of action (Seven of Cups reversed) rather than just vague hopes, that orthodox medicine and therapeutic counseling (the Pope) should be called on, but that X should steer clear of a certain overbearing and heavy-handed doctor (King of Swords reversed), who will only cause X's mother more confusion (Three of Swords reversed). The final card (the Sun) indicates that the prospect for the outcome is one of the best, a complete cure and healthy life.

You may not be able to integrate all the cards in your first attempts at card linking, and that's to be expected. To my way of thinking, it really does constitute advanced work. But with practice, one begins to see how the meaning of one card generates or specifies the meanings of others.

Horoscope Spreads

The card reading method I am about to describe next will constitute our first expedition into the territory of card linking. Because it utilizes the formal layout of horoscope houses, the horoscope spread also happens to be effective for obtaining information on definite points. I believe the method was introduced by Etteilla, then later taken up by a variety of Parisian cartomancers, including the fabled Madame Clément and Edmond. It was subsequently incorporated into the Golden Dawn's complicated five-step process of reading the tarot that they named *The Opening of the Key*. However, the layout comes in all shapes and sizes and is also known as the Astrological Spread, the Zodiac Spread, and the Wheel. Here are a couple of variants. The first is a reputedly Italian layout that I discovered in a book on divination that my father, Richard Carl Huson, edited in 1936.

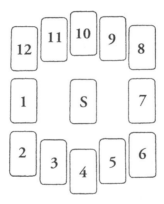

An Italian Method

This method requires the inclusion of the Major Arcana, so be prepared for the possibility of unsettling results. The significator should be placed centrally and the cards shuffled, cut, and fanned out, facedown as usual. The inquirer must now select forty-eight cards at random, making a pile of them, still facedown, one upon the other.

Now, deal the selected cards from the top of their pile—turning them faceup but making sure to preserve their upright or reversed orientation exactly the way it is—into a circle of twelve heaps of four cards each. Begin your first pile at center left and proceed counterclockwise, building up the heaps in rotation as the accompanying illustration indicates. This pattern will, of course, be familiar to students of astrology, representing as it does the chart of the twelve horoscope houses. As we noted in an earlier chapter, each house governs a specific area of human experience. The sentences formed by the cards should be read accordingly:

House 1. The state of mind of the inquirer and the general circumstances surrounding him or her.

House 2. His or her possessions and financial affairs.

House 3. His or her communication skills; also casual travel and neighbors.

House 4. Home life, where he or she lives; also the inquirer's mother.

House 5. The inquirer's creativity, pleasures, love life, or children.

House 6. The inquirer's work; also health.

House 7. The inquirer's marriage or partnerships, sexual or otherwise.

House 8. Possessions gained through others, legacies, or deaths.

House 9. The inquirer's philosophy, deeper quests, travel to distant parts.

House 10. The inquirer's career, self-expression in the world; also the inquirer's father.

House 11. The inquirer's connections, social contacts, friends, image.

House 12. The inquirer's burdens, restrictions, and secret fears.

Edmond's Method

I have adapted this second type of horoscope spread from one proposed by the once-famous nineteenth-century French cartomancer Edmond Billaudot, who was known by only his first name. Here you will select the significator as usual, but leave it *in* the deck. Now have the inquirer shuffle and cut the entire deck of seventy-eight cards. He or she must then draw cards unseen from the fanned deck, distributing them *faceup* and counterclockwise to make a circle of twelve piles, taking care to preserve the order and upright or reversed orientation of each card and noting the location of the significator when it turns up. As indicated in the figure on page 267, your first card should be placed where nine o'clock is positioned on a clock face (the first house), your second at eight o'clock (the second house), and so on until you have used up the entire deck. In this spread each house will end up with a stack of six or seven cards.

The packet containing the significator is now removed and the other eleven heaps discarded.

Having noted the house that the significator was found in and the special field of interest it represents, the packet of cards should now be spread out from left to right, top card first. Now begin linking the cards together as a reading, working in the direction in which the significator is facing, beginning with the farthest card in the line, to the right or left as the case may be. Work your way through all six or seven cards, applying their significance, remember, to the field of interest that the horoscope house represents. If a significator makes its appearance *reversed*, far from indicating something dire for the inquirer, it simply means that the cards should be read in the *opposite* direction from that in which the significator is facing. Should the significator not face in either direction but be presented full face, or have no face at all in the event it's a trump card, then whether or not it's reversed, read the cards from right to left, beginning with the farthest card on the right.

On the other hand, should the significator lead the line of cards, facing away from them, then the reading is to be considered null and void. Another type of reading should be attempted, using a different spread and, if possible, rephrasing any question asked.

Twenty-One-Card Spreads

Somewhat more complex than the foregoing spreads, here are three methods of divining that use twenty-one cards.

Method I

This first spread is another traditional "gypsy" method popular since the 1920s. Like the horoscope spreads presented above, it is equally useful in generating a general reading or a response to a specific question: it utilizes a format compartmentalized into areas indicative of prevailing psychological conditions, home influences, aspirations, expectations, and so on.

Having selected your significator and placed it in front of you, shuffle and cut the deck in the correct manner, and invite the inquirer to select twenty-one cards at random and unseen from the deck. Distribute these facedown in a semicircle from left to right, building seven piles of three cards each as indicated by the figure on page 269. Now turn the piles over, carefully preserving their orientation, and read them in the order in which they were distributed, cards one, two, three, and so on.

The pile of three cards on the far left-hand side of the arc is said to represent the inquirer's personality, specifically his or her present psychological condition. Cards four, five, and six depict present home life. Cards seven, eight, and nine show his or her present desires. Ten, eleven and twelve indicate the inquirer's expectations. Thirteen, fourteen, and fifteen show what is not expected. Sixteen, seventeen, and eighteen show the immediate future, and nineteen, twenty, and twenty-one show more long-term influences.

Method II

Methods II and III are best used for answering a specific question of some importance. Both require that you use the entire deck of seventy-eight cards, so be prepared for input from the Major Arcana.

Select the significator but leave it in the deck. After shuffling and cutting, all the cards should now be distributed, faceup, in six rows of thirteen, whether left to right or right to left doesn't matter, but you should keep them consistent.

You must now find the preselected significator and then, moving in the direction indicated by the gaze of the character on the card, or in the event of this being inapplicable, in the direction in which the cards were laid down, count seven cards along, counting the significator as card number one. The seventh card will become the first card of your reading, which you can lay to one side to facilitate matters. Count seven more cards along now to find the second card of your reading, and lay it beside the first; and so on.

When you come to the end of the row closest to you, return to the beginning of the top row and continue your counting until the full complement of twenty-one has been read as one long "sentence" in answer to the inquirer's question. Begin with the first card you laid aside and end with the twenty-first.

Method III

Method III relies on the same layout as Method II but harks back to the days of the oracle books, requiring that a pair of dice be shaken and cast by the inquirer. The sum of the two dice faces indicates the number of cards to be counted along, starting from the significator, traveling in the direction of its gaze or the order of the cards in which they were laid down, as the case may be. Again, the first card to be read is the first selected by the dice throw, and the reading is complete when twenty-one cards have been selected in this manner.

As I have indicated, in both Methods II and III, it is helpful if the diviner removes the cards as they are counted out and places them away from the bulk of the others for closer scrutiny and linking. Again, this is a method to be applied to answering a single question.

Of course, both methods may be considerably simplified by just counting out the required cards from an upward-facing deck. This detracts from the ritual, however, which I think is an important psychological part of the process.

COMPLEX SYSTEMS

Until you are completely at ease with the practice of linking the cards, my advice is that you stay with the simpler systems. The complex ones are for experts. However, when you are ready, here are three that I believe to be among the most significant. The first is attributed to one of the nineteenth-century interpreters of Etteilla, Julia Orsini, of "Faubourg Saint-Germain" notoriety, whom we encountered in an earlier chapter.

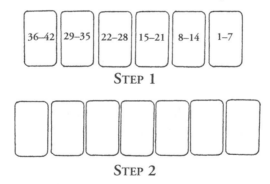

The Oracles of Julia Orsini

Step 1

No significator is to be preassigned in this method. After you have prepared the cards in your usual manner, the inquirer should select forty-two cards at random from the entire deck, sight unseen of course, and distribute them face upward to form a row of six piles, seven cards to each. Selected cards one through seven should be contained in the first pile on the right; eight through fourteen in a pile to the left of the first , and so on. As always, care should be taken as the cards are distributed to preserve their upright and reversed orientations.

Step 2

Take up the first pile on the right and lay it out, right to left, still face-down. Take up the second pile and also deal it out right to left on top of the cards from the first pile, as demonstrated in the figure on page 271. Repeat this process until the six seven-card piles are exhausted and you are now confronted by seven six-card piles.

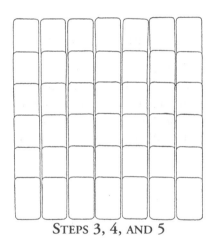

STEPS 3, 4, AND 5

Step 3

Skim off the top card of each pile, shuffle them together, and lay them out, right to left as always, in a new row.

Step 4

Take the next two cards from each pile, shuffle them, and lay them out as two new rows below the first.

Step 5

Gather up the remaining twenty-one cards, shuffle them, and lay them out in three rows beneath your first three. Once again, you are con-fronted by six rows of seven cards.

Step 6

Search for the significator. In this instance, the Pope (Hierophant) must be used for a male inquirer, the Female Pope (High Priestess) for a female. If the card appears within the spread, remove it and place it to the left of the array if it is the Female Pope and to the right if it is the Pope. The inquirer should then draw another card unseen from the remaining deck of thirty-six cards to fill the gap. If the significator does not appear on the table, search the unused deck for it and place it on the left or right as indicated. This traditional step actually makes very little sense, unless we view it as an example of the magical "insertion"of the inquirer into the pack that we mentioned earlier.

Step 7

Read the cards beginning at the top right-hand corner, working right to left, and ending at the bottom left-hand comer.

As you see, this process uses no handy layout. There is no division of the pattern into convenient areas of interpretation, such as "past" and "future." It offers no external support to the diviner, and therefore should be reckoned one of the most advanced processes. The cards must literally "speak" to the cartomancer, who has to rely entirely on intuition as to which cards are the most important and relevant ones.

Etteilla's Method

This is the original method of tarot divination devised by Etteilla toward the end of the eighteenth century. It can actually be divided into two spreads, the first of which I call for convenience the Horseshoe Spread and the second by its traditional name, Etteilla's Great Figure of Destiny. Mathers adapted both of them and published his versions in his 1888 booklet on the tarot. What follow are Etteilla's original methods, however, not Mathers's.

The Horseshoe Spread

Step 1. No significator is required for this method. Having shuffled the entire deck of seventy-eight cards and invited the inquirer to cut the deck three times with the hand that he or she does not use for writing, deal the cards, facedown, into three piles—A, B, and C—of twenty-six cards each. One card must be placed on each of the piles in turn, working from left to right.

STEPS 1–4

Step 2. Pile B, the middle pile, should now be taken and placed off to the right. Piles A and C should then be gathered together and shuffled and cut three times by the inquirer.

Step 3. The shuffled cards of A and C should again be dealt out into three piles, of seventeen cards each—A, B, and C, again—working from left to right, and the remaining single card placed off to the left.

Step 4. Again remove the central pile, B, and place it off to the right, alongside the other B pile. Adding in the remaining single card placed off to the left, gather up piles A and C, which will amount to thirty-five cards, and invite the inquirer to shuffle and cut them three times.

Step 5. Deal these cards into three piles of eleven cards each, leaving two cards undealt. Place the central, B, pile to the right once again and discard the flanking piles A and C, along with the remaining two cards left over from the deal. Now turn your attention to the three remaining B piles off on your right.

Pick up the pile you made first, containing twenty-six cards. Lay out the cards it contains, faceup now, in a large horseshoe shape arcing away from you, placing the top card, which we shall call card number one, in the lower right-hand corner, and the bottom card, card number twenty-six, in the lower left-hand corner.

Then, working from right to left and linking the cards together as you go, begin your reading with card number one and end it on card number twenty-six. Etteilla says this arc refers to the inquirer's soul, which we may take to mean his or her psychological and emotional condition.

Having dispensed with the twenty-six cards, remove them and lay out the pile of seventeen from right to left in exactly the same manner. This arc deals with the inquirer's mind, his or her mental preoccupations, work, affections, abilities, and pastimes.

Now the last pile of eleven cards should be laid out in a small arc

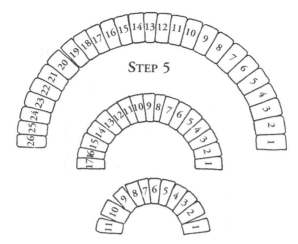

STEP 5

from right to left. This Etteilla refers to as the inquirer's body, his or her material condition, health, monetary situation, and environment.

Etteilla's Great Figure of Destiny

This spread uses sixty-six cards drawn from the full deck and does require the use of a significator.

After selecting your significator, placing it centrally, shuffling, and performing the triple cut, allow the inquirer to draw sixty-six cards one after another, unseen, of course. These should be placed face upward in the pattern illustrated on page 276.

Beginning at the bottom, place cards one through eleven in a column up the right-hand side of the table.

Now place cards twelve through twenty-two up the left-hand side in a similar column, leaving plenty of room in between.

Place cards twenty-three through thirty-three right to left along the top of the table, joining the two columns like a beam.

Now, within the two side pillars, starting toward the bottom and halfway between them, lay cards thirty-four through sixty-six around the significator in a counterclockwise circle. Leave gaps in your circle between cards forty-four and forty-five, between fifty-five and fifty-six, and between sixty-six and thirty-four (where the two ends of the circle join).

Finally, place the remaining eleven cards below the Significator in the circle. They will not be read.

Your spread is now complete.

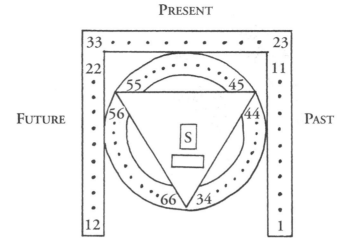

Cards one through eleven and thirty-four through forty-four are said by Etteilla to refer to the past. They must be read in pairs, one and thirty-four, two and thirty-five, and so on up to eleven and forty-four. Cards twenty-three through thirty-three and forty-five through fifty-five represent the present. Again, read them in pairs, twenty-three and forty-five, twenty-four and forty-six, and so on.

Cards twelve through twenty-two and fifty-six through sixty-six represent the future, what is yet to come for the inquirer. But here the cards in the center segment are to be read contrary to the order of their sequence, in pairs twelve and sixty-six, thirteen and sixty-five, and so on. (Both Mathers and Papus give variations at this point, but they don't follow the scheme that Etteilla quite obviously has in mind, so I won't trouble the reader with them).

As you can see, there are a great many cards to deal with here, and unless you have already acquired the knack of linking the meanings of the cards so that they blend together, the best you will achieve is a muddle of ideas and feelings that don't really cohere. So work up to this method. Don't attempt it at first. Your unconscious mind has to be led to the point where it can pick out and enlarge upon what it sees as the relevant tarot symbols, and this requires practice with the simpler spreads. The more card variables you place in your tarot layout, the more at ease with them you have to be.

LAST WORDS OF ADVICE

Don't worry about making a fool of yourself when you start reading the cards. Blurt out your impressions of the cards as you read them, without censoring or trying to edit them—always retaining some caution, however, about delivering destructive interpretations. This may sound like something of a balancing act, but it isn't all that difficult. Essentially what you do is give your unconscious mind free play within a set of limits that you yourself impose, like a rabbit in a pen.

You are bound to make as many errors as hits at first, but you will know when the cards start speaking to you and triggering your intuitions correctly. This can be a very exciting moment. Your concentration will become very intense and your inquirer will begin to find your perception eerily accurate.

Remember, too, that you can always stop if you need a rest; cartomancy can be very taxing at times. Try to empty your mind while you do this, then resume the reading when you're ready. If you go blank on a card, try repeating the card's name over and over to stimulate your associations.

Be aware any session can take one of two general directions: toward a "reading"—with verbal input from the inquirer—or toward a divination, without verbal input. An inquirer's questions will, of course, bend the interpretation you give the cards toward a practical end. This is exactly what is supposed to happen in any "reading" session. Readings rely as much on the cartomancer's common sense and powers of empathy as they do on extrasensory perception. The cards become talking points that inevitably lead to revelatory material. How insightful such readings turn out to be will depend to some degree on how accurate you are as a judge of character. With practice, you'll learn to distinguish between the feel of mere guesses and genuine intuitions. Persistent thoughts will finally strike you with particular impact; these are the ones to take note of.

As for prediction of the future, my feelings about the matter suggest that your accuracy will depend on just how deep your contact is with the collective unconscious. Looking back on card reading sessions, you may be surprised to learn just how much the cards reflected matters that later came to pass. With this in mind, you can ask your inquirers if they would mind your making notes on, or audio taping, their readings. This kind of feedback can be very helpful to your development as a cartomancer.

If you get completely stuck on the meaning or the relevance of a card, try psychometry on it. Lay your hand on it, blank your mind completely, and allow impressions to rise. This is something Waite suggested in his *Pictorial Key,* and it can sometimes work. However, if certain cards persist in making absolutely no sense, say so and skip them. Don't waffle. They may be alluding to something you can't even imagine now but that may well be revealed later.

And finally, here is one last word of very practical advice. You'll be surprised how many people enjoy having their cards read. Once news gets out that you read the tarot, you may find yourself being asked to bring your cards along with you wherever you go, which may or may not become a nuisance, depending on your inclination. Remember, you can always say no, and you *should* decline the request if you don't feel like performing. There's nothing worse than trying to do a reading when you're not in the mood. It won't please you, and it probably won't help the inquirer.

Enough said.

Appendix 1
HISTORICAL TAROT DECKS

Thoth divines the moral status of a human soul at its postmortem Judgment

Here is a selection of some of the historical tarot and tarocchi decks that I deal with in this book that may be used for divination, plus one or two others that I find useful, intriguing, or otherwise worthy of inclusion. Most of them are available today in newly created editions, in some cases as photo facsimiles made from museum or private collections. Bear in mind, however, that these are often considered "specialty" cards created for collectors or cartomancers, not decks created for card play, so many are printed in limited editions. Don't be disappointed if you have to hunt a little to find them. To make your search easier, appendix 2 provides a list of addresses and contact numbers for card publishers and distributors that I have found useful.

STANDARD PATTERNS

The word *pattern* (also *portrait*) used in connection with a deck of playing cards refers to its design. Also be aware that what are known by playing-card historians as "standard patterns," as for example the "Belgian" pattern, don't necessarily refer to the place where the cards were made but to where the pattern was recognized as the standard and used for card play.

The Marseille Tarot

The Marseille pattern is undoubtedly the most popular tarot pattern known today. Although the pattern was also produced in Paris, Belfort, and Avignon, its "Marseille" title was bestowed on the deck only fairly recently by the famous card manufacturer Grimaud. Grimaud CEO Paul Marteau had boldly adjusted the pattern in the 1920s, taking as his model the tarot of Nicholas Conver, an eighteenth-century card-maker from Marseille. Marteau issued his new deck during the 1930s under the title *Tarot de Marseilles,* and the pattern has borne the Marseille name ever since. Prior to Marteau's naming it, the pattern had simply been referred to as the "Italian" tarot. Indisputably deriving from an old Milanese playing-card pattern (see below under "The Tarot of Milan"), the Marseille pattern closely resembles cards from an uncut partial sheet of fifteenth-century Milanese tarots in the Cary Collection at the Beinecke Library, Yale University. It's my belief that something like the Cary-Yale sheet may well have been the pattern that provided the prototype for the painted decks of the Viscontis and D'Estes.

One of the older Marseille-pattern decks, designed by Claude Burdel in 1751, is available today in facsimile from Edizione Lo Scarabeo of Turin. On the other hand, probably the most famous Marseille tarot of all, the 1760 Tarot of Marseille of Nicholas Conver, has also been reproduced in facsimile by Lo Scarabeo, as well as by Héron-Boéchat of Bordeaux, by Edizione Il Meneghello of Milan, and by Dal Negro of Trieste. Piatnik of Vienna offers the Marseille Tarot of Ignaz Grebs, created in 1800. Grimaud's large, primary-colored Tarot of Marseille is still on the market, and as of the time of writing is available from U.S. Games Systems, Éditions Dusserre, and A. G. Müller of Switzerland.

The Marseille pattern was produced not only in France but also in Fribourg, and Neuchâtel, Switzerland. A Swiss Marseille-pattern deck, the 1804 deck of Jean Proche—an intermediate in style between the Marseille and the Besançon patterns—is currently available as the Swiss Tarot (1804) from Edizione Il Meneghello, Milan.

The Lombardy Tarot

Because the areas of northern Italy known as Piedmont and Lombardy lie next door to each other, it's little wonder that a certain amount of confusion exists about the names applied to tarocchi decks that developed in places. However, playing-card historians generally reserve the name "Lombardy" tarocchi for the pattern closely related to the Marseille pattern that appeared during the eighteenth century in Lombardy and used French titles, even though the decks were made by Italian card makers.

Aside from their French titles, you can recognize Lombardy-pattern decks from several characteristic features: the Devil generally wears a pair of furry pants, the Moon is depicted full face, Justice is winged, the Ace of Cups is depicted as a Gothic font, and the King and Queen of Coins wear unmistakable and idiosyncratic crowns. Examples of decks using this pattern were produced by card makers in Bologna, Modena, Padua, and Trieste, among other places. Later, interest in this pattern developed in Milan, where the cards acquired Italian titles. As a standard pattern, it has now been replaced in popularity in Milan by the Piedmont pattern (see below under "The Piedmont Tarot").

There are a large number of Lombardy-pattern tarocchi available today, although they call themselves by a variety of names. An attractive reproduction of the *All'Aquila* Milanese deck of Giacomo Zoni printed in 1780 in subtle earth colors is offered by Edizione Il Meneghello of Milan under the somewhat misleading title of *Gioco di 78 Carte Bologna XVIII Secolo,* and another version is offered by Lo Scarabeo of Turin. Il Meneghello markets a deck produced in Milan around 1840 by the innovative card maker Ferdinando Gumppenberg as *Tarocco di 78 Carte F. Gumppenberg, Milano, 1840c.,* and offers another double-headed deck dating from around 1880, called *Tarocchino Milanese a Doppia Figura.* To use these double-headers for divination, you have to mark the cards to signify a definite upright orientation if you plan to use the reversed-card interpretations.

Meneghello also carries a deck of elegant, tinted engravings that Teodoro Dotti created in 1845, which Meneghello promotes as *Tarocco Italiano Ristama Fedelissima di un Gioco della Fabrica Dotti—Milano—1845.* W. B. Yeats, the poet and an early member of the Order of the Golden Dawn, seems to have used an engraved and color-stenciled Dotti deck for his divinations rather than attempt to create one in the pattern of the official Order deck—an ordeal for a nonartist if ever there was one—as he would have been entitled to do as a high-grade adept.

The Tarot of Milan

Many historians today believe the Milanese pattern of the tarot to have been the first created. The partial sheet of wood-block-printed fifteenth-century cards in the Cary Collection is the only sample we presently have of it. Its iconography indicates a close similarity to the Marseille pattern, which historians theorize derived from it. Cards designed in the Milanese pattern seem to have been used in Milan until the time when production of tarocchi was proscribed under an economically repressive Spanish regime that governed the state from 1535 to 1713.

The so-called Milanese standard pattern to be found today, however, was actually developed from the Marseille pattern by the card manufacturer Ferdinando Gumppenberg, beginning in 1810, after Milan had passed into Austrian hands. Gumppenberg published a pretty deck of tinted engravings that are fussily but delicately drawn in the Neoclassical style typical of the early nineteenth century. This deck substitutes the

southern-Italian and Spanish-style cudgels for the northern-style batons, and straight swords for curved blades. Promoted today as *Antichi Tarocchi Lombardi* (Ancient Tarots of Lombardy), a handsome reproduction of these cards can today be obtained from Lo Scarabeo.

More sophisticated were the designs created later by Carlo della Rocca, an early-nineteenth-century artist who worked for Gumppenberg. His tarot decks from 1823 to 1840 are more obviously based on the Marseille pattern, reverting to batons and curved swords, all interpreted in a florid Victorian manner. A fine facsimile reprint of della Rocca's 1835 tarot and a very similar deck dating from 1880 are also available from Lo Scarabeo. Della Rocca's splendid and practically identical "*Soprafino*" deck (1835) and his 1840 deck are available from Meneghello of Milan.

The Piedmont Tarot

The Piedmont standard pattern or Tarot of Piedmont was also originally a variant of the Marseille pattern. Confusingly, this deck can also go by the name of the Tarot of Venice.

Produced by French card manufacturers during the eighteenth century, probably at Lyons, the Piedmont Tarot was exported to Nice and to Piedmont in Italy, where it gained an individuality all its own. It strayed from the Marseille pattern in a number of ways—by putting a face on the Devil's belly, by showing the Moon as a half-moon in profile, and by giving a caption, *La Morte,* to the Death trump, a card generally left unnamed. At the end of the nineteenth century the Piedmont Tarot adopted double-headed cards to aid in card play, and modern Piedmont trumps tend to have Arabic numerals rather than the roman numerals of the old ones.

Double-headed *Tarocchi Piemontese* printed by Masenghini of Bergamo are available, as is a facsimile of the full-length deck designed in 1860 by Giovanbattista Guala in soft blues, golds, and reds, to which fortune-telling interpretations printed in Italian have been added at the base of each card. This deck is published by Lo Scarabeo of Turin as *Antichi Tarocchi Divinatori*. Modiano of Trieste and Dal Negro of Trieste publish the widely available modern, double-headed plastic-coated decks.

The Besançon Tarot

A further Marseille-derived tarot pattern is that designated the Tarot of Besançon, a French town lying on the border of Switzerland, just above Geneva. This is one of the patterns that contain the eighteenth-century, papally correct substitutes Juno and Jupiter in place of the Female Pope and Pope. Although it still carried French captions, the Besançon Tarot was once used by German-speaking card players in eastern France, Switzerland, and parts of Germany.

A beautiful and subtly colored facsimile of a Besançon Tarot is available today from Edizione Il Meneghello, Milan.

The Swiss Tarot

A Besançon tarot offspring that you might consider owning is the Swiss pattern, also known as the "JJ" pattern, alluding to the initial letters of

Juno and Jupiter. This tarot was introduced in the mid-nineteenth century, as is apparent from the dress style of the figures on the cards. A beautifully engraved example of this pattern is available in a facsimile edition from A. G. Müller, and U. S. Games Systems.

The Tarot of Jacques Viéville

Although accounted by some a Belgian pattern, playing-card and games historian Thierry Depaulis conjectured that the Jacques Viéville deck represents a seventeenth-century combination of the Marseille and Bologna patterns.

A fine photographic facsimile of this deck with a commentary and set of tarot game rules by Depaulis was published by Heron-Boéchat of Bordeaux. I bought a deck in Belgium a few years ago, and I recently saw decks being advertised at the playing-card museum in Issy-les-Moulineaux, Paris. It's worth trying to get hold of a deck if you can, as the images are very striking.

The Tarot of Bologna

The Bolognese pattern of tarocchi has been around since the middle of the fifteenth century, possibly 1459, and is probably the oldest pattern still in active use as a game. The deck is restricted, consisting of only sixty-two cards: the suit cards two through five have been dropped. Navigators often appear on the Moon trump, and a spinner with her distaff on the Sun trump. The four cards that so frequently gave offense to church authorities, namely the Pope, Female Pope, Emperor, and

Empress, were replaced by four spear-carrying Moors or Satraps in 1725, after Bologna fell under papal influence. At one time—but no longer, apparently—these decks were called *tarocchini,* meaning "little tarocchi," and some say this term referred to the cards' narrowness rather than the curtailment of the suit cards.

Since the second half of the eighteenth century, the standard Bolognese-patterned decks meant for card play have included double-headed court cards and trumps.

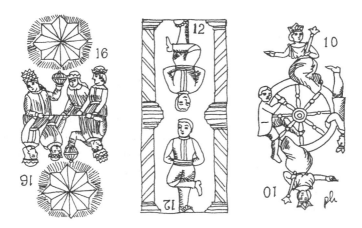

Today the modernized Bolognese pattern can be bought in a slim and elegant double-headed deck printed by Modiano of Trieste. Cambissa of Trieste has also published a deck, as has Dal Negro of Trieste. Dal Negro and Il Meneghello have also published beautiful reproductions of the *Tarocchini di Gioseppe Maria Mitelli,* a set of twenty-two trumps and forty suit cards that first appeared as six book plates in 1664 and were designed by the renowned engraver Mitelli. The trumps are uncaptioned and unnumbered, and among other changes, the Female Pope has been transformed into another male Pope, and the Emperor and Empress into the Western and Eastern Emperor.

The Belgian Tarot

The Besançon-pattern tarot, in its turn, gave rise to the eighteenth-century Belgian pattern, produced exclusively in Belgium. Incongruously, the Belgian pattern replaces the Female Pope with a card captioned the "Spanish Captain Fracasse" (misspelled "Eracasse" in some decks), depicting a

character borrowed from the commedia dell'arte, sixteenth-century Italian improvisational theater of a farcical nature. The Pope is charmingly replaced by Bacchus astride a wine barrel. Hmm . . .

In the Belgian pattern, The Hanged Man now dangles by his neck and not his foot, and the Tower is replaced by a shepherd under the tree—as we noted earlier, perhaps a reference to the *Mystery Play of the Shepherds.* The eighteenth-century Brussels card maker F. I. Vandenborre produced a deck that is currently available as a quaint and wonderful reprint by A. G. Müller in conjunction with Carta Mundi.

The Minchiate of Florence

According to the pioneering playing-card collector Sylvia Mann, the word *minchiate* translates roughly as "to play at trumps." As we have seen, the minchiate deck contains ninety-seven cards, which include the twelve

signs of the zodiac and the four elements, plus various substitutions, additions, and omissions from the "regular" tarot trump sequence. The pattern was introduced in Florence in the sixteenth century and had spread to Genoa and Sicily by the late nineteenth. Various reproductions of this standard pattern are now available.

Lo Scarabeo has produced an elegant *"Etruria"* edition of delicately tinted engravings from 1725 Florence. Another deck—similarly from 1725 and also entitled *"Etruria"* (maybe they're from the same original?) but with richer, duskier tones—has been published by Edizione Il Meneghello. This company also offers the *"Fiorentine"* deck, whose colors are brighter still, though of clumsier design, being printed from a woodblock dated 1850.

Unique Decks

Obviously, the patterns listed above do not embrace "one-off" decks that were specially commissioned by certain people or families like the Viscontis, D'Estes, or Sola-Buscas. Facsimiles of the most famous of these unique decks are now available. With these I also include certain mixed-parentage decks and decks produced solely for divination.

Bembo's Visconti-Sforza (Morgan-Bergamo) Tarot

Several versions of the Visconti-Sforza deck are currently available, photographically reproduced from the original cards in the collections of the Pierpont Morgan Library, the Casa Colleone, and the Accademia Carrara, Bergamo. U.S. Games Systems. has published one version, A. G. Müller another, Edizione Il Meneghello a third, Dal Negro a fourth. Lo Scarabeo has also published a striking deck painted by the Bulgarian artist Atanas Alexander Atanassov, very closely following the Visconti designs and incorporating brilliant gold backgrounds similar to those of the originals. I had not realized quite how dazzling those backgrounds have remained through all the centuries until I saw some of the original cards in the Accademia Carrara in Bergamo recently.

Bembo's Visconti Cary-Yale/Modrone Tarot

As far as I know, only U.S. Games Systems. has published a facsimile edition of the Visconti Cary-Yale/Modrone Tarot, an important deck also attributed to Bonifacio Bembo. Several of the cards are missing, and there are extra court cards, including female Pages, female Knights, and extra Virtue trumps. The cards are believed to have been painted for Francesco Sforza of Milan, sometime between 1440 and 1450. The facsimiles tend to be a bit dim, and the silver and gold illumination does not photograph well, but they of enormous historical interest.

The Tarocchi of Mantegna

Facsimiles of the extremely interesting set of fifteenth-century black-and-white Mantegna engravings that we examined in chapter 3 (it's not really a deck of cards) are available from both Il Meneghello and Lo Scarabeo. As noted, it has particular relevance to Renaissance philosophical and Hermetic issues.

The Sola-Busca Tarot

Lo Scarabeo issued a colorful rendition (not facsimile) of the wonderfully eccentric fifteenth-century Sola-Busca cards under the title *Illuminating Ancient Tarots,* and U.S. Games Systems. currently carries them in the United States. They're difficult to use for divination unless you associate specific meanings to them. For a tarot enthusiast like me, however, it's a treat to own a deck. They're very curious and special, being for the most part surrealistically conceived or grotesque images of Worthies, heroines, and villains, historical, biblical, and legendary. As we have seen, Pamela Colman Smith used several of them as starting points for her designs for Waite's Minor Arcana.

Mulûk Wanuwwâb, the Mamlûk Cards

The historically pivotal Mamlûk cards were photographically reproduced some years ago in a limited edition of 750 copies by Carta Mundi, published by Aurelia Books of Brussels and Louvain. The original cards in the Topkapi Sarayi Museum are from a partial deck, itself augmented by cards from other old decks. The Carta Mundi edition supplied simulations to fill in the missing originals. Altogether, these are a prize, if you can get hold of a set, but again, no use for divination. U.S. Games Systems. used to carry them, but the secondhand market may be your only recourse now.

The Tarot of Paris

In 1985 the illustrious playing-card company B. P. Grimaud published a beautiful facsimile edition of the famous early- seventeenth-century Tarot of Paris, using photographs of the deck possessed by the Bibliothèque

Nationale, Paris, and offering an informative booklet by Depaulis. The bookstore of the Bibliothèque used to carry it, and may still. It is another collector's gem. A mixture of French, Italian, and Spanish themes, the Tarot of Paris remains in its way as much of an enigma as the early painted decks.

Etteilla's Tarot

As we have seen, Etteilla's cards, and the decks based on them, came in a variety of versions. They still do. These are extremely important to the history of cartomancy, providing as they do most of the Minor Arcana cartomantic interpretations that became standard. However, as I indicated earlier, the Etteilla decks took gross liberties with the order, names, and even identities of the historical trumps.

If you do wish to use them or simply add them to your collection, a selection of decks is available. Grimaud offers the quaintly bourgeois *Grand Etteilla ou Tarots Egyptiens,* in which the designs match Etteilla's original deck; Éditions Dusserre publishes a facsimile of a set in the Bibliothèque Nationale, the altered and gothicized *Tarot Egyptien–Grand Jeu de l'Oracle des Dames.* Lo Scarabeo of Turin has also published a version of an Etteilla deck entitled Esoteric Ancient Tarots, which first saw the light of day between 1870 and 1880 under the odd name of *Jeu de la Princesse Tarot* (Game of the Princess Tarot). By far the most "thorough" deck available, I suppose, is one entitled *Tarocco Egiziano* from Dal Negro, Trieste, which covers its bases on each card with an image of an Etteilla *Tarot Egyptien,* a Hebrew letter, a tiny Italian tarot card, and a French suit card! Etteilla packs are available from a variety of sources, including U.S. Games Systems, Llewellyn, and France-Cartes.

The Papus Tarot

The Papus Tarot cards are very handsome, facsimiles of the designs created by Gabriel Goulinat for Papus's 1909 book, *Le Tarot Divinatoire.* They are published by Éditions Dusserre and are a must for the diligent collector of fine tarot cards. If you use them for divination, you will note that Papus reverted to Etteilla's original interpretations.

The Golden Dawn Tarot

U.S. Games Systems has published one version of the Golden Dawn Tarot, Llewellyn Publications, another. Based upon notebooks and records of the Order, the U.S. Games Systems cards were painted by Robert Wang in collaboration with Israel Regardie, who brought practical experience to the project as an initiate of the Stella Matutina—a later development of the Golden Dawn. The Llewellyn deck was created by Sandra T. Cicero, also apparently with the encouragement of Regardie. Be aware, however, that there are decks on the market with "Golden Dawn" in their titles that have little or nothing to do with the Order or its tarot. So before you buy, make quite sure what you're getting. As previously noted, Darcy Küntz has published, in booklet form, facsimiles of the black-and-white line drawings of the original Golden Dawn court cards only, which he has entitled "As Drawn by William Wynn Westcott and Moïna Mathers." These rather crudely executed drawings are, presumably, the genuine articles.

Thoth Tarot Cards

The Golden Dawn cards were the inspiration for illustrations by painter Frieda Harris for a book about tarot written by the ex–Golden Dawn magician Aleister Crowley, which he entitled, not entirely originally, the *Book of Thoth: A Short Essay on the Tarot of the Egyptians*. The book was published on March 21, 1944. Llewellyn subsequently published the illustrations by themselves as a deck of cards in the late 1960s; U.S. Games Systems has since published a deck, as have A. G. Müller and several other publishers. Though of great occult interest, the Thoth cards bear very little similarity to historical tarot decks, although many cartomancers enjoy using them. They reflect Crowley's own personal philosophy, which some consider an advantage.

The Rider-Waite Tarot

Probably the most well-known divinatory tarot deck today, the cards designed to A. E. Waite's specifications by Pamela Colman Smith in 1909 may be obtained at almost any bookstore. They may be found in their original 1910 color scheme—reprinted in Belgium and published by Rider and Co., England, and by U.S. Games Systems—as The Original Rider Waite Tarot Deck. They have also been produced in many versions, in all colors, shapes, and sizes, by U.S. Games Systems, A. G. Müller, Dal Negro, and Lo Scarabeo.

Appendix 2
WHERE TO BUY
YOUR CARDS

Unfortunately, the reproductions of old tarot and tarocchi decks that used to be available at bookstores and Italian tobacconists have often been edged out by new, catchier cartomantic decks with designer-generated imagery so idiosyncratic that it frequently has little to do with historical tarot at all. So, aside from checking with your local or online bookstores and tarot sites, you may wish to write, fax, or Web site e-mail any of the sources listed below if you're in search of a particularly hard-to-find historical tarot deck. Publishers Llewellyn and U.S. Games Systems and card distributors Somerville, Il Trigono, and Alida have (as of the time of writing) good selections of the older decks.

UNITED STATES

Llewellyn Publications

P. O. Box 64383-052
St. Paul, Minnesota 55164-0383
Phone: 651 291 1970
Fax: 651 291 1908
Web site: www.llewellyn.com/

U.S. Games Systems

179 Ludlow Street
Stamford, CT 06902
Fax: 203 353 8431
Web site:
http://www.usgamesinc.com/

UNITED KINGDOM

InterCol

43 Templars Crescent
London N3 3QR
England
Phone: 011 20 8349 2207
Fax: 011 20 8346 9539
Web site: www.intercol.co.uk

Rider Books

Random House
20 Vauxhall Bridge Road
London SW1V 2SA
United Kingdom
Phone: 011 20 7840 8400

Fax: 011 20 7840 8406
Web site: www.randomhouse.co.uk
(The formerly titled Rider-Waite, now
Waite–Colman Smith, deck is obtain-
able through U.S. Games Systems)

EUROPE

A. G. Müller
Bahnhofstrasse 21
CH 8212, Neuhausen am Rheinfall,
Switzerland
Phone: 011 41 (0) 52 674 03 30
Fax: 011 41 (0) 52 674 03 40
E-mail: info@agm.ch
Web site: http://www.agm.ch/

Alida
Salita alla Rocca, 4
47890 Repubblica di San Marino,
Italy
Web site: http://www.alidastore.com/

Carta Mundi
Visbeekstraat 22
B-2300 Turnhout, Belgium
Phone: 011 32 (0) 14/42 02 01
Fax: 011 32 (0) 14/42 82 54
Web site: http://www.cartamundi.com/

Dal Negro
Fabbrica Carta da Gioco
Piazza Cavazerani, 9
31030 Carbonera
Treviso, Italy
Phone: 011 39 0422 6922
Fax: 011 39 0422 397625
Fax: 011 39 0422 692490
E-mail: info@dalnegro.com
Web site: www.dalnegro.com

Éditions Dusserre
4 rue Nansouty
75014 Paris, France

Phone: 011 (1) 45 89 40 21
Fax: 011 (1) 45 89 76 31

France-Cartes
49, Rue Alexandre 1er, BP 49
54130 Saint-Max Cedex,
France
Phone: 011 33 03 83 21 32 32
Fax: 011 33 03 83 21 99 39
E-mail: contact@frances-cartes.fr
Web site: http://www.france-cartes.fr/

Grimaud is now published by
France-Cartes.

Héron-Boéchat is now distributed in
France by France-Cartes; in Italy by
Dal Negro.

Il Meneghello
Edizioni di Osvaldo Menegazzi
Via Fara, 15
Milano, Italy
Phone: 011 39 02/ 670 28 17
Phone: 011 39 02/ 670 31 85

Il Trigono
Via Roma 112
Vicofertile
43040 Parma, Italy
Phone: 011 39 0521 674000
Fax: 011 39 0521 672733
Web site:
http://www.trigono.com/tarots/index
.htm

Lo Scarabeo
Via Varese 15c
10152 Torino, Italy.
Phone: 011 39 011 283793
Fax: 011 39 011 280756
E-mail: info@loscarabeo.com
Web site: www.loscarabeo.com

Masenghini
Fabbrica da Gioco
Jolly Joker S.r.l
Piazza Cavazerani, 9
31030 Carbonera
Treviso, Italy
Phone: 011 39 0422 398406
Fax: 011 39 0422 699374
E-mail: info@masenghini.it
Web site: www.masenghini.it

Modiano
Via Travnik, 21
San Dorligo della Valle
34018 Trieste, Italy
Phone: 011 39 040 389311
Fax: 011 39 040 827716
E-mail: info@modiano.it
Web site: www.modiano.it/

Piatnik
Wiener Spielkartenfabrik
Ferdinand Piatnik & Söhne
Hütteldorfer Str. 229-231
Postfach 79
A-1141 Wien, Austria
Phone: 011 43 1 / 914 4151
Fax: 011 43 1 / 911 1445
E-mail: info@piatnik.com
Web site: www.piatnik.com

R. Somerville (Playing Cards)
Place de la Mairie
F-31420 ALAN, France
Phone: 011 33 (0)5 61 98 76 61
Fax: 011 33 (0)5 61 98 76 10
Web site:
http://www.playingcardsales.com

Appendix 3
WHERE TO SEE
THE ORIGINALS

The original decks mentioned in the text are possessed by the museums listed below. Before trying to see any, however, contact the museum to ascertain viewing days and hours, whether they currently have the cards you want on view, and whether you need to make an appointment. Most large libraries, such as the Bibliothèque Nationale in Paris, require you to obtain a reader's card before you can consult their private collections. So get in touch with them by mail or e-mail beforehand, explaining who you are and the nature of your visit, what you need to see, and whether it is for research purposes or simple interest. Be aware that you will often be asking to view priceless treasures, so the library staff needs assurance that you are honest, responsible, and genuine in your interest.

UNITED STATES

The Beinecke Rare Book and Manuscript Library

Yale University, 121 Wall Street, New Haven, Connecticut 06511, USA
Mailing address: P.O.Box 208240, New Haven, CT 06520
Phone: 203 432 2972
E-mail: ellen.cordes@yale.edu
  Partial printed tarocchi sheet from Milan (prototype of the Marseille pattern), old catalog no. I-1010.
  The Cary-Yale Visconti di Modrone tarocchi, partial deck consisting of sixty-seven cards, painted by Bonifacio Bembo.

The Metropolitan Museum of Art

1000 Fifth Avenue, New York, New York 10028-0198, USA
Phone: 212 570 3756
Fax: 212 570 3972

E-mail: education@metmuseum.org
Three uncut printed tarocchi
sheets from Ferrara or Venice.
Catalog no. 26.101.5, Harris
Brisbane Dick Collection.

The National Gallery of Art
600 Constitution Avenue NE,
Washington DC 20002, USA
Phone: 202 737 4215
E-mail: der-info@nga.gov
The Rosenwald Tarot Cards, uncut
printed sheet from Florence.
Rosenwald Collection, catalog
no. B.19823.
The fifty tarocchi of Mantegna
engravings, E-series. The Ailsa
Mellon Bruce Fund.
The fifty tarocchi of Mantegna
engravings, S-series. The
Rosenwald Collection.

The Pierpont Morgan Library
29 East 36th Street, New York, New
York 10016, USA (under reconstruc-
tion, scheduled for reopening 2006)
Phone: 212 685 0610
E-mail: media@morganlibrary.org
The Pierpont Morgan Visconti-
Sforza tarocchi, partial deck of
thirty-five cards painted by
Bonifacio Bembo.

UNITED KINGDOM
The British Museum
Great Russell Street, London WC1B
3DG, England
Phone: 011 (44) 020 7323 8299
E-mail:
information@thebritishmuseum.ac.uk
The Sola-Busca tarocchi, seventy-
eight uncolored engravings.

The Swiss Tarot of Johann Georg
Rauch.
The Albrecht Dürer tarocchi
engravings. Sloan Collection.

The Warburg Institute
Woburn Square, London WC1H 0AB,
England
Phone: 011 44 020 7862-8949
E-mail: Warburg.Library@sas.ac.uk
The Thoth Tarot, original water-
color designs by Frieda Harris
for Aleister Crowley's tarot.

EUROPE AND TURKEY
Accademia Carrara
Piazza Giacomo Carrara 82, 24121,
Bergamo, Italy
Phone: 011 39 035399640
Fax: 011 39 035224510
E-mail:
segr@accademiacarrara.bergamo.it
The Visconti-Sforza tarocchi,
partial deck of twenty-six
cards painted by Bonifacio
Bembo and an unknown artist
(identified by the museum as
Antonio Cigognara).

The Albertina Museum
Albertinaplatz 1, 1010 Vienna,
Austria
Phone: 011 43(0)1 534 83 0
Fax: 011 43(0)1 533 76 97
E-mail: info@albertina.at
The fifty Sola-Busca tarocchi
designs, uncolored engravings

Bibliothèque Municipale de Rouen
3 Rue Jacques Villon, 76043 Rouen,
CEDEX 1, France
Phone: 011 33 02 35 71 28 82
Fax: 011 33 02 35 70 01 56

E-mail: bm.villon@rouen.fr
> Partial deck of thirty Italian taroc-
> chi with Latin captions, printed
> and hand painted, probably
> from sixteenth-century Venice.
> Leber Collection, catalog
> no. 1352-XIV.

Bibliothèque Nationale
Département des Estampes et de la
Photographie, 58 rue de Richelieu, F-
75084 Paris, CEDEX 02, France
Phone: 011 (33) 01 53 79 83 80
Fax: 011 (33) 01 53 79 83 07
E-mail: estampes-photo@bnf.fr
> The so-called Charles VI partial
> deck, composed of seventeen
> hand-painted cards.
> The Egyptian Tarot of Etteilla.
> The Tarot of Jacques Viéville.
> The "Mantegna" tarocchi (S-series),
> fifty engravings.
> The Tarot of Marseille, Nicholas
> Conver, 1761.
> The Tarot of Paris.

Musée du Louvre
25058 Paris, CEDEX 01, France
Phone: 011 (33) 01 40 20 50 50
Fax: 011 (33) 01 40 20 54 42

E-mail: info@louvre.fr
> Uncut printed tarocchi sheet from
> Bologna (Rothschild Collection).

Museé Français de la Carte à Jouer
Galerie d'Histoire de la Ville, 16 rue
Auguste Gervais, 92130, Issy-les-
Moulineaux, France
Phone: 011 33 01 41 23 83 60
Fax: 011 33 01 41 23 83 66
E-mail: musee@ville-issy.fr
> Various tarot decks and tarocchi.

Musei Civici del Castello Visconteo
Viale XI Febbraio 35, 27100 Pavia,
Italy
Phone: 011 39 0382 – 33853/304816
Fax: 011 39 0382 – 303028
E-mail: museicivici@comune.pv.it
> Minchiate from Florence.

The Topkapi Sarayi Museum
Sultanahmet, Eminonu, Istanbul,
Turkey
Phone: 011 90 212 512 0480
Fax: 011 90 212 528 5991
E-mail: history@ee.bilkent.gov.tr
> The Mamlûk cards.

ABOUT THE ILLUSTRATIONS

Frontispiece: The Wheel of Fortune, after a ninth-century manuscript in the John Rylands Library, Manchester.

Page 9, left: King David. After an illustration of the Nine Worthies from *Le chevalier errant*, 1394, MS 12559, fol. 1. Bibliothèque Nationale, Paris.

Page 9, right: King Arthur and the Emperor Charlemagne. After an illustration of the Nine Worthies from *Le chevalier errant*, 1394, M.S. 12559, fol. 1. Bibliothèque Nationale, Paris.

Page 10: Death, the Devil, the Tower, the Star, the Lovers, Temperance, Justice, Fortitude, the Queens of Cups, Swords, and Coins, and the Juggler. After a partial sheet of printed woodcut tarocchi, Florence, fifteenth century. Rosenwald Collection, National Gallery of Art, Washington DC.

Page 12: Mars, after the fifteenth-century Mantegna engraving.

Page 13: The Female Pope, the Emperor, the Empress, the Moon, the Star, and the Juggler, after a partial sheet of woodcut tarocchi, probably from Milan, fifteenth century. Cary Collection, Beinecke Library, Yale University.

Page 15: The Mamlûk suit signs and their European derivatives.

CHAPTER 1

Page 21: "The Great King," Darius I of Persia, after a sixth to fifth century B.C.E. relief from Persepolis.

Page 23: Clockwise from the top left, the angels of Prudence, Justice, Temperance, and Fortitude, after Luca della Robbia, the ceiling of the Cardinal of Portugal's chapel, San Miniato al Monte, Florence.

Page 27: A Persian Magus, after a gold votive plaque in the British Museum, seventh to sixth century B.C.E.

CHAPTER 2

Page 34, top: Limbo and Hell-Mouth, after a sixteenth-century manuscript by Hubert Cailleau, showing the setting for the mystery play at Valenciennes, 1547. The blazing towers of limbo and hell lie at the far right of the stage. Lucifer rises above the tower of hell, mounted on a dragon.

Page 34, right: The Devil trump, after a card in the Tarot of Jacques Viéville, Paris, 1650.

Page 35, left: After an original devil's costume for a fifteenth-century mystery play, formerly in the possession of Count Dr. Hans Wilczek at Castle Seebarn, Korneuburg, Austria.

Page 35, right: After devils' masks for the mystery play at Sterzing, originally in the Ferdinandeum collection, Innsbrück.

Page 36: After the *Dance of Death,* by the sixteenth-century painter Jakob von Wyl. Death comes for the Emperor, the Pope, and the King.

Page 37: Dame Fortune, blindfolded and holding her ever-turning wheel, enthroned opposite Dame Wisdom (Prudence), holding her mirror and seated on her throne of virtues. Sixteenth-century French engraving.

Page 38: Pope Joan with her child, after a woodcut from the *Chronicle of Hartmann Schedel,* Nüremberg, 1493.

Page 40: Engraving by Erhard Schön in Leonhard Reymann's *Nativität Kalender,* Nüremberg, 1515, showing horoscope house images similar to six tarot trumps: the Wheel of Fortune, the Emperor, the Pope, Death, the Lovers, and the Sun.

CHAPTER 3

Page 43: Thoth, the Egyptian god of wisdom and writing, after the papyrus of Taukherit, twenty-first dynasty, Rijkmuseum van Oudheden, Leiden.

Page 46: After images from *Eyn Loszbuch ausz der Karten gemacht,* an early-sixteenth-century German oracle book involving the use of playing cards.

Page 47: After a Wheel of Fortune illustration from *Il libro di ventura overa il libro de la sorte, di Lorenzo Spirito, Milan, 1501,* an early-sixteenth-century Italian oracle book.

CHAPTER 4

Page 74: Trump 0, the Fool, after a card from the Tarot of Marseille of Nicholas Conver, 1761, Bibliothèque Nationale, Paris.

Page 75, right: Court Fool in his official costume, after a woodcut, *Cosmographie Universelle* of Münster, Basel, 1552.

Page 75, bottom: The Fool disports himself with a child's windmill to which is attached a balloon. His right arm and leg bear metal restraints or cuffs, and from the cuff on his arm dangles a broken chain. After an engraved illustration of Bolognese tarocchini, Giuseppe Maria Mitelli, 1664.

Page 77: Trump I, the Juggler, after a card from the Tarot of Marseille of Nicholas Conver, 1761, Bibliothèque Nationale, Paris.

Page 78, top: Uncaptioned Juggler, after a partial sheet of woodcut tarocchi, Milan, probably fifteenth century.

Page 78, bottom: A juggler performing his tricks, after *Luna and her Children,* wood engraving from an astrological almanac, *Wirkungen der planeten,* 1470.

Page 79, top: *The Conjuror* is eyed very narrowly by a disbelieving peasant woman. After Hieronymus Bosch, Musée Municipal, Saint-Germain-en-Laye.

Page 79, bottom left: Trump I, the Juggler, after a card from The Tarot of Paris, seventeenth century, Bibliothèque Nationale, Paris.

Page 79, bottom right: Seventeenth-century Harlequin, after an engraving by Giuseppe-Maria Mitelli.

Page 81: Trump II, the Female Pope, after a card from the Tarot of Marseille of Nicholas Conver, 1761.

Page 82: The Female Pope trump, after an uncaptioned card painted by Bonifacio Bembo for the fifteenth-century Visconti-Sforza deck. Pierpont Morgan Library, New York.

Page 83: Pope Joan holding a book, after a woodcut made by Jacobus Philippus Forestus for *De plurimis claris sceletisque Mulieribus,* Laurentius de Rubeis, Ferrara, 1497.

Page 86, top: Trump III, the Empress, after a card from the Tarot of Marseille of Nicholas Conver, 1761.

Page 86, bottom : The Empress, after an uncut sheet of woodcut trumps, Milan, fifteenth-century. Cary Collection, Beinecke Library, Yale University.

Page 87: The Empress, after a trump painted by Bonifacio Bembo for the fifteenth century Visconti-Sforza deck.

Page 89: Trump IV, the Emperor, after a card from the Tarot of Marseille of Nicholas Conver, 1761.

Page 90, top: The Emperor, after an uncut sheet of woodcut trumps, Milan, fifteenth century. Cary Collection, Beinecke Library, Yale University.

Page 90, bottom: Detail of the tenth horoscope house of Erhard Schön (see entry for page 40).

Page 92: Trump V, the Pope, after a card from the Tarot of Marseille of Nicholas Conver, 1761.

Page 93: Detail of the ninth horoscope house of Erhard Schön (see entry for page 40).

Page 95, top: Trump VI, the Lovers, after a card from the Tarot of Marseille of Nicholas Conver, 1761.

Page 95, bottom: The Lovers, after a trump painted by Bonifacio Bembo for the fifteenth-century Visconti-Sforza deck.

Page 96, left: Love, after an engraving by Giuseppe-Maria Mitelli in 1664 to illustrate the tarocchini of Bologna.

Page 96, bottom: Detail of the seventh horoscope house of Erhard Schön (see entry for page 40).

Page 98: Trump VII, the Chariot, after a card from the Tarot of Marseille of Nicholas Conver, 1761.

Page 99: The Chariot, after a card from a partial sheet of wood-block tarocchi, Florence, fifteenth century. Rosenwald Collection, National Gallery of Art, Washington DC.

Page 100: After Éliphas Lévi's design for the Chariot, *Rituel de la Haute Magie,* 1856.

Page 101: Trump VIII, Justice, after a card from the Tarot of Marseille of Nicholas Conver, 176l.

Page 102: The Cardinal Virtue Justice, after a fifteenth-century painted card in the Charles VI set.

Page 104, top: Trump IX, the Hermit, after a card from the Tarot of Marseille of Nicholas Conver, 1761.

Page 104, bottom: Saturn, after the fifteenth-century Mantegna engravings.

Page 105: Time, after an engraving by Giuseppe-Maria Mitelli in 1664 illustrating the tarocchini of Bologna.

Page 107: Trump X, the Wheel of Fortune, after a card from the Tarot of Marseille of Nicholas Conver, 1761.

Page 108: The Wheel of Fortune, after the card painted by Bonifacio Bembo for the fifteenth-century Visconti-Sforza deck.

Page 109: Detail of the eleventh horoscope house of Erhard Schön (see entry for page 40).

Page 111, top: Trump XI, Fortitude, after a card from the Tarot of Marseille of Nicholas Conver, 1761.

Page 111, left: Fortitude, after a twelfth-century mosaic, St. Marks Cathedral, Venice.

Page 111, right: The Cardinal Virtue Fortitude, after a fifteenth-century painted card in the Charles VI set.

Page 112: The Cardinal Virtue Fortitude, after a card painted by an unknown artist for the fifteenth-century Visconti-Sforza deck.

Page 113, top: Trump XII, the Hanged Man, after a card from the Tarot of Marseille of Nicholas Conver, 1761.

Page 113, right: The Traitor, after an engraving by Giuseppe Maria-Mitelli in 1664 illustrating a pack of tarocchini of Bologna.

Page 113, left: The Hanged Man, after a painted card in the fifteenth-century Charles VI set.

Page 115: Detail of the twelfth horoscope house of Erhard Schön (see entry for page 40).

Page 117: Trump XIII, Death, after a card from the Tarot of Marseille of Nicholas Conver, 1761.

Page 118, top: Death and the Lawyer, after the *Dance of Death,* fifteenth-century block-book.

Page 118, bottom: Unnumbered and uncaptioned Death trump, after a partial sheet of woodcut tarocchi, Florence, fifteenth century.

Page 119: Detail of the eighth horoscope house of Erhard Schön (see entry for page 40).

Page 121, top: Trump XIV, Temperance, after a card from the Tarot of Marseille of Nicholas Conver, 1761.

Page 121, bottom: Temperance, after Etteilla, *Manière de se recréer avec le jeu de carte nommé les tarots* Paris, 1783.

Page 124, top: Trump XV, the Devil, after a card from the Tarot of Marseille of Nicholas Conver, 1761.

Page 124, bottom left: Lucifer devouring Judas Iscariot, after *Opere del divino poeta Danthe,* Venice, Bernardino Stagnino, 1512.

Page 124, bottom right: Unnumbered and uncaptioned Devil trump, after a card from a sheet of fifteenth-century tarocchi of Bologna, Rothschild Collection, Musèe Louvre, Paris.

Page 125: The Devil, after a card from a partial sheet of woodcut tarocchi, Florence, fifteenth century. Rosenwald Collection, National Gallery of Art, Washington DC.

Page 126, left: *The Sabbatic Goat,* after Éliphas Lévi, *Rituel de la haute magie,* 1856.

Page 126, right: Trump XV, the Devil, after Pamela Colman Smith's design for A. E. Waite's tarot, 1910.

Page 129, top: Trump XVI, the Tower, after a card from the Tarot of Marseille of Nicholas Conver, 1761.

Page 129, right: The Lightning-Struck Tower, after a card from a sheet of woodcut fifteenth-century tarocchi from Venice or Ferrara. Metropolitan Museum of Art, New York.

Page 129, left: The Tower, after a fifteenth-century card from a sheet of Bolognese tarocchi. Rothschild Collection, Musèe Louvre, Paris.

Page 130: Unnumbered and uncaptioned Tower trump, after an eighteenth-century Florentine minchiate card.

Page 132, left: The Thunderbolt, after a seventeenth-century card from the Tarot of Jacques Viéville, Paris.

Page 132, right: Shepherds celebrate the birth of Christ. After a fifteenth-century woodcut in a Book of Hours printed by Antoine Verard.

Page 135: Trump XVII, the Star, after a card from the Tarot of Marseille of Nicholas Conver, 1761.

Page 136, top: *Crepuscolo della mattina* (Morning Twilight), after Cesare Ripa, *Iconologia*, 1603.

Page 136, bottom: The Three Magi, after a sixth-century mosaic in the church of Saint Apollinare Nuovo, Ravenna.

Page 137: The Star, after a card in a sheet of uncut fifteenth-century Bolognese tarocchi. Rothschild Collection, Musèe Louvre, Paris.

Page 139, top: Trump XVIII, the Moon, after a card from the Tarot of Marseille of Nicholas Conver, 1761.

Page 139, left: Unnumbered and uncaptioned Moon trump, after a card painted by an unknown artist for the fifteenth-century Visconti-Sforza deck. Pierpont Morgan Library, New York.

Page 139, right: The Moon, after a card in a partial sheet of fifteenth-century Milanese tarocchi. Cary Collection, Beinecke Library, Yale University.

Page 140, left: The Moon, after a card designed in 1770 by F. I. Vandenborre.

Page 140, bottom: The Moon, after a painted card in the fifteenth-century Charles VI set. Bibliothèque Nationale, Paris.

Page 142, top: Trump XIX, the Sun, after a card from the Tarot of Marseille of Nicholas Conver, 1761.

Page 142, left: The Sun: depicting the philosopher Diogenes, who lives in a barrel, asking Alexander to move out of his sunlight. After a card painted by an unknown artist for the fifteenth-century D'Este tarocchi. Cary Collection, Beinecke Library, Yale University.

Page 143, top left: The Sun, after a standard Belgian Tarot pattern of the eighteenth-century.

Page 143, top right: Trump XIX, the Sun, after Pamela Colman Smith's design for A. E. Waite's tarot, 1910.

Page 143, bottom: Detail of the fifth horoscope house of Erhard Schön (see entry for page 40).

Page 144: The Sun, after a card painted by an unknown artist for the fifteenth-century Visconti-Sforza deck. Pierpont Morgan Library, New York.

Page 145: Trump XX, Judgment, after a card from the Tarot of Marseille of Nicholas Conver, 1761.

Page 146: Judgment, after a card from the fifteenth-century Cary-Yale Visconti deck painted by Bonifacio Bembo. Cary Collection, Beinecke Library, Yale University.

Page 148, top: Trump XXI, the World, after a card from the Tarot of Marseille of Nicholas Conver, 1761.

Page 148, left: Trump XXI, the World, after a card from the Tarot of Jacques Viéville, 1650. Bibliothèque Nationale, Paris.

Page 149, left: Christ in Majesty, after the Stavelot Bible, 1097, British Library.

Page 149, top right: Paradise, after a sixteenth-century manuscript by Hubert Cailleau, showing the setting for the mystery play at Valenciennes, 1547. The tower representing paradise stood at the far left of the stage.

Page 149, bottom: The World, after a card painted by an unknown artist for the fifteenth-century Visconti-Sforza deck. Accademia Carrara, Bergamo.

Page 150 left: The Angel (the World), after a card from an uncut sheet of fifteenth-century woodcut tarocchi. Rosenwald Collection, National Gallery of Art, Washington DC.

Page 150, right: The World? After an uncaptioned card from the Charles VI set. Bibliothèque Nationale, Paris.

CHAPTER 5

Throughout this chapter: Figures at left following the card name are based on the version of the card in the Marseille-pattern deck of Nicholas Conver, 1761. **Figures at right following the card name** are based on the version of the card in A. E. Waite's deck, designed by Pamela Colman Smith, 1910.

Page 155: The Cardinal Virtue Prudence, after an engraving in Cesare Ripa's *Iconologia,* 1603.

Page 156: After Éliphas Lévi, the Pantacle of Ezechiel, the key to all pantacles, *Dogme de la Haute Magie,* 1855.

Page 171, right: Lancelot, *Valet de Trèfle,* after an eighteenth century French suit card.

Page 171, left: Lancelot agrees to knight his son Galahad, after a manuscript of the *Lancelot-Graal* cycle. Hill Monastic Manuscript Library, Collegeville, Minnesota.

Page 174, lower left: *Argine, Dame de Trèfle,* after an eighteenth-century French suit card.

Page 176, lower left: *Alexandre, Roi de Trèfle,* after an eighteenth-century French suit card.

Page 177: Alexander borne aloft by griffins, after a twelfth-century floor mosaic, Otranto Cathedral.

Page 179: The Cardinal Virtue Temperance, after a trump in the fifteenth-century Visconti-Sforza deck.

Page 182, left: Two of Cups, twin dragon-head detail, after the Tarot of Jacques Vièville, Paris, 1650.

Page 182, right: Twin-dragon head detail, after a Mamlûk card in the Topkapi Sarayi Museum, Istanbul.

Page 193, bottom right: *La Hire, Valet de Coeur,* after an eighteenth-century French suit card.

Page 194: After a *Valet de Coeur* circa 1500, shown carrying the torch of Hymen, the Greek god of marriage.

Page 197: *Judic* (Judith), *Dame de Coeur,* after an eighteenth-century French suit card.

Page 198, bottom left: Charlemagne in coronation robes, after François Hottenroth.

Page 199: *Charles* (Charlemagne), *Roi de Coeur,* after an eighteenth-century French suit card.

Page 200: The archangel Michael carrying the sword and scales of Justice.

Page 205: Three of Swords, after a card from the Sola-Busca deck, Venice, 1491 or 1523.

Page 211, top: Seven of Swords, after a card from the Sola-Busca deck, Venice 1491 or 1523.

Page 211, bottom: Maugis d'Aigremont casts a sleeping spell over Charlemagne and his knights in order to steal their swords. After a miniature by Loyset Liédet, c.1460, MS *Renaut de Montaubon,* Bibliothèque de l'Arsenal, Paris.

Page 217, top: *Hogier, Valet de Pique,* after an eighteenth-century French suit card.

Page 217, bottom: Ogier with his sword Cortante, after a seventeenth-century French suit card.

Page 220, middle left: *Pallas, Dame de Pique,* after an eighteenth century French suit card.

Page 220, bottom: Joan of Arc, *"La Pucelle,"* chasing off three whores with her sword, breaking it in the process. After a fifteenth-century manuscript.

Page 222, left: King David playing the harp, surrounded by four jongleurs. After a thirteenth-century manuscript in the Bibliothèque Nationale, Paris.

Page 222, right: *David, Roi de Pique,* after an eighteenth-century French suit card.

Page 224: Fortitude, after the fifteenth-century "Mantegna" engraving.

Page 240: *Hector, Valet de Carreau,* after an eighteenth-century French suit card.

Page 243: *Rachel, Dame de Carreau,* after an eighteenth century French suit card.

Page 244, middle right: *Cezar* (Caesar), *Roi de Carreau,* after an eighteenth-century French suit card.

Page 244, lower left: French suit card *Roi de Carreau* circa 1490, carrying the Roman fasces insignia (Batons), and identified as Julius Caesar.

CHAPTER 6

Page 246: *Die Fraw von Herz* (the Queen of Hearts), after a German playing-card oracle book, 1543.

Page 256, top: The Melancholy Temperament, after a woodcut in a German calendar, Augsburg, circa 1480.

Page 256, bottom: The Phlegmatic Temperament, after a woodcut in a German calendar, Augsburg, circa 1480.

Page 257, top: The Sanguine Temperament, after a woodcut in a German calendar, Augsburg, circa 1480.

Page 257, bottom: The Choleric Temperament, after a woodcut in a German calendar, Augsburg, circa 1480.

Page 276: Etteilla's Great Figure of Destiny.

APPENDIX 1

Page 279: The god Thoth weighing the Heart of the Deceased against the Feather of Truth, after the Funerary Papyrus of the Royal Scribe and Steward of King Sety I, Memphis, Egypt, circa 1310 B.C.E., British Museum papyrus 9901.

Page 282: The Fool, after a card from the *Tarocco Soprafino* of F. Gumppenberg, Milan, 1835.

Page 283: Juno (Female Pope substitute) and Jupiter (Pope substitute), after the Tarot of Besançon, eighteenth century.

Page 284, left: The Chariot, after a card from the Tarot of Jacques Viéville, Paris, 1650.

Page 284, right: Justice, after a card from the Tarot of Jacques Viéville, Paris, 1650.

Page 285: The Star, the Hanged Man, and the Wheel of Fortune, after a double-headed modern deck of tarocco Bolognese published by Modiano.

Page 286, top left: The Spanish Captain Fracasse, used as a substitute for the Female Pope in Belgian decks after the seventeenth century. After a card designed by F. I. Vandenborre in 1770.

Page 286, center: The Spanish Captain Fracasse of the sixteenth-century commedia dell'arte. After a sixteenth-century manuscript in the Bibliothèque Nationale, Paris.

Page 286, top right: The Bacus (Bacchus) Trump, used as a substitute for the Pope in Belgian decks after the seventeenth century. After a card designed by F. I. Vandenborre in 1770.

Page 286, bottom: Trump cards Sagittarius and the element water, after an eighteenth-century minchiate deck from Florence.

BIBLIOGRAPHY

Here is a list of the material I have consulted in writing this book. Gertrude Moakley's groundbreaking work, the tarot encyclopedias of Stuart Kaplan, and the painstaking works of Dummett, Decker, and Depaulis have been of fundamental importance to me, as they should be to anyone interested in the history or occult development of tarot cards. Robert V. O'Neill's book is also of great value for its careful exploration of tarot symbolism from a divergent number of points of view. Regrettably, many of the other, rarer works are available only in major libraries, although some are included in more recent texts, which I have indicated where applicable.

CARD DECKS

Antichi Tarocchi Lombardi. Milano: F. Gumppenberg, 1810; Turin, Italy: Lo Scarabeo.

The Cary-Yale Visconti Tarocchi Deck. New York: U.S. Games Systems, 1984.

The Complete Tarot Cards Authentic. Designed by Pamela Colman Smith and Arthur Edward Waite. New York: University Books, n.d.

Grand Etteilla Egyptian Gypsies Tarot. Saint-Max Cedex, France: Cartomancie Grimaud, France-Cartes.

I Tarocchini Gioseppe Maria Mitelli, Sec. XVII. Edizione Speciale per la BIASS. Bergamo, Italy: Grafica Gutenberg, n.d.

The Minchiate Fiorentine "Etruria." Milan: Edizioni Il Meneghello, 1994.

Mulûk wanuwwâb (Mamlûk Cards from Istanbul). Brussels and Louvain, Belgium: Aurelia Books, 1972.

The Original Rider Waite Tarot Deck. Stamford, Conn: U.S. Games Systems; London: Random House, Rider Books, 1999.

Petit Etteilla. Saint-Max Cedex, France: B. P. Grimaud, France-Cartes, 1994.

Sola-Busca Illuminating Ancient Tarots. Turin, Italy: Lo Scarabeo, 1995.

Swiss Tarot 1JJ. Neuhausen am Rheinfall, Switzerland: A. G. Muller.

Tarocchi del Mantegna. Lissone, Italy: Edizione del Solleone, 1981.

Tarocchi Gioco di 78 Carte Bologna XVIII Sec. Milan: Edizione Il Meneghello, 1986.

Tarocchino Milanese a Doppia Figura 1880c. Milan: Edizione Il Meneghello, 2000.

Tarocco di Besançon Sec. XVIII. Milan: Edizione ristampata da Il Meneghello, 2000.

Tarocco di Besançon XIX Sec. Milan: Edizione Il Meneghello, 1986.

Tarocco di Marsiglia da Nicola Conver. Trieste, Italy: Boéchat Frères, Dal Negro.

Tarocco di 78 Carte F. Gumppenberg, Milano, 1840c. Milan: Edizione Il Meneghello, 1995.

Tarocco "Soprafino" di F. Gumppenberg. Milan: Edizioni Il Meneghello, 1992.

Tarot de Jacques Viéville. Bordeaux: Héron-Boéchat, n.d.

Tarot de Paris. Paris: B. P. Grimaud, 1984.

Le Tarot Divinatoire par le Dr. Papus. Paris: Éditions Dusserre, n.d.

Tarot Egyptien—Grand Jeu de l'Oracle des Dames: Methode d'Etteilla et du Livre de Thot. Paris: Éditions Dusserre, n.d.

Tarot of Marseilles. Paris: B. P. Grimaud [1930?]

Thoth Tarot Cards. St. Paul: Llewellyn Publications, n.d. Also *Aleister Crowley Thoth Tarot.* Stamford, Conn.: U.S. Games Systems, 1988.

Vandenborre Tarot. New York: Aurelia Books, U.S. Games Systems, n.d.

Visconti-Sforza Tarocchi Deck. New York: U.S. Games Systems, 1975.

PRINTED WORKS AND WEB SITES
Tarot and Playing-Card History

Bauwens, Jan. *Mulûk wanuwwâb* (Mamlûk Cards). Issued in combination with a reproduction of the Istanbul deck. Leuven (Louvain): Aurelia Books, 1972.

Benham, W. G. *Playing-Cards.* London: Ward Lock, 1931; Spring Books, 1950.

Berry, John. "'The Nine Worthies' and French Cards." *Playing-Card* (International Playing-Card Society) 27, no. 218 (1999).

Berti, Giordano, and Andrea Vitali. *Le carte di corti: I tarocchi, Gioco e Magia alla Corte degli Estensi.* Ferrara, Italy: Nuova Alfa Editoriale, 1987.

Berti, Giordano, Marissa Chiesa, and Giuliano Crippa. *Antichi Tarocchi Bolognese.* Torino, Italy: Lo Scarabeo, 1995.

Berti, Giordano, Sofia Di Vincenzo, and Maria Chiesa. *Antichi Tarocchi Illuminati: Sola-Busca.* Torino, Italy: Lo Scarabeo, 1995.

D'Allemagne, Henry René. *Antique Playing-Cards: A Pictorial History.* New York: Dover Publications, 1996.

———. *Les cartes a jouer du quatorzième au vingtième siècle.* Paris: Librairie Hachette, 1906.

Decker, Ronald. "Number Symbolism and the Tarot Trumps." *Playing-Card* (International Playing-Card Society) 27 (1999).

———. "The Tarot: An Inquiry into Origins." *Gnosis* (San Francisco) (winter 1998).

———. "Who's Who in Court Cards." *Playing-Card* (International Playing-Card Society) 16 (1988).

Decker, R., and M. Dummett. *A History of the Occult Tarot 1870–1970.* London: Duckworth, 2002.

Decker, R., T. Depaulis, and M. Dummett. *A Wicked Pack of Cards.* New York: St. Martin's Press, 1996.

Depaulis, Thierry. *The Paris Tarot.* Issued with the *Tarot de Paris.* Marseille: Societé le Jeu de Marseille, 1984.

———. *Tarot, jeu et magie.* Exhibition catalog. Paris: Bibliothèque Nationale, 1984.

Dummett, Michael. *The Game of Tarot from Ferrara to Salt Lake City.* London: Duckworth, 1980.

———. *Twelve Tarot Games.* London: Duckworth, 1980.

Dummett, Michael, and K. Abu-Deeb. "Some Remarks on Mamlûk Playing Cards." *Journal of the Warburg and Courtauld Institutes* (London) 36 (1973).

Hargraves, Catherine Perry. *A History of Playing-Cards.* New York: Dover, 1966.

Hoffman, Detlef. *The Playing-Card.* New York: New York Graphic Society, 1973.

Husband, Timothy B. *The Cloisters' Playing Cards and Other Hand-Painted Packs of the Fifteenth Century.* Issued with *The Flemish Hunting Deck.* Vienna: Piatnik, 1994.

Kaplan, Stuart R. *The Encyclopedia of Tarot.* Vol. 1, New York: U.S. Games Systems, 1978; vol. 2, New York: U.S. Games Systems, 1986; vol. 3, Stamford, CT: U.S. Games Systems, 1990.

Little, Tom Tadfor. *The Hermitage.* Tarot history web site, www.Tarothermit.com.

Mann, Sylvia. *Collecting Playing-Cards.* New York: Bell Publishing, 1966.

Mayer, L. A. *Mamlûk Playing-Cards.* Leiden, Netherlands: E. J. Brill, 1971.

McLeod, John. *Card Games.* Web site, http://www.pagat.com.

Merlin, R., *L'Origine des cartes à jouer.* Paris, 1869.

Moakley, Gertrude. *The Tarot Cards Painted by Bembo.* New York: New York Public Library, 1966.

Morley, H. T. *Old and Curious Playing-Cards.* Secaucus, New Jersey: Wellfleet Press, 1989.

Olsen, Christina. *The Art of Tarot.* New York: Abbeville Press, 1995.

O'Neill, Robert V. *Tarot Symbolism.* Lima, Ohio: Fairway Press, 1986.

Pollett, Andrea. *Andy's Place.* Playing card history Web site, www.geocities.com/a-pollett/.

———. "Tûmân, or the Ten Thousand Cups of the Mamlûk Cards." *Playing-Card* (International Playing-Card Society) 31 (2002).

Pratesi, Franco. "Italian Cards: New Discoveries #2." *Playing-Card* (International Playing-Card Society) 15 (1987).

———. "Italian Cards: New Discoveries #9." *Playing-Card* (International Playing-Card Society) 27 (1989).

Revak, James W. *Villa Revak.* Tarot history Web site, www.villarevak.org.

Rijnberk, Gerard Van. *Le Tarot, historie, iconographie, esoterisme.* Paris, 1947. Reprint, Paris: Éditions de la Maisnie, 1981.

Steele, Robert. "A Notice of the Ludus Triumphorum and Some Early Italian Card Games." *Archaeologia* (London) 57 (1900): 185–200.

Medieval and Renaissance Drama

Allerdyce, Nicoll. *Masks, Mimes, and Miracles.* London and New York: Harrap, 1931. Reprint, 1963.

Axton, Richard. *European Drama of the Early Middle Ages.* London: Hutchinson, 1974.

Beadle, Richard and Pamela King. *York Mystery Plays: A Selection in Modern Spelling.* New York: University Press, 1984.

Bevington, David. *Medieval Drama.* New York: Houghton Mifflin, 1975.

Chambers, Edmund. *The Medieval Stage.* New York: Dover, 1996.

———. *The English Folk-Play.* New York: Oxford University Press, 1969.

Clark, James Midgley. *The Dance of Death in the Middle Ages and Renaissance.* Glasgow: Jackson, 1950.

Davidson, C., and J. H. Stroupe, eds. *Iconographic and Comparative Studies in Medieval Drama.* Kalamazoo, MI: Western Michigan University, 1991.

Duchartre, Pierre Louis. *The Italian Comedy.* Translated by R. T. Weaver. New York: Dover, 1966.

Gassner, John. *Medieval and Tudor Drama.* New York: Bantam, 1971.

Kahrl, Stanley J. *Traditions of Medieval Drama.* London: Hutchinson, 1974.

Konigson, Elie. *La Représentation d'un mystère de la passion a Valenciennes en 1547.* Paris: CNRS, 1969.

Mantzius, Karl. *A History of Theatrical Art in Ancient and Modern Times.* London: Duckworth, n.d.

Nagler, A. M. *Source Book of Theatrical History.* New York: Dover, 1952.

Rose, Martial, ed. *The Wakefield Mystery Plays.* New York: W. W. Norton, 1969.

Rossiter, A. P. *English Drama from Early Times to the Elizabethans.* New York: Barnes and Noble, 1967.

Walker, Greg, ed. *Medieval Drama, an Anthology.* Walden, MA: Blackwell, 2000.

Wickham, Glynne. *A History of the Theatre.* London: Phaidon Press, 1985.

———. *The Medieval Theatre.* London and New York: Cambridge University Press, 1974. Reprint, 1987.

Classical, Medieval, and Renaissance Literature and Art

Albertus Magnus. *"Postilla in Isiam,"* in Opera Omnia ad Fidem Codicum Manuscriptorum Edenda. Vol. 19, edited by F. Siepmann. Monasterii Westfalorum: Aschendorff, 1952.

Apuleius of Madaura. *The Apologia and Florida.* Translated by H. E. Butler. 1909. Reprint. Westport, CT: Greenwood Press, 1970.

Ariosto, Ludovico. *Orlando furioso.* Translated by Guido Waldman. New York: Oxford University Press, 1983.

Augustine of Hippo. *Confessions*. Book 8, chapter 12, p. 29. (See Appleton, *The Catholic Encyclopedia*.)

Baring-Gould, Sabine. *Curious Myths of the Middle Ages*. New York: University Books, 1967.

Bernardo, A. S. *Petrarch, Laura, and the Triumphs*. Albany, NY: State University of New York Press, 1974.

Berthelot, Anne. *King Arthur, Chivalry and Legend*. Translated by Ruth Sharman. London: Thames and Hudson, 1997.

Boccaccio, Giovanni. *Famous Women* (De mulieribus claris). Translated by Virginia Brown. Cambridge: Harvard University Press, 2003.

Boethius. *The Consolation of Philosophy*. Translated by P. G. Walsh. New York: Oxford University Press, 1999.

―――――. *The Consolation of Philosophy*. Translated by V. E. Watts. London: Penguin Books, 1969.

Boiardo, Matteo Maria. *Tarocchi*. Edited by Simona Foà. Rome: Salerno Editrice, 1993.

Bolte, Johannes. *Geschichte der Losbücher*. In *Georg Wickrams Werke*, vol, 4, edited by Johannes Bolte. Tübingen, Germany: Litterarischer Verein Stuttgart, 1903.

Brewer, E. Cobham. *Brewer's Dictionary of Phrase and Fable*. London: Cassell, 1977.

Carruthers, Mary. *The Book of Memory: A Study of Memory in Medieval Culture*. Cambridge: Cambridge University Press, 1990.

Cartari, Vincenzo. *Le imagini colla sposizione degli dei degli antichi*. Venice: Marcolini, 1556. (See Volpi, *Le imagini degli dei di Vincenzo Cartari*.)

Casanova, Giacomo. *History of My Life*. Translated by W. R. Trask. Vol. 3. Baltimore: Johns Hopkins University Press, 1977.

The Catholic Encyclopedia, 1908. Robert Appleton Company. Online Edition Copyright 1999 Kevin Knight: http://www.newadvent.org/cathen/

Cavendish, Richard. *King Arthur and the Grail*. New York: Taplinger, 1979.

Cirlot, J. E. *Dictionary of Symbols*. New York: Philosophical Library, 1962.

Cocai, Merlini. (Teofilo Folengo). *Il caos di triperuno* (The Chaos of Three for One). Venice, 1527. (See Kaplan, *The Encyclopedia of Tarot*, vol. 2, pp. 8–9.)

Cusa, Nicholas de. *De Ludo Globi: The Game of Spheres*. Translation and introduction by P. M. Watts. New York: Abaris Books, 1986.

Dante Alighieri. *The Divine Comedy.* Translated by R. Pite and H. Cary. New York: Everyman Paper Classics.

De Troyes, Chretien. *Arthurian Romances.* Translated by W. W. Kibler and C. W. Carroll. London: Penguin, 1991.

Engels, I. J. "Hector." In *A Dictionary of Medieval Heroes,* translated by Tanis Guest. Suffolk, England, and Rochester, New York: Boydell and Brewer, 1998.

Evans, M. W. *Medieval Drawings.* New York: Paul Hamlyn, 1969.

Gerritsen, W. P., and A. G. van Melle, eds. *A Dictionary of Medieval Heroes.* Translated by Tanis Guest. Suffolk, England, and Rochester, New York: Boydell and Brewer, 1998.

Hall, James. *Dictionary of Subjects and Symbols in Art.* London: John Murray, 1974.

Heninger, S. K. *The Cosmographical Glass: Renaissance Diagrams of the Universe.* San Marino, CA: Huntington Library, 1977.

Hibbert, Christopher. *The Rise and Fall of the House of Medici.* London: Allan Lane, 1974.

Hind, Arthur M. *An Introduction to a History of Woodcut.* New York: Dover, 1963.

Holbein, Hans. *Dance of Death.* Introduction and notes by James M. Clark. London: Phaidon Press, 1947.

Hottenroth, François. *Le costume chez les peuples anciens et modernes.* Paris: Armand Guerinet, n.d.

Homer. *The Iliad and the Odyssey.* Translated by W. J. Black. New York: Barnes and Noble, 1999.

Husband, T. B. *The Medieval Housebook and the Art of Illustration.* New York: Frick Collection, 1999.

Kaplan, Aryeh. *Sefer Yetzirah.* New York: Samuel Weiser, 1990.

Kircher, Athanasius. *Oedipus Aegyptiacus.* Rome, 1642–44.

Lacroix, Paul. *Moeurs, usages et costumes au Moyen Age.* Paris, 1871.

Lehner, Ernst. *Symbols, Signs and Signets.* New York: Dover, 1950.

Leland, Charles Godfrey. *Aradia, or The Gospel of the Witches.* London: David Nutt, 1899.

———. *Etruscan Magic and Occult Remedies.* New York: University Books, 1963.

Lollio, Flavio Alberto. *Invettiva contra Il Gioco del taroco, in Rime piacevoli.* Venice, 1550. (See Kaplan, *The Encyclopedia of Tarot,* vol. 1, p. 30.)

Luck, Georg. *Arcana Mundi, Magic and the Occult in the Greek and Roman Worlds.* Baltimore: Johns Hopkins University Press, 1985.

Malory, Thomas. *Le morte d'Arthur* in *The Works of Thomas Malory.* Edited by E. Vinaver. Oxford and New York: Oxford University Press, 1977.

Martin, Ruth. *Witchcraft and the Inquisition in Venice, 1550–1650.* Oxford and New York: Blackwell, 1989.

Ovid. *The Metamorphoses.* Translated by M. M. Innes. London: Penguin Books, 1971.

Patch, Howard Rollin. *The Goddess Fortuna in Medieval Literature.* Cambridge: Harvard University Press, 1927.

Petrarca, Francesco (Petrarch). *Rerum memorandarum libri.* Edited by G. Billanovich. Florence: Sansoni, 1945.

——. *The Triumphs of Francesco Petrarch, Florentine Poet Laureate.* Translated by Henry Boyd, with an introduction by Guido Biagi. London and Cambridge, Mass.: The University Press, 1906. (See Kaplan, *The Encyclopedia of Tarot*, vol. 2, pp. 142–47.)

Paton, Lucy Allen. *Studies in the Fairy Mythology of Arthurian Romance.* New York: Burt Franklin, 1960.

Philo. *On the Virtues.* Vol. 8, book 4. Loeb Classical Library. Cambridge: Harvard University Press, 2000.

Picatrix. See Pingree.

Pingree, David. *Picatrix: The Latin Version.* London: Warburg Institute, 1986.

Piton, Camille. *Le costume civil en France du XIII au XIX siècle.* Paris: L. Maretheux, n.d.

Plutarch. *Lives of the Noble Greeks.* New York: Dell, 1968.

Portoli, Attilio, ed. *Le opere maccheroniche de Merlin Cocai.* Vol. 3. Mantua, Italy: 1890.

Puhvel, Jaan, ed. *Myth and Law among the Indo-Europeans.* Berkeley and Los Angeles, CA.: University of California Press, 1970.

Ragghiante, Carlo L., ed. *Le vite di Giorgio Vasari.* Vol. 1. Milan: Rizzoli Editore, 1945.

Ringhieri, Innocenzio. *Cento giuochi liberali et d'ingegno; novellamente da M. Innocentio Ringhieri, gentilhuomo Bolognese ritrovati e in dieci libri descritti, impresa per Anselmo Giaccarelli.* Bologna, 1551. (See Kaplan, *The Encyclopedia of Tarot*, vol. 1, p. 30.)

Ripa, Cesare. *Iconologia.* 1593. Milan: I tascabili degli Editori Associati, 1992.

Rodriguez de Montalvo, Garci Ordonez. *Amadis of Gaul.* Translated by H. C. Behm and E. B. Place. Lexington, KY: University Press of Kentucky, 1974–75.

Rudwin, Maximilian. *The Devil in Legend and Literature.* La Salle, Illinois: Open Court Publishing, 1959.

Santi, Bruno. *The Marble Pavement of the Cathedral of Siena.* Florence: Scala, 1982.

Schelling, Michael. "Rota Fortunae: Beziehungen zwischen Bild und Text in mittelalterichen Handschriften." In Wolfgang Harms and L. Peter Johnson, *Deutsche Literatur des späten Mittelalters.* Hamburger Colloquium 1973. Publications of the Institute of Germanic Studies, University of London, vol. 22. Berlin: Erich Schmidt Verlag, 1975.

Scholem, Gershom. *Kabbalah.* New York: New York Times Books, 1974.

———. *Origins of the Kabbalah.* Princeton, NJ: Princeton University Press, The Jewish Publication Society, 1987.

Schröder, Horst. *Der Topos der Nine Worthies in Literatur und bildender Kunst.* Göttingen: Vandenhoek and Ruprecht, 1971.

Scott, Walter, ed. and trans. *Hermetica: The Ancient Greek and Latin Writings Which Contain Religious or Philosophic Teachings Ascribed to Hermes Trismegistus.* 4 vols. Boulder, CO: Hermes House, 1982; Boston: Shambala Publications, 1985.

Seznec, Jean. *The Survival of the Pagan Gods.* Translated by Barbara Sessions. New York: Harper Torchbook, 1961.

Stanford, Peter. *The Legend of Pope Joan.* New York: Henry Holt, 1998.

Thomas Aquinas. *Summa Theologica.* Translated by the Fathers of the English Dominican Province. Chicago: Thomas More Press, 1997.

Virgil. *The Aeneid.* Translated by Robert Fitzgerald. New York: Random House, Vintage Books, 1990.

Volpi, Caterina. *Le imagini degli dei di Vincenzo Cartari.* Rome: Edizione De Luca, 1996.

Wace and Layamon. *Arthurian Chronicles.* Translated by E. Mason. London: J. M. Dent, 1977.

Wade, Elizabeth I. "A Fragmentary German Divination Device: Medieval Analogues and Pseudo-Lullian Tradition." In *Conjuring Spirits: Texts and Traditions of Medieval Ritual Magic,* edited by Claire Fanger. Pennsylvania: Pennsylvania State University Press, 1998.

Waite, A. E. *The Holy Grail.* New York: University Books, 1961.

———. *The Holy Kabbalah.* New York: University Books, n.d.

Wolfegg, Christoph Graf zu Waldburg. *Venus and Mars: The World of the Medieval Housebook.* Munich and New York: Prestel Verlag, 1998.

Yates, Frances A. *The Art of Memory.* London: Routledge and Kegan Paul, 1966.

———. *Giordano Bruno and the Hermetic Tradition.* London: Routledge and Kegan Paul, 1964.

Persian and Islamic Literature

Arifi of Herat. *The Ball and the Polo Stick, or The Book of Ecstasy.* Translated by R. S. Greenshields. London: Octagon Press, 1980.

Browne, E. G. *A Year amongst the Persians.* London: Adam and Charles Black, 1893.

The Dabistan, or School of Manners. Author unknown. Translated by D. Shea, and A. M. Troyer. New York: Walter Dunne, 1901. Also see Joseph H. Peterson's Web site on Zoroastrianism, http://www.avesta.org.

Ibn Khaldûn. *The Muqaddimah, an Introduction to History.* Translated by Franz Rosenthal, abridged and edited by N. J. Dawood. London: Routledge and Kegan Paul and Secker and Warburg, 1967.

The Koran. Translated by N. J. Dawood. New York: Penguin Books, 1983.

Mayer, L. A. *Saracenic Heraldry: A Survey.* Oxford and London: Oxford University Press, 1933, 1999.

Nicholson, R. A. *Studies in Islamic Mysticism.* London: Routledge and Kegan Paul, 1998.

Omar Khayyám. *The Rubaiyat of Omar Khayyam.* Translated by Peter Avery and John Heath-Stubbs. London: Penguin Books, 1979.

———. *The Rubaiyat of Omar Khayyam.* Translated by Edward Fitzgerald. New York: Dover, 1991.

Shah, Sayed Idries. *The Sufis.* New York: Doubleday, 1964.

Cartomancy, Symbolism, and the Occult Sciences

Agrippa, Henry Cornelius. *Three Books of Occult Philosophy.* Antwerp, 1531; Hastings, England: Chthonios Books, 1986; St. Paul: Llewellyn Publications, 1993.

Angelus, Johannes. *Astrolabium planum in tabulis ascendens.* Augsburg, 1488; Venice, 1502.

Bertozzi, Marco. *La tirannia degli astri: Gli affreschi astrologici di Palazzo Schifanoia.* Bologna, Italy: Cappelli di Bologna, 1985; Livorno, Italy: Sillabe, 1999.

The Chaldean Oracles as Set Down by Julianus. Translated by Francesco Patrizzi and Thomas Stanley. Gillette, New Jersey: Heptangle Books, 1989.

Chambers, Robert. *Book of Days.* 2 vols. London and Edinburgh: R. Chambers, 1864.

Christian, Paul. *Histoire de la magie, du monde surnaturel et de la fatalité à travers les temps et les peuples.* Paris, 1870.

———. *The History and Practice of Magic.* Edited by Ross Nichols. Translated by James Kirkup and Julian Shaw. New York: Citadel Press, 1969.

———. *L'Homme rouge des Tuileries.* Paris, 1863; Paris: Éditions de la Maisnie, 1977.

Court de Gébelin, Antoine. *Le monde primitif analisé et comparé avec le monde moderne.* Paris, 1781.

Crowley, Aleister (The Master Therion). *The Book of Thoth: A Short Essay on the Tarot of the Egyptians.* New York: Samuel Weiser, 1969.

D'Ambly, Paul Boiteau. *Les cartes a jouer et la cartomancie.* Paris: Hachette, 1854; Bologna: Arnaldo Forni Editore, 1980.

De Givry, E. G. *A Picture Museum of Sorcery, Magic and Alchemy.* Translated by J. C. Locke. New York: University Books, 1963.

Devore, Nicholas. *Encyclopedia of Astrology.* New York: Philosophical Library, 1947.

D'Odoucet, M. M. *Science des signes, ou Médecine de l'esprit, connue sous le nom d'art de tirer les cartes.* 3 vols. Paris, 1804–7.

Encausse, Gérard (Papus). *Le tarot divinatoire: clef du tirage des cartes et des sorts.* Paris, 1909; Paris: Éditions Dangles, 1969.

———. *The Tarot of the Bohemians.* Translated by A. P. Morton. Edited and with a preface by A. E. Waite. North Hollywood, CA: Wilshire Book Company, 1978.

Etteilla. *Dictionnaire synonymique du Livre de Thot ou Synonymes de significations primitives tracées sur les feuillets du Livre de Thot.* Paris, 1791.

———. *Manière de se recréer avec le jeu de cartes nommées tarots.* Paris, 1783–85; Paris: Éditions Jobert, 1977.

Etteilla, ou L'art de lire dans les cartes. Paris, 1791.

Fachan, Zoé. *L'homme zodiaque.* Marseille: Agep, 1991.

Fanti, Sigismondo. "Triompho di Fortuna." In Grazia Mirti, *La Forza delle immagine in astrologia.* Transcript of the first International Congress of the Astrological Federation of Southern Europe, Mykonos, June 10, 2000. Mirti@mbox.venco.it.

Fortune, Dion. *The Mystical Qabalah.* London: Williams and Norgate, 1948.

———. *Practical Occultism in Daily Life.* London: Aquarian Press, 1976.

Gettings, Fred. *Dictionary of Astrology.* London: Routledge and Kegan Paul, 1987.

Gilbert, R. A. *The Golden Dawn Scrapbook.* New York: Samuel Weiser, 1997.

Giles, Cynthia. *The Tarot: History, Mystery, and Lore.* New York: Simon and Schuster, 1994.

Gleadow, Rupert. *The Origin of the Zodiac.* New York: Castle Books, 1968.

Grand Orient (A. E. Waite). *A Handbook of Cartomancy, Fortune-Telling and Occult Divination.* London and Edinburgh: G. Redway, 1889.

———. *A Manual of Cartomancy, Fortune-telling and Occult Divination.* 4th ed., revised and enlarged, with plates. London: Rider, 1909. (Also available as *A Manual of Cartomancy and Occult Divination,* republished by Kessinger Publishing Company, Kila, Montana, n.d.)

Halbronn, Jacques. *Etteilla: L'astrologie du Livre de Thot (1785), suivie de recherches sur l'histoire de l'astrologie et du tarot.* Paris: Éditions de la Grande Conjonction, 1993.

Hoffmann, Detleff, and Erika Kroppenstedt. *Wahrsagekarten, ein Beitrag sur Geschichte des Okkultismus.* Bielefeld: Deutsches Spielenkarten Museum, 1972.

Hone, Margaret E. *The Modern Text-Book of Astrology.* London: Fowler, 1973.

Howe, Ellic. *The Magicians of the Golden Dawn.* London: Routledge and Kegan Paul, 1972.

Huson, Richard, ed. *The Complete Book of Fortune: A Comprehensive Survey of the Occult Sciences and Other Methods of Divination.* London: Associated Newspapers, Northcliffe House, 1936.

Hutton, Ronald. *The Triumph of the Moon: A History of Modern Pagan Witchcraft.* Oxford and New York: Oxford University Press, 1999.

King, Francis. *Ritual Magic in England (1887 to the Present Day)*. London: Neville Spearman, 1970.

Küntz, Darcy. *The Golden Dawn Court Cards as Drawn by William Wynn Westcott and Moïna Mathers*. Edmonds, WA: Holmes Publishing, 1996.

Lévi, Éliphas (Alphonse-Louis Constant). *The History of Magic*. Translated by A. E. Waite. London: Rider, 1813; New York: Weiser, 1999.

————. *Transcendental Magic*. Translated by A. E. Waite. London: Rider, 1896; New York: Weiser, 1999.

Losbuch in Deutschen Reimpaaren. Vollständige Faksimile ausgabe im original-format des Codex Vindobonensis Series Nova 2652 der Österreichischen Nationalbibliothek. Graz, Austria: Akademische Druck u. Verlagsanstalt, 1973.

Magoni, Gianluigi. *Le cose non dette sui Decani di Schifanoia, una lettura astronomica*. Accademia delle Scienze di Ferrara. Ferrara: Corbo Editore, 1997.

Marcolino da Forlì, Francesco. *Le sorti de Francesco Marcolino da Forlì, intitolate Giardino di Pensieri allo Illustrissimo Signore Hectore Estense, Duca di Ferrara*. Venice, 1540, 1550. (See de Givry, *A Picture Museum of Sorcery*, pp. 290–93.)

Mathers, S. L. M. *The Greater Key of Solomon*. Chicago: De Laurence, 1914.

————. *The Kabbalah Unveiled*. London: Routlege and Kegan Paul, 1954.

————. *The Tarot*. New York: Occult Research Press [1888?]

McIntosh, Christopher. *Éliphas Lévi and the French Occult Revival*. New York: Weiser, 1974.

McLean, Adam. *The Magical Calendar of Tycho Brahe*. Magnum Opus Hermetic Sourceworks Number 1, Edinburgh, 1980.

Orsini, Julia. *L'art de tirer les cartes*. Paris, 1850; Paris: Éditions Dusserre, n.d.

Papus. See Encausse, Gérard.

Raine, Kathleen. *Yeats, the Tarot and the Golden Dawn*. Dublin: Dolmen Press, 1976.

Regardie, Israel. *The Complete Golden Dawn System of Magic*. Phoenix: Falcon Press, 1984.

————. *The Golden Dawn: An Account of the Teachings, Rites and Ceremonies of the Order of the Golden Dawn*. 4 vols. Chicago: Aries Press, 1937–40. Also St. Paul: Llewellyn, 1992.

Revak, James W. *The Influence of Etteilla and His School on Mathers and Waite.* Online article version 1.1 (8/19/00). (See Revak, *Villa Revak.*)

Seligman, Kurt. *The History of Magic.* New York: Pantheon Books, 1948.

Spirito, Lorenzo. Il Libro della Ventura overo Il Libro de la Sorte. Milan, 1501.

Thorndike, Lynn. *A History of Magic and Experimental Science.* Vols. 1–4. New York: Columbia University Press, 1964–66.

Vaillant, J.-A. *Les Rômes: Histoire vraie des vrais bohémiens.* Paris, 1857.

Waite, A. E. *The Key to the Tarot: Being Fragments of a Secret Tradition under the Veil of Divination.* London: William Rider and Son, 1910.

———. *The Pictorial Key to the Tarot.* 1910. New York: University Books, 1959.

———. *Shadows of Life and Thought.* London: Selwyn and Blount, 1938.

Webb, James. *The Occult Underground.* La Salle, IL: Open Court Publishing, 1974.

Weston, Jessie. *From Ritual to Romance.* Princeton, NJ: Princeton University Press, 1993.

Psychology, Divination, and the Paranormal

Beloff, John. "Parapsychology and Philosophy." In *The Handbook of Parapsychology.* Edited by Benjamin Wolman. New York: Van Nostrand Reinhold, 1977.

Eisenbud, Jule. *Paranormal Foreknowledge.* New York: Human Sciences Press, 1982.

Geiser, L., and M. I. Stein, eds. *Evocative Images: Thematic Apperception Test and the Art of Projection.* Arlington, Va.: American Psychological Association, 1999.

Hardy, A., and A. Koestler. *The Challenge of Chance.* New York: Random House, 1973.

Jung, Carl Gustave. *The Archetypes and the Collective Unconscious.* Translated by R. F. C. Hull. Princeton, NJ: Princeton University Press, Bollingen Series, 1981.

Koestler, Arthur. *The Roots of Coincidence.* New York: Random House, 1972.

Loewe, M., and C. Blacker. *Oracles and Divination.* Boulder, CO: Shambala Publications, 1981.

Nadeau, R., and M. Kafatos. *The Non-Local Universe: The New Physics and Matters of the Mind.* New York: Oxford University Press, 1999.

INDEX

Page numbers in italic indicate illustrations.